Unhealthy Cities

The purpose of this book is to show the important role that space and place play in the health of urban residents, particularly those living in high-poverty ghettos. The book brings together research and writing from a variety of disciplines to demonstrate the health costs of being poor in America's cities. Both authors are committed to raising awareness of structural factors that promote poverty and injustice in a society that proclaims its commitment to equality of opportunity. Our health is often dramatically affected by where we live; some parts of the city seem to be designed to make people sick. This book is intended for students and professionals in urban sociology, medical sociology, public health, and community planning.

Kevin Fitzpatrick is Professor and Jones Chair in Community, Department of Sociology at the University of Arkansas. As Director of the Community and Family Institute, Dr. Fitzpatrick continues his work on homelessness, health of special populations, at-risk behaviors among minority youth, and community. Dr. Fitzpatrick was recently awarded a grant from the Wal-Mart Foundation to begin working on the development of mobile health care in Northwest Arkansas.

Mark LaGory is Professor and Chair of Sociology and Social Work at the University of Alabama at Birmingham. He is an urban sociologist whose current research explores the role of place and social capital in mediating stressful environmental circumstances such as poverty and homelessness. He teaches courses in theory, urban ecology, religion, and homelessness. He is an ordained Episcopal deacon, and a member of the clergy staff at St. Luke's Episcopal Church in Birmingham.

Unhealthy Cities
Poverty, Race, and Place in America

Kevin Fitzpatrick
University of Arkansas

Mark LaGory
University of Alabama at Birmingham

Routledge
Taylor & Francis Group

NEW YORK AND LONDON

First published 2011
by Routledge
270 Madison Avenue, New York, NY 10016

Simultaneously published in the UK
by Routledge
2 Park Square, Milton Park, Abingdon, Oxon OX14 4RN

Routledge is an imprint of the Taylor & Francis Group, an informa business

© 2011 Taylor & Francis

Typeset in Caslon and Copperplate Gothic by Swales and Willis Ltd, Exeter, Devon
Printed and bound in the United States of America on acid-free paper by
Sheridan Books, Inc.

Library of Congress Cataloging in Publication Data
Fitzpatrick, Kevin.
  Unhealthy cities: poverty, race, and place in America /
  Kevin Fitzpatrick, Mark LaGory. — 1st ed.
    p. cm. — (Metropolis and modern life)
  Includes bibliographical references and index.
  Rev. ed. of: Unhealthy places, 2000.
  1. Inner cities—Health aspects—United States. 2. Urban poor—Health and
  hygiene—United States. 3. Minorities—Health and hygiene—United States.
  4. Urban health—United States. I. La Gory, Mark, 1947-
  II. Fitzpatrick, Kevin. Unhealthy places. III. Title.
  RA566.3.F58 2010
  362.109173'2—dc22
  2010015832

ISBN: 978-0-415-80516-2 (hbk)
ISBN: 978-0-415-80517-9 (pbk)
ISBN: 978-0-203-84376-5 (ebk)

DEDICATION

To my family, and most importantly, my wife, Mary for her love, encouragement and support. —Kevin Fitzpatrick

To all people in need, mindful not only of their needs but of the gifts they can give, and to Mary Sue and my family, who give encouragement and support. —Mark LaGory

TABLE OF CONTENTS

PREFACE   X

ACKNOWLEDGMENTS   XII

ABBREVIATIONS   XIII

CHAPTER 1   THE IMPORTANCE OF PLACE   1

Place Matters   3

Why an Urban, Place-Based Approach to Health?   6

Ghetto Poverty Tracts: A Definition   8

Place as Life Chance and Risk   9

Place as Social Resource   12

A Framework for the Book   16

CHAPTER 2   HUMANS AS SPATIAL ANIMALS   21

The Meaning of Place   22

Territorial Behavior in Animals   23

Territorial Diversity in Humans   25

The Nature of the Environment-Behavior Relationship   28

Basic Spatial Needs in Humans   31

Conclusion   41

CHAPTER 3   THE ECOLOGY OF EVERYDAY URBAN LIFE   42

Micro Environments   44

Macro Environments: Cities as Unique Environments for Living   51
The Dimensions of the Urban Mosaic   56
Capitalism and Landscapes of Hazard and Despair   64
How Spatial Structures Affect Our Choices:
   A Constrained-Choice Approach   68
Conclusion   78

CHAPTER 4   THE SOCIOLOGY OF HEALTH   79
The Healthy Society   80
Health Beliefs   83
Health Lifestyles   85
Risk and Protective Factors   88
Psychosocial Resources   91
Neighborhood Disadvantage and the Ecology of Health   95
Conclusion   100

CHAPTER 5   CITIES AS MOSAICS OF RISK AND
             PROTECTION   102
Physical Hazards and Risks in the Residential Environment   104
Sociocultural Hazards and Risks in the Residential Environment   106
Blankets of Protection   108
Physical and Mental Health Consequences for the Urban Dweller   119
Conclusion   123

CHAPTER 6   HEALTH RISKS AMONG SPECIAL
             POPULATIONS IN THE CITY   125
The Homeless   126
Risk and Hazard among the Homeless   127
Health among the Homeless   129
Racial and Ethnic Minorities   130
Theories of the Underclass   131
Context and Health Differences   133
Needs and Health Risks of the Young and Old   136

Youth at Risk 137

Elders at Risk: Physical and Mental Health Aspects of Aging 146

Conclusion 152

CHAPTER 7 PROMOTING HEALTH: PLACE-BASED
SOLUTIONS TO PLACE-BASED PROBLEMS 153

Removal Strategies 159

Community Development Strategies 164

Healthy Places: Building a Healthier America Programs 184

Planning for the Future: Minimizing the Urban Health Penalty 187

REFERENCES 189

INDEX 223

PREFACE

Unhealthy Cities offers new insight into understanding the complex relationship between place and health. Our first book, a decade ago, forged new ground by bringing together a then rather scattered literature documenting place-based effects on health, in a theoretically and policy-relevant manuscript. Now with an up-to-date, focused examination of the city and its high-poverty ghettos, we revisit and reexamine this complicated relationship using the latest theory and research. We are convinced that until the public's view of health encompasses a basic understanding that where we live affects how we live and die, the health status of certain segments of the population cannot improve. Our physical address may be the single most important health-related number that our doctor needs to know.

Unhealthy Cities is an excellent teaching and research resource. The comprehensive bibliography serves both the student and instructor as they explore the issues of health and place in greater detail. Whether interested in environmental justice, the place-based effects on youth and elderly, homelessness or housing design, *Unhealthy Cities*, unlike any other book, provides the reader with a thematically consistent, theoretically and empirically up-to-date, and comprehensive examination of the place–health relationship. *Unhealthy Cities* should prove a valuable resource in both undergraduate and graduate courses in urban sociology, public health, medical sociology, urban planning, and environmental studies.

The chapters detail both historical and current literatures that provide new insight into an old problem—how understanding the ecology of cities helps us to understand the well-being of urban residents. We argue that a place-based approach to health is a promising perspective from which to address significant health disparities and plan for the healthy society—a major objective in the federal government's health goals for the new millennium. Without a comprehensive place-based strategy to address the health needs of the at-risk, underserved, and unprotected in the urban core, America will continue to be a society plagued by the contradiction of great wealth and mediocre health. From the first chapter documenting the significance of place for health to the final chapter outlining place-based solutions, this book serves as a useful guide for students and researchers alike.

ACKNOWLEDGMENTS

This book represents the outgrowth of our first book, *Unhealthy Places*, which started to take shape nearly twenty years ago. Since then an extremely fruitful and vibrant professional and personal relationship has evolved, enabling this project to be both enjoyable and intellectually satisfying.

We acknowledge the support, assistance, insight, criticism, and thoughtful reflection of several people and organizations important to the development of this project. We would like to thank the University of Arkansas, Fulbright College of Arts and Sciences, and the Department of Sociology and Criminal Justice, and the University of Alabama at Birmingham, School of Social and Behavioral Sciences, and the Department of Sociology for creating the intellectual environments that make writing a book like this so much easier.

We would like to extend a special thanks to our research assistants, Anne Kearney and Wendie Choudary, for their help throughout various phases of this project. In addition, we would like to express our appreciation to the staff at Taylor & Francis/Routledge, our editor, Stephen Rutter, and editorial assistant, Leah Babb-Rosenfeld, for making what seemed like a monumental task a doable one.

Finally, we would like to single out and thank our wives, Mary and Mary Sue, for the many roles they play, their encouragement, and their love and support, without which this project would not have been possible.

ABBREVIATIONS

CPH   Congregations for Public Health
HCP   Healthy Cities Project
HLM   hierarchical linear modeling
HUD   Housing and Urban Development
MSA   Metropolitan Statistical Area
MTO   Moving to Opportunity
OSAP   Office of Substance Abuse Prevention
SAD   seasonal affective disorder
SBC   school-based clinic
SES   socioeconomic status
STI   sexually transmitted infection
VOC   volatile organic compound

THE IMPORTANCE OF PLACE

Like those of other living things, our structure, development, and behavior arise from a genetic foundation sunk in an environmental context. Yet while we readily accept that a healthy seed can't grow into a plant without the right soil, air, light and water, and that a feral dog won't behave like a pet, we resist recognizing the importance of environment in our own lives.

Winifred Gallagher

Flames leaped 200 feet into the air. A thick pillar of black smoke loomed over Birmingham, Alabama, on October 2, 1997 as a fire, punctuated by a series of explosions, consumed a large downtown warehouse complex. The warehouse, which burned for three days, contained heavy concentrations of hazardous chemicals. A 15-square-block area near the warehouse was evacuated because of the health risks. Hours after the fire started, ash continued to rain down from the sky onto pedestrians. Millions of gallons of water used to douse the fire flooded the sewer system and washed into Village Creek, a stream that periodically floods low-income neighborhoods on the western side of Birmingham, near the downtown.

Uncertainty surrounding the dangers posed by the fire and by pollutants released into the air and water continued for nearly a week after the fire began. Initially, state and county officials denied that hazardous materials had leaked from the warehouse. As early as the day after the fire's start, however, newspapers reported that nearly 5,000 gallons of a highly concentrated form of Dursban (80 times the over-the-counter concentration) had been released into the water and air. Dursban is an organophosphate pesticide, a low-level nerve agent, known to cause health problems ranging from birth defects, chronic headaches and neuromuscular pain, short-term memory loss, nausea and vomiting, and breathing problems, to a condition known as multiple chemical sensitivity (U.S. Environmental Protection Agency 1997). Concerns over the safety of Dursban raised by the Environmental Protection Agency (EPA) led its manufacturer, Dow Chemical, to voluntarily restrict its marketing and revise instructions for application and use.

In the first few days after the fire began, residents living in the low-income, mainly African American neighborhoods near Village Creek reported smelling noxious fumes and experiencing a variety of physical symptoms including headaches and nausea. Dying fish and other signs of serious environmental problems were noticed in the stream that flows through their neighborhoods. It took almost a week, however, before any official response to residents' complaints. Six days after the fire, "no fishing" signs were posted, the Alabama Department of Environmental Management finally released test results on water and air samples. By then, the seriousness of the contamination was obvious. Village Creek had become a flowing stream of dead, rotting fish. Residents living along the creek complained to EPA lawyers about the slow response of local officials to their concerns. They believed that the spill would have been taken more seriously if the damage had occurred in a better-off neighborhood where residents were White. Indeed, it was only after the polluted waters began to wreak devastation further downstream, near those better-off residential areas, that more serious measures were taken. A temporary filtration dam was built to protect these areas from pollutants, but it failed. In a span of three weeks, almost 30 miles of waterway near residential areas were contaminated and hundreds of thousands of fish killed. The first legal actions were taken only after pollution began to wash ashore near higher-income, mostly White residential areas. Civil suits were filed on behalf of local residents in two of these areas (a residential area near Bay View Lake and one near the Black Warrior River).

These suits raised concerns about damage to the water supply and housing values.

Six months after the fire and the largest Dursban spill in history, contamination levels in some areas remained high, although the waterways showed signs of a slow recovery. While a number of reports of medical problems connected with Dursban poisoning have been received by the County Health Department, little is known about the long-term public health consequences of the spill. Blood samples taken from residents along Village Creek were lost, with few repercussions. Despite media coverage, surprisingly little consideration has been given to the mental or physical health consequences of the event in the Village Creek area. This spill represented a dramatic ecological event, but it was only one instance in a long history of environmental problems. Village Creek is a dumping ground for industrial waste, prone to other environmental problems such as periodic flooding. Residence here is stressful and dangerous.

The natural history of this disaster reflects a larger public health issue in the United States that continues to be pervasive in America's central cities. Persons living in neighborhoods with large concentrations of poor minorities are exposed to serious physical and mental health risks (Andrulis 1997; Charles 2003; Conrad 2009; Corburn 2009; Kawachi and Berkman 2003; Williams and Collins 2001). With limited resources to address these risks, residents have found existing agencies incapable or unwilling to deal with the wide range of problems encountered. Risky environments are not usually the ones where politically effective responses occur or where the greatest public efforts are made to address the problem. Yet, in this ineffective response to serious health needs, the health and well-being of the greater whole is affected. As Dr. Martin Luther King Jr. once reminded us: "Of all the forms of inequality, injustice in health is the most shocking and the most inhumane."

Place Matters

Place is a key element in our identity. Who we are is reflected in the places we occupy and the spaces we control. These places range from nation to region, state, metropolitan area, community, neighborhood, block, and residential dwelling. Each location has profound social meaning for us, and in a literal sense defines not only who we are, but also how we live and die. Despite the evolution of cyberspace technologies capable of transforming "theres" into "heres," residence continues to have dramatic consequences for individual health and well-being. The prevalence and incidence of risks for a variety of physical and mental health conditions within metropolitan areas range widely by residential area. Most notably, life and death experiences in the inner city are more similar to those living in the Third World than to the experience of suburbanites living just a few miles away (Geronimus et al. 2001). Perhaps the most notorious examples of this situation are the neighborhoods of Harlem in New York City and Roxbury in Boston. Mortality rates in these places for Black men under 65 are more than double the rates of U.S. Whites and 50 percent higher than the rates for all U.S. Blacks (McCord and Freeman 1990, 2009).

For certain segments of the population, being in the wrong place is not a matter of timing or accident, *but rather a function of the social structure.* The places we live, work, and play are fundamental resources, like time or money. The access we have to these resources dramatically affects our well-being. All human beings live in a spatial world where everything and everybody has its place. Everyday lives are spatially structured. At the heart of this structure is a simple fact—there is distance between ourselves and the other actors and objects in our environment. To satisfy basic needs and interests we must either find ways of getting objects or actors we are interested in to come to us, or find ways of getting to them. Hence, where people live is of great importance.

Place matters in the contemporary world, but for different reasons than in the past. Our ancestors were place-bound by necessity. Indeed, for most of human life on earth we lived as hunters and gatherers, living off the land in small bands so isolated from each other that strangers were met with great suspicion and alarm.

Dramatic technological revolutions eroded this isolation in ever intensifying waves of change—first, an agricultural revolution 10,000 years ago, then an industrial-urban revolution 9,700 years later. During this vast period of time, the spatial horizons of people broadened as transportation and communication technologies improved, trade expanded, and cities attracted large numbers of culturally heterogeneous populations. We are now in the midst of an information revolution. This third wave of change is technically capable of ending the isolation between people; yet spatial barriers persist in highly segregated cities with distinct inner-city and outer-city areas. Thus, as we progress through a new millennium, space is redefined and reshaped, and for some takes on heightened significance.

The enduring significance of place is truly remarkable, for technologies now exist to move people and resources vast distances in very short times, while information can be transported almost instantaneously to the most remote regions of the world. Distant places have attained a kind of "hereness" that was unimaginable just a century ago. Marshall McLuhan (1965) describes this new world as a "global village," but this place has a more distant potential for certain segments of the population. Indeed, when surveying the urban geography, with its vast neighborhood differentials in health risks, the more appropriate spatial analogy may be that of an expanding universe of places moving farther away from each other, rather than closer.

There is good news and bad news contained in the reality of evolutionary trends. While technological developments in transportation, communication, and information processing give humans new capacities to break down spatial barriers, a socially structured spatial environment produces new barriers. These structures are the modern-day equivalent of the medieval city's walls—separating portions of society from one another and preserving vast differences in levels of living and overall well-being. Awareness of the impact of these invisible barriers for the health and well-being of large numbers in our society may make it possible to develop programs to alleviate this spatial penalty. As Melvin Webber has suggested (1964), we have the technological capacity to live in a "non-place urban realm" where the friction of distance is minimized. At present, however, we live in a bifurcated world of possibility and actuality. There is the potential for a non-place urban realm, but at the same time there is the reality of a highly segregated city perpetuating an ecology of disadvantage.

Why an Urban, Place-Based Approach to Health?

There is an ecology of disadvantage in America, and one of its most significant outcomes is the "urban health penalty" (Greenberg 1991). This penalty is important to understand for several reasons. First, we live in an urban society. While a century ago only 25 percent of the population resided in urban areas, now three-fourths live in a metropolitan area consisting of one or more principal cities and a ring of suburbs. Second, experts generally agree that the single most important global environmental influence in this century is the process of urbanization itself (Gallagher 1993). A majority of the world's population now lives in cities, and in the next three decades nearly three-fourths of the world is likely to be urban (Galea et al. 2005; Mercado et al. 2007). The impact on the ecosystem of such an event is potentially serious, with dramatic increases in pollution, consumption of non-renewable resources and irretrievable losses of millions of known and unknown animal and plant species (Meadows et al. 1972). Third, the city is a distinct social environment that over time has accentuated great inequities between peoples. Within its boundaries dramatic variation exists in material wealth, personal well-being, and overall quality of life. Finally, the city is an artificially constructed environment, an "intentional" or "built" environment, and thus it can be re-engineered to promote more desirable health outcomes. Unlike natural disasters, the disasters befalling some of our inner cities are preventable.

Data on the largest cities in the United States (Andrulis 1997; Benbow 2007) suggest the health costs of urban residence. Among the most striking observations are:

- The murder rate in America's large cities is more than 2½ times the national average.
- The infant mortality rate in large cities is 25 percent higher than the U.S. average.
- Of the 880 most disadvantaged neighborhoods identified by the Child Welfare League, 99 percent were located in cities.
- Forty percent of urban children live below the poverty level.
- The HIV mortality rate is over 3 times higher in large cities.

- The incidence rate for tuberculosis in large cities is 2¼ times the national average.
- The mortality rates for cancer, heart disease, and diabetes are considerably higher in the nation's large cities.

The health problems of urban residents are most severe in the inner city and some of the city's aging suburbs. Here the circumstances of poverty and minority status are exacerbated by segregation; the spatial concentration of these two characteristics intensifies the disadvantages of low income and minority status. Indeed, the American College of Physicians concludes: "One of the most important characteristics [of the health care challenge] is the interrelationships among health and social and environmental problems. The so-called 'urban health penalty'—the confluence of circumstances such as poor nutrition, poverty and unemployment with deteriorating housing, violence and loss of services—has created a deepening health crisis in the inner city." A medical approach, in other words, can no longer be sufficient to reduce the differentials that exist in American health because health risks are spatially and socially structured. Indeed, there is growing realization within medicine and public health that societal forces shape and create the disease patterns experienced by a society, and that successful health interventions require addressing the social factors that produce them (Cockerham 2007; Link 2008). Place is a critical social factor.

While the concepts of place and environment are essential to understanding physical and mental health outcomes in society, they are broad, multidimensional constructs. Place can be defined as a portion of space regarded as measured off or distinct from other spaces. It can be conceptualized as a position or location in space. The environment can be thought of as the totality of surrounding conditions, as an area in which something exists. Both concepts imply a force, which is more than physical in character. As an environment, a place can be seen as a container whose characteristics derive primarily from what is contained within its recognized boundaries. These contents involve physical, cultural, and social components.

As a point or portion of space, spatial coordinates can define a place, and hence it has physical qualities. But it is also a space, which is socially, culturally, economically, politically, and psychologically defined. The places occupied by individuals are thus not just physical entities characterized by physical positions in space or by the characteristics of those elements contained within the spaces. They are also mental constructs, psychologically defined by individuals who occupy certain social positions and possess a particular set of cultural values. Each person carries around a set of mental maps that are a product of personal experiences, cultural stereotypes, preferences, and objective information. We live in personal worlds, so that the very same places may be understood and defined very differently by persons with different sociocultural backgrounds and personal experiences. One person's heaven may be another's hell. Understanding the relationship between environment and health thus requires a careful analysis of environments in all their complexity, for place is a multidimensional construct.

Ghetto Poverty Tracts: A Definition

This book deals with the impact of place on health, specifically poor urban neighborhoods and their importance for residents' health. The term *inner city* is used frequently in both the popular and scientific literature on urban areas, yet that concept is deceptive because not all poor urban neighborhoods are centrally located; metropolitan poverty is sometimes concentrated in aging suburbs. Perhaps the closest thing to a formal designation for the spatial concentration of poverty is contained in the work of urban researchers such as Wilson (1996) or Jargowsky and Bane (1991), who use U.S. census data to designate "ghetto poverty census tracts." Ghetto poverty areas are census tracts within Metropolitan Statistical Areas (MSA) where the household incomes of at least 40 percent of residents are below the poverty line. Researchers have noted several significant trends in these ghetto areas over the last four decades: (1) the number of ghetto areas more than doubled during the 1970s and 1980s; (2) the ratio of poor to non-poor in ghetto areas increased dramatically; (3) the African American presence in ghetto tracts grew substantially; (4) while these trends tended to reverse themselves in the

1990s, they began to re-escalate in the first decade of the twenty-first century (Jargowsky 2003; Kneebone and Berube 2008; Wilson 1996). Today, nearly half of metropolitan-area Blacks live in ghetto tracts that increasingly isolate the metropolitan Black poor from Whites and non-poor Blacks.

While there is considerable debate over the issue (Massey and Denton 1993), Wilson (1980, 1987, 1996) believes that the growing concentration of Black poor in ghetto tracts represents a new trend in urban minority poverty. Wilson argues that the recent trends in ghetto poverty tracts are more than just an outgrowth of the processes of racial and class segregation. He believes that as jobs left the central city during the 1970s and 1980s, so did non-poor Blacks, and as jobs and middle-class Blacks left, both the ghetto economy and ghetto community collapsed. He contends that the current concentration of minority poor occurs faster and for different reasons. In the past, ghettos and slums, while products of dramatic racial segregation, were more organizationally stable because they contained a wide range of economic institutions and a sizable population of non-poor who served in positions of leadership in the community.

> Though they may have lived on different streets, blacks of all classes in inner-city areas . . . lived in the same community and shopped at the same stores. Their children went to the same schools and played in the same parks. Although there was some class antagonism, their neighborhoods were more stable than the inner-city neighborhoods of today; in short, they featured higher levels of what social scientists call "social organization."
>
> (Wilson 1996:20)

While Wilson uses the concept *inner city* to describe concentrated urban minority poverty, *ghetto poverty tract* is more technically accurate and so we choose to use the latter term.

Place as Life Chance and Risk

Every place we live in has certain levels of *hazard* and *risk* associated with its various social, cultural, and physical components. A hazard is a situation that, under particular circumstances, could lead to damage or harm to a human being or a population. It is thus a collection of situations and circumstances. An example might be the situation of a curving, deteriorating road, which, under the circumstances of heavy traffic and light rain, could result in a multicar accident. Or in the case of the Birmingham warehouse fire, the situation was an unprotected stream, Village Creek, which frequently received runoff from the industries located around it. The circumstances which, in combination with this situation, led to the potential for serious environmental damage and human loss were: (1) a warehouse without adequate fire safety features, (2) heavy concentrations of dangerous chemicals stored in that warehouse, and (3) a metropolitan area and state with an ill-prepared emergency response team. Risk is defined as: "the probability of damage or harm in a specified period [and place]" (Royal Society Study Group 1992:3). In essence, risk is the likelihood of a hazard causing harm to an individual or population.

Beck (1995) has argued that risk and hazard are of particular importance in advanced modern societies ("risk societies") where a system of rules has developed to deal with industrially produced risks and insecurities. The calculus of risk, developed in the work of physical scientists, engineers, and public health professionals, has become the "mathematical morality of the technological age." In this form of reckoning, the risk of a decision or activity is calculated as a mathematical probability and is no longer defined as potential harm to individual human beings. That is, risks are borne by a population rather than by individuals. After scientists calculate risks, they are judged to be either more or less acceptable, and strategies are devised to contain risk within some acceptable range.

Once risks are established, a series of protections can theoretically be devised to reduce the probabilities of harm or loss attached to certain decisions and the circumstances that surround them. In an advanced, high technology society such risks can be very high. Some people will be more affected by the growth of these risks than others; that is, what Beck (1995) calls "social risk positions" develop which follow the inequalities of place and class standing. In the "risk society," levels of hazard and risk are differentially distributed in the urban landscape, and the distribution of risk and hazard in turn differentially affects health outcomes. Each level of residential place from nation to region, state, metropolitan area, community, neighborhood, block, and dwelling can be assessed in terms of health risks and hazards.

Places are environments consisting of physical, cultural, political, economic, and social components, with each component contributing in complex ways to the differential risks experienced by a population. At one level, place can be seen as a means of objectifying the complex set of risks that come together to affect a population's health—in short, a method for reporting health risk data. But it is clearly more than just a unit by which the health of a population can be reported and analyzed. Place is a meaningful unit, not simply because a population uses various places as the stage on which to carry out its behaviors and actions, but because the stage (or place) itself shapes these actions and experiences. We are who we are, and we experience what we do on a daily basis in part because of where we find ourselves. Our physical and mental health is a product of not only how we live, but also where we live.

Environments are *risk spaces*. The most obvious place-based health risks are associated with physical aspects of an environment. These include such things as harmful chemical agents, pollutants, viruses, and bacteria contained in a local space as well as the quality and arrangement of built and natural physical features in a place (architecture, building deterioration, building materials, paint, landscape, etc.) that may present seen and unseen hazards for the occupants. But places also contain psychological and social risks as well. Some areas are decidedly more stressful, with too much noise, too many people, or just an overload of stimuli. Other places expose individuals to strangers where interactions are less secure and predictable, or to situations where hostile, aggressive interactions are possible. In many cases, the risks associated with place are heavily concentrated in just a few areas. Not surprisingly, such areas tend to occur where residents are least equipped to respond to the challenges imposed by place—such as Village Creek in Birmingham, the Roxbury area of Boston, or New York's Harlem.

Place as Social Resource

Just as the areas of a city can be viewed as risk spaces containing differing levels of hazard, cities are *resource spaces* where the goods and services capable of protecting inhabitants from harm are also differentially distributed. That is, cities have a topography both of risk and of protection. This topography, as Beck (1995) notes, tends to follow the shape and structure of the larger society, with the most visible distinctions occurring at the opposite ends of the system of stratification. Each metropolitan area reflects the contours of the society, with risk heavily concentrated in the inner zones of the metropolis where there are significant concentrations of low-income, underemployed minorities. At the same time, protection from risk, in terms of availability of health professionals, community resources, and supportive social networks, tends to be inversely related to risk and risk locations. These are not merely matters of material differences between people but reflect a larger fabric of inequality only partially related to income. This inequality has become more obvious as the geography of inequality has become more apparent in America's cities. Historically, slums were so successfully hidden from the daily activities of middle-class consumers of the city space that they seemed non-existent. Indeed, the term *slum* is believed to derive from the word *slumber*, because slums were composed of "unknown, back streets or alleys, wrongly presumed to be sleeping or quiet" (Partridge 1958). While patterns of residential segregation still permit most metropolitan residents to avoid slums on a daily basis, the geographical spread of the high-poverty ghetto and its multiplicity of problems make such places hard to ignore. They are certainly not sleeping or quiet, and the long-term implications of such concentrated risk for the society as a whole are significant.

Wilson (1996), in his discussion of the inner city, notes a substantial change in the character of the areas where minority poverty concentrates. Lower levels of "social organization" characterize the inner-city neighborhoods of today. He notes several optimal dimensions of neighborhood social organization: (1) the prevalence, strength, and interlocking of social networks; (2) the degree to which neighbors take personal responsibility for neighborhood problems; (3) the extent of surveillance done by neighbors; and (4) the degree of participation in formal and voluntary organizations tied to the neighborhood and to the larger community. Social organization in this sense is a critical protection against hazard and risk. Areas where there is a concentration of weak social networks, limited feelings of personal responsibility for neighbors, low levels of surveillance, and limited participation in the institutional network of the community are also areas where vulnerability to the risk of environmental *hazard* is concentrated. This susceptibility to risk becomes all the more important in areas with limited economic and political resources and high levels of *hazard* to begin with. The risks themselves are cumulative; that is, the hazardous nature of a given environmental circumstance intensifies under the absence of protection. Strong organizational structures in an area can serve as a form of inoculation against stress and ill health. Neighborhood context can promote a culture of vigilance and responsibility that mitigates against local hazards and risk, while at the same time empowering individuals to take action against the hazards present in local spaces.

Place is a force in the lives and health of a population apart from the individuals and risks associated with that place; it is a real factor in personal well-being. Individual choices and actions take place in spaces which in turn shape and structure those choices and actions. Places are the stages upon which social and cultural forces in the larger society affect individuals. In this sense, the spatial division between high-poverty ghetto areas and the rest of the metropolis is a reflection of the U.S. society's structure itself; the spatial distance between populations reflects their social distance, their position within the larger society (LaGory and Pipkin 1981). The existence of the high-poverty ghetto is geographic testimony to the dramatic socioeconomic divide that persists between certain minority groups (most notably African Americans and Hispanics) and mainstream America. Cities from their very origins were founded on differences, just as the societies, which contained them, involved a system of stratification. In preindustrial cities, these differences were primarily between the urban resident and the peasants. Walls were erected to regulate access to the city's resources and to protect the system of differences that prevailed in society. The social distance between citizen and peasant was dramatically symbolized and reinforced by the city walls. The contemporary city is heterogeneous, yet real barriers exist between residents.

The contemporary city's walls are not like the physical structures of the preindustrial city, but there are real physical and mentally constructed barriers between the populations that reside there. The barriers are reflected in pervasive patterns of segregation, with those groups at the bottom of the social system most highly segregated from others. As groups assimilate into the larger society they are less likely to be concentrated in certain areas and tend to disperse across the urban landscape. This does not mean, however, that minority groups, which scatter across the metropolis, are any less likely to be segregated. For example, while middle-class African Americans have dispersed spatially, they remain highly segregated from Whites. Indeed the most significant feature of U.S. residential patterns in the last 60 years has been the concentration of Blacks in central cities and Whites in suburbs (Booza et al. 2006; Charles 2003; Massey and Denton 1993). While Black suburbanization has occurred, only a small percentage of Blacks live in suburbs, and most of those live in highly segregated, older suburbs.

Segregation is a powerful spatial force protecting the status quo and separating groups from one another. Highly segregated groups find themselves isolated from the organizational structures and resources necessary to promote health and well-being (Mitchell and LaGory 2002). Thus, segregation ensures that neighborhoods with limited resources for protection against risk will be particularly vulnerable, since their isolation restricts their access to the range of resources available in the larger community. Places with weak social organization that are also highly segregated promote an existence very different from the rest of the society. This type of segregation creates walls as real and impermeable as those in ancient preindustrial cities.

Insularity is likely to promote cultural differences across the urban landscape as well. Places in which outside contact is restricted become fertile ground for the promotion of subcultures and lifestyles associated with high-risk behaviors. There is strong evidence that pursuing a healthy lifestyle can enhance health and life expectancy (Cockerham 2007). It is also well known that certain lifestyles have negative health consequences. Unprotected sex, promiscuous sexuality, and intravenous drug use increase the risk of contracting AIDS. Smoking is linked to lung cancer and heart disease, alcoholism to cirrhosis of the liver. Participation in gangs increases the exposure to violence and risk of physical injury, while high-fat diets accelerate the risk of heart disease and atherosclerosis. Segregation may be linked to the promotion of unhealthy lifestyles by creating the conditions in which access to mainstream role models is highly constrained and access to deviant institutions and deviant subculture is intensified. In criminology, differential association theory (Sutherland and Cressey 1960; Taylor 1988) suggests that individuals develop deviant lifestyles because of their exposure to certain contexts. Certain lifestyles, in other words, are more likely to be learned because individuals in highly segregated settings experience greater exposure to deviant subcultures and greater isolation from more traditional health lifestyles.

Besides promoting subcultural differences in health lifestyles, segregation can enhance the negative circumstances of already stressful high-poverty environments. Since the mental well-being of individuals undergoing stress is in part a function of their social resources, it stands to reason that the range of these resources will have an impact on health. People living in spatially constrained communities have spatially constrained support systems, and hence may be more likely to experience the negative consequences of stress (Haines and Hurlbert 1992).

The Multidimensional Nature of Place

The neighborhood is an important place for the provision of protection against risk, and much of our discussion focuses on that spatial level. Aspects of protection and risk, however, manifest themselves in a variety of environmental layers. These layers range from the home, to the neighborhood, the community, the metropolitan area, region, nation, and globe. Place is a multidimensional, hierarchical phenomenon. All human action occurs in space, but this space is more than a physical container; it is a social and cultural phenomenon as well. Barker (1967) portrays places as "behavior settings." A behavior setting is bounded in space and time and possesses a structure that interrelates physical, social, and cultural properties in a particular way so that certain patterns of behavior are likely to be elicited. Place involves far more than a physical setting. While a place's character is a function of physical qualities, it is also a product of risks and opportunities, the nature of the social organization attached to the locale, its political, social, and economic relationships with other places, the psychosocial characteristics of the individuals occupying the space, and the local cultural milieu. We learn to act in specific ways in certain places; we don't genuflect in bars or drink beer or eat popcorn in churches. Hence, our actions in various places are conditioned by a number of factors, all of which may operate on the individual to affect not only their behavior, but also their health. This relationship between place and health has not been adequately explored. Its importance, however, is undeniable. The complexity of this relationship is equally indisputable. Places are more than spaces. They are both real geographic units with physical, social, and cultural properties as well as personally defined places—both aspects of place matter for health.

A Framework for the Book

As our discussion suggests, residential areas are more than a simple reflection of the existing system of inequality. Place, and the process of segregation that creates it, actually plays a role in the health and well-being of its occupants. The purpose of this book is to understand that role. In doing this, we explore the nature of residential space, with our focus on the high-poverty ghetto and the impact it has on individual and social life. At the same time, we review existing social science theories of health and suggest how they might be incorporated into a broader understanding of the ecology of health and its implications for the "urban health penalty."

The Birmingham case study, introduced at the beginning of this chapter, is not an isolated event. It is evidence of a recurring theme in American public health that reminds us of the power of place. While the

Village Creek Dursban spill received considerable media attention, it is but one episode in a more complicated daily drama reproduced across many American high-poverty neighborhoods. Over the past several decades, poverty has become a distinctly urban problem with growing numbers of very poor minority neighborhoods bearing the burden of the "risk society." Throughout the book we link specific aspects of this trend with broader themes of place and health contained in the chapters.

Chapters 2 and 3 discuss general issues related to human territory and the organization of residential space. Chapter 2 addresses the question of territorial behavior in humans. In what sense are humans ecological actors? Since all human thought and action takes place in physical and social contexts, how do the socially ordered spaces in which we reside affect human thought and action? Do humans have basic spatial needs?

Chapter 3 introduces the reader to the importance of space for everyday urban life, exploring both micro and macro environments. It begins with a discussion of how various features of the built environment shape our experiences. Winston Churchill observed that once we have built our buildings they begin to shape us. What features of architectured spaces affect us, and how does the design of residential space relate to the nature of individuals contained within it? Are there such things as "healthy" and "unhealthy" buildings, and if so, what features distinguish them from one another?

Considering the macro environment, what features of the city differentiate it from other residential areas? We detail these basic dimensions of the urban residential space, which include segregation, density, size, and opportunity. In addition, we show how the social sciences describe the city's basic structure and form, and the pattern of health resources made available to different subgroups within the city. Finally, this chapter also examines how the urban structure influences choice and action for the average resident.

Chapter 4 provides an overview of the major social science models of health: health beliefs, health lifestyles, risk and protective factors, psychosocial resources, and neighborhood disadvantage. These models represent current understanding of the possible social influences on health. While each model has the potential to provide insight into the role of context on health outcomes, only the urban disadvantage perspective has explicitly looked at the role of context on health. To detail the consequences of spatial structure for physical and mental health, we explore the following: (1) the relationship between place variables and various aspects of culture, including health beliefs and health lifestyles; (2) the relationship between place and an individual's access to health resources; (3) the impact of place on risky circumstances; (4) a place's influence on social networks and supports, and an individual's access to protection against risk; and (5) the confluence of neighborhood physical and social deterioration and its impact on behavior and important health risk outcomes. In so doing, we develop a synthetic model of the ecology of health. This chapter provides the springboard for developing a place-based understanding of the health disparities that exist among persons living in highly developed urbanized societies.

Chapters 5 and 6 take the synthetic theory developed in the previous chapter and apply it to specific health-related issues for high-poverty ghetto populations. Beginning with Chapter 5, we review an extensive empirical literature that shows the city to be a mosaic of risks and protection. Typically, the risk and protective factors model has been used to explain health-compromising behaviors among adolescents; here we explore its applicability to a variety of other subpopulations. Chapter 5 begins with a discussion of the physical and sociocultural aspects of risk and their consequences for urban residents. In addition, we consider the role of informal networks and formal services in providing a layer of protection, particularly for those residents who lack the full range of resources available to the average citizen. Specific physical and mental health outcomes are inventoried as consequences of the risk-laden circumstances present in the high-poverty ghetto. This inventory of health outcomes is applied to a set of special at-risk populations in the following chapter.

Chapter 6 examines the needs and risks of the socially disadvantaged. It begins with an exploration of the work of Wilkinson (1996) on the role that social inequality plays in the general health and well-being of populations in highly developed societies. Wilkinson shows that the least-healthy developed societies are those with the widest gaps between the advantaged and disadvantaged, and those with the greatest sociocultural separations between groups. To show how this relationship plays out in the residential areas of American society, we look at two special populations—the homeless and racial and ethnic minorities. The homeless are a particularly important population to consider when studying the ecology of health. They are by definition persons without place. The absence of place, and more particularly control over residential space, has specific physical and mental health consequences. In addition, we look at the so-called underclass from various theoretical perspectives, showing how segregation intensifies their disadvantaged status, and then showing the role that high-poverty ghetto areas play in promoting specific health outcomes related to health beliefs, lifestyles, and risks and protections.

In a later section of Chapter 6, age-related at-risk populations are identified at the two extremes of the life cycle—the young and the old. We first describe characteristics of the young and the old as ecological actors, suggesting the significance these characteristics have for an ecology of health. Both groups find their access to places somewhat constrained by their location in the age stratification system. The discussion of youth focuses on the impact that growing up in the high-poverty ghetto has on development, and the particular physical and mental health challenges associated with residence in such places. We explore the qualities of the individual and the social network necessary for resilience in this challenging environment.

For elders, place is imbued with great meaning, so that social psychological factors such as place memories, perceived risk and fear, neighborhood satisfaction, and mental maps can play an important role in healthy aging. The impact of age segregation on health is a particular focus. Segregation by age in urban areas structures risk and protection and shapes the role these two factors play in the health of place-bound elders.

Chapter 7 concludes by proposing an ecological strategy for health promotion in the high-poverty ghetto. We begin by suggesting that the literature on context-based health effects could leave readers with a misunderstanding of the most appropriate health promotion policy. This literature routinely concludes that while there is a contextual effect on health, individual-level effects, in the form of health beliefs, risk-taking behaviors, genetic predisposition, and so on, are considerably stronger. Although these conclusions are accurate, they have the potential of misdirecting health policy. The fact that individual-level effects are stronger by no means implies that individual-based strategies are the most effective ways to promote health and deliver services in the urban area. Well-designed place-based approaches to health can serve the dual purpose of promoting healthy places, while also efficiently delivering information and services to high-risk individuals.

We believe that a place-based approach to health is a promising perspective from which to address significant health disparities and plan for the healthy society—a major objective in the federal government's health goals for the new millennium (U.S. Department of Health and Human Services 2000). Without a comprehensive place-based strategy to address the health needs of the at-risk, underserved, and unprotected in the urban core, America will continue to be a society plagued by the contradiction of great wealth and mediocre health.

In this final chapter, we review two types of strategies for addressing place-based problems—removal strategies and community development strategies. We conclude that comprehensive community-based approaches to health are likely to be most successful, and we urge that they be local efforts based on the federal model of the demonstration research and evaluation programs. These community-oriented strategies should invite significant local participation and target the special risks and hazards facing residents while also seeking to identify those individual characteristics that promote resilience.

2

HUMANS AS SPATIAL ANIMALS

Good fences make good neighbors.

Robert Frost

Human existence is about living in the space we fill. Human existence is about granting and denying the same sort of space to others around us.

Peter Petschauer

Residents along Village Creek are conscious of the threat posed to their health and well-being by living there, yet this dangerous place is home and thus has deep significance for them. Perhaps no single inhabitant of the Village Creek area was better known than the acclaimed African American folk artist Lonnie Holley, whose works have been displayed at the White House, the Smithsonian, and numerous art galleries and museums around the Southeast. The saga of Holley's struggle to keep his residence is a strong reminder of the meaning of place. Holley lived for 18 years with his family on a quarter acre tract along Village Creek, near the Birmingham airport. During that time he created an "art environment," taking found objects, assembling them into works of art, and then integrating them into the landscape. To some observers his land resembled a junkyard more than a home or studio. For Holley the link between art, territory, and family heritage involved a deep expression of personal identity—a view familiar to sociobiologists who see a profound link between territory and human nature (Eibl-Eibesfeldt 1989; Wilson 1975).

His rights to this heritage were challenged when the Birmingham International Airport Authority decided to expand airport runways on land adjacent to Village Creek. After a long legal battle Holley was forced to move. With the process played out in public, the artist was able to demonstrate place's significance for self-identity. He endured threats from local officials who not only attempted to seize his property but publicly encouraged poachers to take any "salvageable material" they found on his land. All the while, Holley fought back by explaining the value of his property in human and personal terms to anyone who would listen. Holley was eventually forced to relocate, but in the process people in the Birmingham area were reminded of the deep personal significance this place held for him. As compensation for the loss of his land, the Airport Authority paid Holley $165,000 for property originally assessed at $14,000.

His new home in a rural area outside of Birmingham is an attractive, eight-bedroom, columned house surrounded by cotton fields. Planes no longer roar overhead as they did at his old place, and his family has more room. By all appearances Holley made out well in his territorial dispute. Yet when asked how he felt about the settlement Holley remarked, "I won't say good, but positive. Things down here are quite different than the way they were. I've got to turn everything around completely in my mind to make it work. It's hard to get adjusted. . . . The other place—I knew the people in the neighborhood. Here I'm like a stranger" (Rochell 1998:M8).

The Meaning of Place

Holley's story is one of many that can be told reflecting the deeply ingrained attachment people have with place. Place is more than the stage on which social actions and experiences are played out; it is more than mere geography. For human beings the significance of space and place runs deep. Indeed, the link between individuals and the places they occupy is deeply tied to human biology and culture. Understanding the biological and cultural heritage that binds us to place is essential to fully appreciate the connection between environment and health.

Humans, like other animals, exist in bounded spatial arenas that affect and are affected by the behavior that takes place within them. The pages of human history are replete with bloody, periodic clashes over territory. These international and national disputes, from Africa to the Middle East, from Northern Ireland to portions of the former Soviet Union, serve as constant reminders of the importance of place in everyday life. Closer to home, in many American cities, groups of youth emblazon their territory with gang symbols and graffiti and wear their colors to signify dominance over an area of the community. During the past decade, gang-related crime has plagued high-poverty neighborhoods and schools in the United States. According to recent estimates there are more than 20,000 criminally active gangs, with a million members, committing as much as 80 percent of the crime in many communities (National Alliance of Gang Investigators Associations 2009).

The striking similarity between these territorial behaviors and behaviors across many vertebrate species has led some observers to claim that humans share an instinctive urge to claim and defend territory (Ardrey 1966; Wilson 1975). Others take exception to this idea and suggest that human territorial behavior is much more complicated and not comparable to the rest of the vertebrate world (Klopfer 1969). Whatever the answer to the question of the nature of human territorial behavior, it is undeniable that place has an important role in our everyday actions, choices, and thoughts. Space is a critical sociological and psychological force and as such affects the quality of our lives. In this chapter we examine the nature of the territory–behavior relationship in human actors.

Territorial Behavior in Animals

Typically the term *territoriality* is used to refer to spatial behaviors directed at the active defense of a territory. In ethology, territorial behavior is thus more than the habitual use of a defined area; it is "behavior characterized by recognition of, use of, and some kind of defensive reaction toward a specific area" (Buettner-Janusch 1973:553). Definitions of *territory* also include this link to defensive actions. E. O. Wilson, for example, defines territory as "an area occupied more or less exclusively by an animal or group of animals by means of repulsion through overt defense or advertisement" (Wilson 1975:256). Robert Ardrey describes it as an area that an animal or group of animals defends as an exclusive property primarily against members of their own species (1966).

When dealing with humans, however, the term reflects a more complex relationship between space and behavior. Here territorial behavior is defined as "habitual use of particular spatial locations" and no specific reference is made to defensive behaviors (Sundstrom and Altman 1974). Taylor (1988) uses the term *territorial functioning* to refer to human territorial behavior. Territorial functioning is "an interlocked system of sentiments, cognitions and behaviors that are highly place specific, socially and culturally determined and maintained, and that represent a class of person-place transactions concerned with issues of setting management, maintenance legibility and expressiveness" (p. 6). He is very clear to note that territorial functioning is highly variable across different communities, although it is also essential to a community's long-term health.

Another type of spatial behavior closely linked to territoriality is *individual distance*—a critical area that surrounds the individual animal like a bubble. Unlike territory, this space is not anchored in place, but moves with the individual. In humans, this distance varies culturally and from one social situation to the next. Hall (1966) argues that there are four individual distance zones in American culture—intimate, personal, social, and public. Intimate social relations take place in a range from actual physical contact to about 18 inches. The behaviors occurring in this zone vary from lovemaking or physical aggression to conversations in which touching is permitted. Personal distance extends from 18 inches to four feet. It is the arena within which personal or so-called primary group relationships occur. It is the normal space for conversation at informal gatherings. Often times the closeness of the tie is reflected by the distance between the interactants. Social distance is the zone in which secondary or more businesslike relationships take place. According to Hall, this varies from 4 to 12 feet. The more impersonal the relationship, the greater the distance between parties. Highly formal ties occur in public distance, where one or more speakers are separated from an audience by large distances. These distances are likely to promote one-way communication.

While humans display territorial behavior, there is no convincing evidence that these behaviors are innate. Humans are cultural animals; culture conditions the human experience of place. As such, it is not likely that a species-specific pattern of behavior linked to territory can be identified; rather, it is more probable that each culture displays different responses to the same behavioral stimuli. While territoriality is a "phylogenetically acquired trait," it manifests itself "in diverse cultural forms dependent upon specific ecological and historical conditions" (Eibl-Eibesfeldt 1989). Thus, it is both genetically and culturally transmitted. The significance of this fact for territorial diversity and the environment–behavior relationship is explored in the rest of this chapter.

Territorial Diversity in Humans

To say that humans are cultural is to assume that our response to spatial stimuli differs from that of other animals. Human relationships with the environment are mediated by symbols and, above all, by language. All of our experiences are interpreted with a socially learned symbol system, and all of our interactions involve symbolic exchange. As W. I. Thomas notes, "If men define situations as real they are real in their consequences" (Volkart 1951:81). That is to say, it is the meanings we attribute to the situation that affect our responses to it, rather than the objective circumstances of the situation itself. The effect of the learned symbol system (culture) on our spatial behavior is threefold: (1) it affects what we experience; (2) it assigns values and preferences to the things we experience; and (3) it creates greater variability in territorial behaviors.

Regarding the effect of culture on experience, we tend to perceive only those aspects of place that we are culturally conditioned to see. Culture acts as a filter, letting through only selected elements of the more complex environment. Language, for example, codes experience into unique meaning categories. The Sapir-Whorf hypothesis suggests that language essentially determines reality for us (Newman 1997). This can affect our understanding of space. The Zulu of South Africa, for example, have no words for squares or rectangles. Their doors, windows, houses and villages are round (Ittelson et al. 1974). Research suggests that they also lack the linear perspective and sense of perpendicularity which others acquire from early childhood (LaGory and Pipkin 1981). Seeing is essentially learned. Colin Turnbull's (1961) account of the "forest people," a group of African Pygmies, provides another example of this. Turnbull took a group of Pygmies out of the forest they occupied to visit a nearby plain for the first time. When they arrived on the plain, herds of buffalo were grazing far in the distance. One of the Pygmies asked Turnbull, "What insects are these?" and refused to believe that they were buffalo. Pygmy culture provided no understanding of perspective.

Besides shaping our experiences, culture also influences our evaluation of these experiences by assigning relative values to spatial encounters. For example, individual distance is highly variable from one culture to another. What might be seen as an invasion of an individual's personal space in one culture could be the distance of everyday interaction in another. Edward Hall (1966) notes the potential for conflict when persons of different cultures occupy the same social space:

> As I waited in the deserted lobby, a stranger walked up to me where I was sitting and stood close enough so that I could not only easily touch him, but I could hear him breathing. . . . If the lobby had been crowded with people I would have understood his behavior, but in an empty lobby his presence made me exceedingly uncomfortable.
>
> (p. 151)

How people feel about their spatial arrangements and the places they occupy matters greatly for their spatial behavior. As Taylor (1988) notes, "How people feel about a location is often reflected in how they act there" (p. 81).

Culture's impact on the experience and evaluation of place suggests that territorial functioning will be highly variable. This is particularly evident in density patterns and concepts of territory. Density patterns in societies tend to be linearly related to the level of cultural development.

The more advanced and extensive a society's technology, the better it can absorb large concentrations of population and the more densely populated its communities.

Territorial constructs and defense also vary culturally. In hunting and gathering societies, territory was communally owned. In these societies, war was seldom waged for territorial gain, and the warfare that resulted from territorial disputes was highly ritualized. It was more aggressive display than overt aggression. A concept of individually owned private property began to emerge only as food surpluses developed in agricultural societies. As this occurred, more technologically sophisticated and highly organized warfare was used to expand and defend territory. About 5,000 years after the emergence of agriculture, the state developed as a new territorial unit. Through the Middle Ages and Renaissance the state was generally localized, and conflict was organized according to dynastic and feudal alliances in which the concept of nation was absent. In the modern period, on the other hand, territorial defense is generally organized around the nation state.

This level of variability attests to the significance of culture and social structure for territorial functioning. While we are territorial by nature, the way we function within a given place and how we define that place are highly variable. Culture gives human populations some flexibility in dealing with the environment that allows some populations to significantly modify the predisposition to fixed territory (Casimir and Rao 1992).

Territorial behavior varies from one culture to the next, but this variation signifies our adaptive capacity rather than our tendency to be cultural robots subjected to culturally programmed behavior. By nature we are adaptive creatures. We can and often do adapt to dysfunctional environments. But such adjustments can be at great cost to our health and well-being. Our adaptive ability often allows us to dismiss deplorable, yet changeable environments. Since we can endure even pathological contexts, we often underestimate the significance of environment for our general well-being. There are clearly healthy and unhealthy neighborhoods and buildings. While humans who live in such settings may define them as home and may even feel comfortable there, in order to arrive at this level of comfort they have to expend great energy and develop cultural, social, and psychological adaptations that may have decidedly negative consequences for their well-being.

> It requires energy to move to a new level of adaptation and it requires energy to stay there. Environmental factors that do not conform to some model value . . . are expensive to live with, we pay for tuning them out by using more energy or by being less effective in our work and play.
>
> (Wheeler 1967:4)

People who live in such settings do so at a cost to their health. If they adapt by using more energy and effort to protect their spaces, they are likely to experience health-threatening stresses. On the other hand, if they adjust to the pathologies of a place by becoming indifferent to their neighborhood they contribute to its disorganization.

Healthy environments are congruent with the basic goals and needs of the culture, the group, and the individual. In this sense, the setting places certain constraints on the choices and actions of people in a given social and cultural context. It makes some actions and choices more possible than others, and it makes some expectations and preferences more plausible. At the same time, the relationship between environment and behavior is indirect, with social and cultural forces mediating it. Culture and social structure are more important in determining behaviors and experiences than is the immediate environment. Nonetheless place does play a significant role in our behaviors and experiences; it does more than merely reflect structure and culture.

The Nature of the Environment–Behavior Relationship

Place and behavior are interwoven in a complex fashion. As we have just seen, human spatial functioning cannot be captured by purely biological models portraying territorial behavior as instinctual or genetically structured. Place is an interpreted setting. It is far more than a collection of physical stimuli, and as such, the territorial behavior which occurs there is also more than a programmed response. How people feel about a place often affects how they act there. People with strong feelings about a given setting are likely to be more protective of it. Human territorial functioning thus involves person–place transactions (Taylor 1988) that are mediated by cultural expectations, as well as social interactions and ties, which take place within an area. Hence, territorial experience and the level of territorial functioning depend on the fit between the individual and the environment.

Michelson (1976) argues that this fit occurs at two levels—*mental congruence* and *experiential congruence*. If places satisfy mental congruence they accommodate the person's values, lifestyle, and expectations. That is, persons who experience mental congruence believe that a particular place or type of place accommodates their needs. For example, in the United States, there is a general belief that suburbs are better suited for raising a family than central cities, hence persons raising families are likely to feel congruence with a suburban setting. At the same time, because places are the stages for behavior (*behavior settings*), experience to a certain extent is constrained by the physical aspects of the place, the cultural expectations about appropriate behavior within the place, and the social experiences possible there. Physical qualities of place make some behaviors and choices more possible than others, and some preferences and expectations more plausible than others. The implication of this congruence approach to territorial behavior is that if the environment is incongruent with the expectations and behaviors of the individual, it manifests itself as an environmental stressor. It also makes it likely that people will not function territorially in such a place. Incongruence diminishes the adaptive functions of territory as well as the personal significance of the territory for identity. Incongruent places do not feel like home.

In addition to Michelson's (1976) notion of the importance of congruence between place and the person's ideals and needs, Stokols (1972) points to the importance of *environmental controllability* for person–environment fit. Certain settings make high demands on the individual, limiting his or her control over the environment. Places with such limited controllability can thwart or block place-related needs and expectations.

When these needs and expectations are thwarted, the individual's health and well-being are likely to be affected.

Geographers capture the complicated nature of the human spatial experience in their distinction between space and place. Up to this point, while we have used those two words almost interchangeably, in geography each has a distinct meaning. Space typically refers to the measurable, objective aspects of geography. It is a material phenomenon, a commodity characterized by what it contains; a set of objects and locations at certain distances from one another. It has formal properties that can be described and measured in a variety of ways including economic, cartographic, geophysical, and demographic. As a wide range of theorists from Lefebvre (1974) to Relph (1976), Tuan (1977), and Logan and Molotch (1987) have noted, however, this concept does not capture the full complexity of the geographic experience. Space as a material commodity is an incomplete, even deceptive conception of the lived space. Indeed, territory can play a more active role, structuring people's perceptions, interactions, and sense of well-being (Zukin 1991). The word *place* is used by contemporary geographers to capture this aspect of the human territorial experience.

Sense of place involves an interactive relationship between the daily experience of local spaces and a perception of one's place in the world. It is simultaneously a center of lived meaning and social position. Place is more than the sum of its parts (Eyles 1985); it is qualitatively different from space and landscape. Relph (1985) attempts to distinguish *space* from the broader, more phenomenological term *place* as follows:

> [Spaces are] part of any immediate encounter with the world, and so long as I can see I cannot help but see them no matter what my purpose. This is not so with places, for they are constructed in our memories and affections through repeated encounters and complex associations.
>
> (p. 26)

He further elaborates the distinction by locating place at the very essence of human identity and existence.

To have roots in a place is to have a secure point from which to look out on the world, a firm grasp of one's position in the order of things, and a significant spiritual and psychological attachment to somewhere in particular.

(p. 38)

Places are locations of felt value. Attachment to place is a basic human need, integral to self-identity and self-definition. For human beings, places are much more than territories that supply physical needs; they are imbued with deep personal and cultural meaning; they are holistic and multilevel. The distinction between place and space is much like the notion in urban sociology of the difference between exchange value and use value. Individual attachments to place are often intense and signify such basic issues of identity and meaning that persons often resort to extra-market mechanisms to fight for their right to place (Logan and Molotch 1987). The measurable aspects of the space often cannot predict the intensity of response. Such is the nature of human territorial relations.

Basic Spatial Needs in Humans

Despite the complexity of our spatial relationships, and the inability to capture this complexity in purely physical terms, we can talk about specific aspects of space that are essential to human existence. Thus, we believe there are basic human spatial needs, whose fulfillment gives us a sense of place or rootedness in the world. By need we mean an objective universal requirement to avoid a state of illness (Casimir and Rao 1992). The most basic human needs are for a stable supply of food, water, and shelter. But are there spatial needs that go beyond these? While culture conditions our spatial expectations and territorial behaviors, creating cultural variation, modernization and globalization have permeated world cultures. Hence, spatial expectations may be less and less diverse over time, making these needs more universal. Writings in environmental psychology support this idea (LaGory and Pipkin 1981) and suggest that for contemporary cultures basic requirements may include the need for privacy, the related requirement of personal space, the need for easy access to social interaction, and the need for safe and defensible spaces. Together these four may supply the sense of place and rootedness that Relph (1985) described as essential to human identity.

Privacy

Privacy constitutes a critical aspect of environmental control in modern cultures supporting norms of individuality and freedom. Sundstrom (1986) describes it as the "ability to control access to one's self or group." It provides a sense of self and an opportunity for self-development (Eibl-Eibesfeldt 1989; Petschauer 1997). By withdrawing from social settings, individuals have the opportunity for reflection, integration, and assimilation of information derived from earlier interactions. This information is used to prepare the self for future behaviors. Private places are the spaces in which people get ready for the presentation of self in "front stage" performances (Goffman 1959).

Besides self-development, privacy provides freedom and opportunities for intimacy (Westin 1967). It permits the individual to choose avoidance or engagement in group experiences, giving them the ability to elude public scrutiny and control. As such, it allows the person a sense of autonomy. Privacy also offers opportunities to maintain or attain intense personal relationships between primary group members, limiting and protecting communication, and enabling individuals to share confidential information with persons they trust. It provides a means of temporarily cutting off communication with outsiders, so that total attention can be devoted to a single relationship.

Simple societies did not provide much privacy or autonomy to the individual. In these societies, which Durkheim ([1893] 1933) referred to as mechanical solidarities, the collective conscience (the shared values, beliefs, and sentiments of the culture) almost completely blanketed individual ways of thinking and evaluating. It was only as societies evolved, becoming organizationally and economically more complex (*organic solidarity*), that the collective conscience weakened and independence and individuality were encouraged. As the individual shifted from being a social object to be controlled to a social unit whose rights were pro-tected, privacy became a critical spatial construct. In the modern world, privacy becomes a basic human need; its absence in the places where indi-viduals live and work produces stress.

Personal Space

In addition to privacy, there also are minimum distance requirements necessary for the healthy functioning of the individual and the group. Eibl-Eibesfeldt (1989) suggests that all human interactions have dis-tance expectations whose trespass is experienced negatively. Edward Hall's (1966) work in proxemics shows, however, that optimal behavior densities vary from one social situation and subculture to the next. That is not to say that crowding has an insignificant effect on social behavior, but that its relationship to behavior and health is complex. High densi-ties are not a sufficient condition for crowding. Crowding is not a physi-cal phenomenon but a cognitive state, wrought by the interaction between physical circumstances, cultural expectations, and the social actors coinciding in a particular space (Hinde 1987).

Most social scientists have, in the past, viewed high densities as unnatural, conflicting with the basic biological needs of the species (Freedman 1975). Simmel ([1905] 1964) was perhaps the first sociolo-gist to address the issue of density. He argued that density produced excessive "nervous stimulation." More than 90 years of accumulated evidence suggests, however, that density has no simple association with pathology (Freedman 1975; Frumkin 2003; Regoeczi 2003). For example, at the neighborhood level, once socioeconomic status of residents is controlled, the relationship between neighborhood density and various forms of social pathology often disappears. Choldin and associates (Choldin and Roncek 1976; Choldin 1978) found that neighborhood density had no independent effect on pathology apart from the effects of slum life, poverty, and discrimination. That is, densely populated poor neighborhoods had higher rates of illness, distress, and crime, but densely populated better-off neighborhoods did not.

On the other hand, at the household level, the impact of density on everyday life is more straightforward. High density in the home "increases opportunities for disagreement, aggression, frustration, and general dissatisfaction among household members" (Baldassare 1981; Gove et al. 1979; Regoeczi 2008). High household density appears to be a stressor for individuals with limited control over the domestic setting. Baldassare (1981) finds that household crowding is particularly stressful to mothers, to parents living in a household where they are not the head or married to the head, and to parents of young children or adolescents. The chronic stress produced by overcrowding in the home has its greatest impact on parent–child relationships. Booth and Edwards (1976) note that in an American sample, high densities apparently increased parents' use of physical punishment. In a sample of residents of Hong Kong, one of the most crowded cities in the world, Mitchell (1971) finds that while residents in crowded housing were more likely to be unhappy and worried (general indicators of strain), they showed no specific indications of stress (such as mental illness, depression, psychosomatic symptoms). The high densities were related only to children's behavior. High densities forced children into the street and away from the surveillance of their parents, creating a potentially unhealthy environment for socialization. While no American studies have found such effects, it is certainly plausible that in overcrowded, unpleasant physical circumstances lower-income urban children spend more time outside in the streets—and hence less time under surveillance.

One way in which people can adjust to household crowding is by relying on an agreed social order to reduce the stressful effects of this negative circumstance. Research findings suggest that while this adjustment benefits some, it creates disadvantages for less powerful members of the family. Age stratification is a basic form of social order in all societies. Apparently in high-density settings this stratification is exaggerated to maintain order. People less able to control the environment, most often children and youth, experience the greatest costs of this adaptation process.

Freedman (1975) describes this phenomenon in terms of a *density-intensity hypothesis*. Crowded conditions exaggerate traditional role relationships, particularly gender roles. Using various role-playing situations in a controlled laboratory setting, he finds that gender roles are intensified in high-density settings. In a competitive setting, when crowding is high, women tend to become less competitive, while men become more so. Similarly, in a simulated jury deliberation, women give less severe sentences in the crowded jury room, while men give more severe ones. With crowding, men become more "manly" and women more "feminine." This intensification of roles can work to the disadvantage of those with limited power in the household such as children and their stay-at-home mothers (Baldassare 1981; Booth and Edwards 1976; Edwards 1994; Mitchell 1971).

In addition to the importance of social control for determining individual crowding experiences, persons with reduced physical or cognitive competence are apparently less capable of responding to the stressors present in a crowded setting. Physical or mental health conditions, or limited social or psychological resources, may reduce an individual's capacity to adapt to challenging circumstances (Hinde 1987; Lawton 1980). Such persons are *environmentally docile* (Lawton 1980), and more likely to experience pathology from a highly demanding environment such as a condition of crowding (LaGory and Fitzpatrick 1992). The docility hypothesis suggests that in areas where crowding is high, the health penalty will be particularly great for those already experiencing physical and mental health problems.

The impact of the madding crowd is highly variable. For many, density has few if any pathological consequences, yet high densities do take their toll on some segments of the population. Most notably, these tend to be the most vulnerable segments of a community or household. Those with fewer resources (limited power, or reduced physical or cognitive ability) find themselves most vulnerable to the stresses involved in an environment.

Access to Social Interaction

While too much social contact, in the form of high densities, can be dysfunctional, too little contact can be particularly harmful. Humans are naturally social, requiring contact with others (Eibl-Eibesfeldt 1989). The linkages between the individual and the group have long been seen as essential to the health of both the person and the social system (Kawachi 2001; Putnam 2000). Ever since Durkheim ([1893] 1933), the extent of social ties has been conceived as a critical barometer of social and moral integration, which in turn directly affects personal well-being.

More than 20 years of research demonstrates the critical role of affiliation in health and general well-being (Kawachi and Berkman 2001; Link and Phelan 1995; Thoits 1995). Persons with substantial social networks have better physical health (Berkman and Breslow 1983) and lower mortality rates (Umberson 1987). In addition, social ties promote and encourage good health practices by providing health assistance in various forms as well as providing the individual with caring others who monitor one another's health and health practices (Kawachi et al. 2008; Tausig 1986a; Umberson 1987). As expected, social ties can be significant in times of physical crisis, and indeed most health care, particularly for the chronically ill, is provided informally (Brody 1985).

Social support also plays an important role in allaying depressed mood (Kawachi and Berkman 2001; Lin et al. 1986). Mood, in turn, is related to self-reported health symptoms (Hagglund et al. 1988); anxiety and depression seem to sensitize the individual to physical symptoms such as pain. Social support generally is linked to the well-being of the individual (Lin 2001). It provides not only instrumental assistance to individuals in times of need, but also a sense of being loved and cared for. Even under the direst of environmental conditions, social ties are critical sources of well-being. For example, among the homeless, affiliation reduces depression and increases personal satisfaction (Irwin et al. 2008).

One's level of social affiliation is a function of degree of access to sources of interaction. Spatial arrangements are important factors in access. Some spatial arrangements bring people together for interaction (sociopetal spaces) while others separate people (sociofugal) (LaGory and Pipkin 1981). These qualities are products of social and physical characteristics attached to a given space. There is variation between cultures in just what constitutes an appropriate space for interaction with acquaintances. For example, in America, front areas often draw people into interaction with one another. In the suburbs, front lawns receive much attention from homeowners, and thus often serve as an arena for neighborly interaction (Whyte 1956). In older urban neighborhoods, low-rise tenements with fronts and stoops closer to the street promote a great deal of neighboring (Jacobs 1961). These behavior patterns encourage friendly conversations and friendship formation along and across the street, whereas back regions are more often used as private living areas.

Besides social definitions of appropriate interaction spaces, access to social affiliation is a function of physical proximity and physical features of the spaces themselves (Porteous 1977; Whyte 1990). Festinger and associates' classic study (1950) demonstrated the impact of proximity on social networks and patterns of interaction. They asked students in 17 low-rise dormitories to identify their friends and to say whom they saw more often socially. The study concluded that: (1) friends were more likely to live in close proximity to one another; (2) friendship choices that included people from different floors were more likely between people closest to stairways; and (3) people at the bottom and top of the stairs were more likely to choose each other as friends than they were to choose people from their respective floors. Thus, features of building design as well as actual physical proximity are important aspects of friendship formation. Cooper's (1975) study of a low-income housing project further supports the role of design and proximity in promoting social affiliations. Because homes were not individually owned, neighbor contacts tended to be enhanced by the placement of shared spaces. Casual neighboring was fostered where common spaces were traversed on the way to parking lots, play areas, laundry facilities, and so forth. In addition to promoting ties, Taylor (1988) notes that physical aspects of the neighborhood, such as vacant buildings or heavy pedestrian or vehicular traffic, can disrupt neighborhood interaction and discourage public socializing.

Just as with the designed environment, access can influence affiliation in the larger metropolitan space. In places where population densities are high, there is a wider choice of friends and acquaintances, leading to a high probability that residents will have and maintain social affiliations in the immediate area (LaGory 1993). Access is, of course, not enough to ensure affiliation. While people's chances of meeting are a function of access and design features, contact is not a sufficient condition for maintaining social ties. According to Blau and Schwartz (1984) and Gans (1967), friendships are a function of neighborhood homogeneity and the ability of the person to move about freely. Propinquity brings people together, but social similarity and commonly shared interests also keep them together (Blau 1977; LaGory 1993). In this sense, perceived social distance is more important than physical distance in promoting the formation of social bonds.

Further research has qualified this finding, suggesting the complicated nature of the relationship between distance and friendship. Athanasiou and Yoshioka (1973) note that physical distance is a critical factor promoting friendships, and that some forms of social similarity are more salient in promoting proximal relationships. For example, at a given distance, people of similar ages are more likely to associate with each other than are people of similar classes. Class, however, becomes significant when race enters into the equation. While race, like age and class, is a salient social identifier, interracial friendship formation, under conditions of high proximity, is probable when socioeconomic statuses are equal (Blau and Schwartz 1984; Deutsch and Collins 1951). That is, the racial barrier to association breaks down when people of similar socioeconomic statuses live close to one another.

Safe and Defensible Spaces

Maslow (1954) argues that the need for security is very basic, ranking just below physiological needs such as hunger and thirst. Security is perhaps most critical in the individual's home, where people expect to relax and let down their defenses (Goffman 1959; Newman 1973a; Taylor 1988). Since basic needs must be filled first, it is crucial that individuals feel a modicum of safety and security in their environments if they hope to satisfy higher-order needs such as affiliation (love, group membership), esteem (personal satisfaction), actualization (achievement), and learning. Without such security, people are likely to become socially isolated and lose contact with the groups and institutions capable of satisfying higher goals.

Unquestionably, poor neighborhoods are inherently less secure places, just as they are also places where basic needs are less likely to be met. In particular, many inner-city neighborhoods are less safe and secure than other residential places in the metropolitan area, with more street traffic, higher crime rates, more exposure to pollutants, more violence, more problems with high vacancy rates and aging buildings (Palen 1997). Under such conditions, Maslow's theory (1954) suggests that insecure residential environments impede the fulfillment of essential human needs such as affiliation, esteem, actualization, and cognitive development. Thus, it is possible that a destructive subculture of poverty will flourish in such places. Wilson (1996) is a strong proponent of this position:

> [The] sharp rise in violent crime among younger males has accompanied the widespread outbreak of addiction to crack-cocaine. The association is particularly strong in inner city ghetto neighborhoods plagued by joblessness and weak social organization. . . . Violent persons in the crack-cocaine marketplace have a powerful impact on the social organization of a neighborhood. Neighborhoods plagued by high levels of joblessness, insufficient economic opportunities and high residential mobility are unable to control the volatile drug market and the violent crimes related to it. As informal controls weaken, the social processes that regulate behavior change. As a result, the behavior and norms in the drug market are more likely to influence the action of others in the neighborhood, even those who are not involved in drug activity.
>
> (p. 21)

In his view, unlike earlier American slums described by Suttles (1968), contemporary inner-city neighborhoods are disorganized. They are disorganized because of the high risk of violence and the lack of economic opportunity that characterize new inner-city poverty neighborhoods. This disorganization is likely to further exacerbate the already weakened ability of such areas (with limited resources and limited political influence) to respond effectively to health crises such as the Village Creek chemical spill. Disorganized neighborhoods' cries for help are often heard as angry cacophony, rather than messages of substance meriting a serious response. Is such disorganization a result of spatial circumstances—a lack of safe and secure spaces? While this cannot be argued with certainty, unmet place needs may lead to greater difficulty in addressing environmental challenges. That is, places which concentrate high risk and limited capacity to respond to risk are more likely to require design features promoting security and defensibility.

Ironically, researchers suggest that certain physical features characteristic of inner-city neighborhoods actually reduce defensibility rather than promote it (Cohen and Felson 1979; Newman 1973a and b; Taylor 1988; Yancey 1971). These design features include high vacancies; spaces that can't be monitored; high-rise, anonymous residential structures; absence of manageable territories promoting territorial identity (such as front or back yards, gardens, or courtyards); proximity to dangerous sites; high vehicular traffic; and unattractive architecture that symbolically stigmatizes residents (Sampson et al. 2002; Taylor 1988).

This lack of defensibility discourages territorial functioning. Territorial functioning promotes healthier social environments.

> Small groupings of residents on street blocks, or at the sub block level, generate social forces that result in the establishment of norms. Adherence to, or deviation from these norms, as evident in territorial behavior and marking, allows group members to gauge one another's commitment to locale and potential helpfulness in times of need. They also express group solidarity. Thus . . . territorial functioning emerges from and shapes social dynamics.
>
> (Taylor 1988:197)

Places with higher levels of territorial functioning have higher neighborhood participation and stronger grassroots community organizations. Local areas with improved territorial functioning experience empowerment and improvement in health. The absence of territorial functioning, however, may actually promote a sense of rootlessness, adding to the hopelessness and lack of empowerment already present in certain areas.

Conclusion

Evidence presented in this chapter suggests that while humans display rich variety in their territorial responses, they have certain culturally and socially conditioned place-related needs and expectations. When these needs and expectations are thwarted, health and well-being is affected, since by nature and culture these needs are deeply rooted in the meaning systems and physiology of the individual.

Such place requirements are most critical, yet most likely to be challenged, in special populations with limited resources and extraordinary needs. These populations are characterized as environmentally docile—less capable of coping with challenging ecological circumstances. Thus poor African Americans living along Village Creek, with limited access to health care services and weak ties to City Hall, find themselves particularly vulnerable to an environmental catastrophe like the October 1997 Birmingham Dursban spill. The very territory that is theoretically supposed to order their world becomes a source of dramatic physical and psychological stress. Attempts to defend it from assault fail, and thus place, instead of being a home, becomes an indefensible territory where risk concentrates alongside limited and ineffective resources. Under such circumstances, residential identity and territorial functioning are threatened, further intensifying ecological vulnerability.

Perhaps the worst-case scenario of the ecologically vulnerable is that of the homeless—a spatially dispossessed class in a variety of political and economic systems. What does it mean for humans to be placeless like the homeless are? A gathering body of evidence suggests grave consequences for the health and mental well-being of this group, with levels of criminal victimization, infectious disease, depression, and chronic health conditions many times higher than those of other low-income groups. We review the plight of the placeless as well as other ecologically vulnerable populations in Chapter 6.

3

THE ECOLOGY OF EVERYDAY URBAN LIFE

We shape our buildings and afterwards our buildings shape us.

Winston Churchill

Tell me the landscape in which you live, and I will tell you who you are.

Ortega y Gassett

The emergence of cities 5,000 years ago marked a revolutionary event in our relationship to place, providing convincing evidence of our ability to control and restructure the physical environment. Since their beginnings, cities have been magnets drawing people to promising opportunities, containers of great cultural and material wealth, centers of innovation, and seats of religious influence. Cities are, however, rife with internal contradictions. In addition to being the source of immense accomplishment, they have been sites of the greatest extremes in living conditions, from luxurious palaces to squalid barrios and ghettos, from secure gated communities to crime-riddled slums. While they generated great economic growth and wealth, they also concentrated hazard in the form of pollution, noise, traffic, and infectious agents. These human-created places have been associated with terms like "placelessness," "alienation," and "homelessness." Apparently, the same city air that makes some free from the tyranny of small-town scrutiny and limited opportunity is a nearly impenetrable prison for others.

Place matters greatly in the modern city. Residents along Village Creek know too well the contradictions of the urban landscape. They experienced most intensely the hazards presented by the Dursban spill, yet were not able to evoke concern from those who could help. This story dramatically captures the reality of the urban space—concentrated hazard for those least able to bear its risks and diminished ability to respond to these hazards effectively because of limited assets. Ironically, those places with more diluted concentrations of the harmful chemical, the areas furthest downstream from the original spill, were the first ones to initiate an orchestrated effort to respond to its risks. This is the essence of the ecology of health in urban spaces—concentrated hazard in areas with limited abilities for protection.

Urban contexts have the power to influence our health. Yet, because we are spatial creatures who have the ability to shape and reshape these spaces, we also have tremendous potential to influence everyday life and health (Lefebvre 1991). This has led some social observers to state emphatically that those who manipulate the physical environment—architects, planners, and developers—have great capacity for good or ill. We owe the cultural map of structural change not to novelists or literary critics, but to architects and designers. Their products, their social roles as cultural producers, and the organization of consumption in which they intervene create shifting landscapes in the most material sense. As both objects of desire and structural forms, their work bridges space and time. It also directly mediates economic power by both conforming to and structuring norms of market-driven investment, production and consumption (Zukin 1991:39).

This chapter examines the nature of these constructed environments and the roles they play in everyday life. We explore architectured spaces, how they have changed over time, and the significance of this change on human experience. These interior spaces are particularly important territories because we spend so much time in them, yet we are only beginning to understand their impact on everyday life and health. We then examine urban macro environs, the neighborhoods, communities, and metropolitan regions in which we live with untold and unknown others. While more careful investigations have been done of these macro environs than of interior spaces, their impact on the health of residents has not been systematically explored until recently. In this chapter the significance of these spatial structures for everyday life is described, and the unique aspects of cities that shape the urban experience are identified. Using a traditional definition of the city, we then identify dimensions of the urban space that vary from one area of the city to another, affecting the quality of life experienced there. We also discuss the role of economics and fear in promoting the varying landscape of hazard. The understanding of urban ecology developed in this chapter is used in Chapter 4 to build a synthetic theory of health and place.

Micro Environments

The Evolution of Residence

One of the consequences of the urbanization of societies has been the development of a marked separation between public and private spheres. The emergence of the spatial division between public and private has created new opportunities for self-consciousness and self-development (Braudel 1979; Lofland 1973; Tuan 1982). In turn, these new spatial distinctions between public and private satisfy a basic territorial need presented by modern cultures emphasizing individuality (see earlier discussion in Chapter 2). As such, modern urban persons find new places and opportunities for personal growth and development of "rootedness." In her best-selling memoir *Under the Tuscan Sun*, Frances Mayes (1997) underscores the significance of one form of constructed space—the home as an aspect of self:

> I have just bought a house in a foreign country. . . . The house is a metaphor for the self of course, but it is totally real. And a foreign house exaggerates all the associations houses carry. Because I had ended a long marriage that was not supposed to end and was establishing a new relationship, this house quest felt tied to whatever new identity I would manage to forge.
>
> (pp. 1, 15)

From this point, the book weaves an intriguing account of the author's reflections on house as metaphor for self, providing a personal tale of how a change of scenery can both renew and remake lives. It underscores the notion that we are spatial creatures who seek satisfaction of our needs in places, and have deep personal ties to home territory. More than spatial beings, we are place-oriented creatures. Place is the immediate and intimate portion of the lived environment. It is the site or location for events, but it also has more personal significance than serving as a context for experience. Places are locations of felt value; attachment to place is viewed as a basic human need, important for identity and connection (Eyles and Litva 1998). "To have roots in a place is to have a secure point from which to look out on the world, a firm grasp of one's position in the order of things, and a significant spiritual and psychological attachment to somewhere in particular" (Relph 1976:38). It can be understood as standing for the human interactions which occur in a location, that is, as a representation of lived experience and of the larger life biography of the individual (Fullilove 1996). This link between place and self is thought to have been accentuated with the growth of cities and changes in residential architecture (Tuan 1977, 1982).

The geographer Yi Fu Tuan (1982) suggests that since the eighteenth century in the West, an ongoing process of "interiorization" has occurred in the built environment of cities. In the ancient and medieval city, public and private, exterior and interior, were mixed together in ways we would find quite confusing today. Lofland (1973) describes how we might feel in such spaces:

> Too many people crowded into too small a space; too many odors, most of them offensive; too many sights, most of them vile. You can't get away from the beggars and vendors. They accost you wherever you go. You can't escape the crippled limbs, the scarred faces, the running sores. Your person seems never safe from the constant assault of pickpockets. Everything seems jumbled together. Rich and poor, health and disease, young and old, house and business, public and private. All seems disorder. All seems chaos.
>
> (p. 33)

That seeming chaos was gradually eliminated in the industrial city through the use of barriers, both real and imagined. While this process of erecting barriers and more clearly defining territories touched all aspects of city life, it is best exemplified by the history of housing.

Home spaces have deep-rooted significance for all humans. The home is a "backstage area" where people can relax social conventions and enjoy more intimate social relationships. It provides more than shelter. What a house "does supremely well is to make the character of the human world vividly present to the senses and to the mind" (Tuan 1982:52). By erecting barriers to the outside world, it shields the household from the distractions of open, undifferentiated public spaces. It affords a degree of privacy, which comes to be expected and required in modern culture. In providing privacy, it creates the possibility of a distinctively personal world, not only permitting self-development but also reflecting aspects of the self.

Imagine the tyranny of a home without rooms or privacy. American culture encourages intense self-awareness and a strong, even exaggerated belief in the power of the individual. Such values had no chance for developing in the architecture of the past, and in some homes today, it continues to be difficult to achieve because of overcrowding, or poor or older design. In these spatial circumstances the place of the individual in domestic life may be unclear. Certainly, earlier rural farmhouse architecture and the tenement and townhouse structures of cities earlier in this century did not meet these needs. In the city, heavy concentrations of multistoried dwellings, with shared-wall construction, close proximity to public sidewalks, and severe cooling difficulties made for an environment where public and private space could not be easily distinguished. The often family-constructed farmhouse had a different set of problems. While it focused and concentrated on family life, and effectively sheltered the family from the public eye, it often afforded almost no privacy. The rural home brought family together for entertainment, work, and sleep, but the floor plan of these homes made retreat from other family members difficult. It was an architecture that effectively promoted sharing at the cost of individuality and freedom.

The suburban tract house makes privacy far more accessible to many Americans. Interior spaces are functionally segregated, while exterior spaces are clearly divided into public and private areas, with back yards and front yards serving distinct functions. Public traffic is regulated by limiting through-traffic and by creating natural buffer zones. Additionally, the technology of the modern home permits greater public-space avoidance (TVs, DVD players, video games, cell phones, computers, internet access, e-mail, iPods, etc.) by making it less necessary to leave the home to satisfy needs and desires. It also creates great separation between family members themselves through personalized electronic entertainment. The superiority of suburban living lies in this segmentation of space, which allows the individual to be alone, to explore and deepen their own sense of being. In the isolation of one's house and the privacy of one's room, it is possible to think seriously and at length and to avoid scrutiny (Tuan 1982:181–82).

While increasing spatial segmentation makes for growing self-consciousness and increases personal liberty, there are two potential problems with this feature of modern residential environments. First, as Tuan suggests, this architectured liberty allows the self to turn inward, but in so doing it can also become fragmented and lose its sense of connectedness. A sense of self, after all, comes only with a developed sense of society (Cooley 1922). This growing fragmentation of space in neighborhood and home, while potentially satisfying a basic spatial need of modern culture, can go too far. As communities and families turn more and more inward, there is the potential of losing sight of the whole. In such cases, individual tolerance of others may be threatened. Indeed, evidence suggests that the growing segmentation of urban society has promoted the growth of individualism at the expense of intergroup tolerance, public civility, and social capital at the individual and community levels (Fischer 1981; Putnam 2000).

A second negative outcome of this architecture is that it is not available to everyone. Most notably, persons residing in older, poorer areas of the city are likely to find privacy difficult to obtain. It is uncertain whether this situation in and of itself creates developmental problems for those residing in such households. Evidence presented in the last chapter, however, suggests that in such surroundings, children are likely to spend more time away from home in areas less likely to be under the surveillance of responsible adults (Gove et al. 1979; Mitchell 1971). Under such circumstances, children may be exposed to high environmental risks while at the same time finding typical sources of protection (particularly within the family) less available.

The Artificially Constructed Environment

In addition to the interiorization of urban life and its impact on public and private use of space, the modern industrial period is also characterized by the growing significance of artificially constructed environments. That is, architectured spaces regulate not only social environmental experiences, but physical ones as well. As Ralph Taylor has suggested, however, "nature is a basic human need" (Gallagher 1993:20). Countering that need is the fact that almost all of our time is spent away from the natural world. Indeed, time-use surveys report that, on average, American adults spend a little more than an hour outside in an entire day, with the other 90 percent spent in buildings and vehicles (U.S. Environmental Protection Agency 1999; Robinson and Godbey 1997). That figure represents a significant change from the past, where more time was spent in public places and outdoors to carry out daily activities (Tuan 1982).

What are the consequences for everyday life and health of this shift to a predominantly artificial environment? Winifred Gallagher (1993) suggests that the shift to architectured settings can have great impact on our emotional and physical well-being. This impact is perhaps most pronounced in extreme environmental conditions:

> "You look around Anchorage in July, and you could be in a lot of places," says John Booker. The window of his office at the university duly frames the very picture of the idyllic American campus. . . . "If you saw how much trouble it is to maintain the population here a few months from now, however, you would understand that this is a fairly artificial environment, and the farther north you go, the more that's true. Maintaining a business-as-usual nine-to-five attitude here in December puts us at odds with what's going on outside to an

extreme degree, as well as requiring a lot of money and effort. To keep a half a million people in Alaska year round is something like operating in an outpost on the moon."

(p. 40)

While advanced technologies permit us to live in even the most foreboding circumstances, research suggests that the more a population lives in conflict with what is actually happening in nature, the more cases of seasonal affective disorder (SAD) it is likely to have (Lurie et al. 2006). Persons with seasonal affective disorder experience clinical depression seasonally, most frequently in winter, with some cases recurring in the summer. Researchers link variations in light and temperature to the depressive symptomatology that accompanies SAD (Bernson 2002; Magnusson 2000). The most effective treatment for winter-based SAD is light therapy, in which patients are exposed daily to bright artificial light for brief periods. In many cultures, light is associated with positive qualities, while darkness with negative ones. The Shakers had a deep appreciation of the tie between light and well-being, painting walls white and using groups of large windows to maximize natural light. "Good and evil are typified by light and darkness. Therefore, if we bring light into a dark room, the darkness disappears, and inasmuch as a soul is filled with good, evil will disappear" (Eldress Aurelia Mace, quoted in Gallagher 1993:47). As Shaker architecture suggests, built environments can effectively regulate and supplement lighting conditions and affect mood, but how many buildings in contemporary society do this well? While indoor lighting can easily be regulated, not enough is known yet about lighting design for health promotion, a fact that takes on added significance as new forms of lighting are being introduced to promote energy conservation (Frumkin 2003).

Temperature can also be regulated. This regulation can be important under extreme conditions, because cold has the effect of stimulating behavior, while heat acts as a sedative (Gallagher 1993). When cold, we feel compelled to keep muscles moving in order to stay warm, while heat seems to urge muscles to rest. The interiorization of space use thus can reduce the behavioral consequences of extremes in temperature. But the impact of heat regulation on SAD is unclear at present. While some have argued that summer's heat may trigger mechanisms in the body that mimic symptoms of depression (extreme fatigue, lack of energy, increased need for sleep), this conclusion is controversial (Gallagher 1993; Wehr and Rosenthal 1989). Indeed, some argue that those experiencing depression in summer months may have mood slumps. Their need to escape the heat leads to light deprivation from being indoors for longer periods of time, rather than to a direct physiological response to the heat outdoors.

The interiorization of living environments appears to give a false sense of control over nature, and produces a feeling of being apart from it. Nature is somehow that which is out there. Yet while urbanization and interiorization have effectively removed nature from most of our daily experiences, the human species evolved in a natural world. Nature not only is a human need, it is diminishing in terms of its availability.

The growing separation from the natural world is but one health-related issue wrought by interiorization. As the technology surrounding architectured spaces has expanded, new substances and new mechanical and electronic devices have been introduced into the home. This creates the potential for new, though little understood, health challenges. In recent years worries about building materials have risen, with special concern being given to the materials contained in older homes. Asbestos removal became a national priority as the link between asbestos and cancer was established. Lead toxicity also became a critical public health issue, particularly for children. The negative effects of lead poisoning for children include reading and learning disabilities, lowered IQ, hyperactivity, neurological deficits, kidney and heart disease, as well as speech and language handicaps. These hazards are most highly concentrated in older, poorer neighborhoods (Aldgate et al. 2004; Costello-Wilson et al. 2005; Hack et al. 2005). That concentration is precisely why a known public health problem identified in the 1960s did not begin to be addressed until much later (Harvey 1997). As Harvey notes, economic dynamics fashion a logic of injustice: "The costs of lead removal would either drive rents up or render inner city landlordism for the poor so unprofitable as to exacerbate already serious problems of housing abandonment in inner city areas" (p. 89). Defiance of this logic requires the dissemination of information as well as political action. Getting the word out effectively on the risks associated with these materials, and the testing and treatment available, will depend in part on neighborhood social networks and the level of attachment that people have with certain places.

Growing interest in the "sick building syndrome" has focused attention on indoor air quality as a health determinant (Burge 2004; Frumkin 2003). Air quality is a problem in both old and new buildings (Roodman and Lenssen 1995). Dust in the home and workplace is a significant carrier of toxins. Dust particles contain a range of materials including pet dander and human skin, fibers, insects, mold spores, pollen, dirt, and various soil components and contaminants. It is currently estimated that two-thirds of these noxious materials come from sources outside the home (Layton and Beamer 2009). In recent years, however, the issue of indoor air quality has focused on materials incorporated into new home construction. Evidence is accumulating that a range of building materials can have a significant negative impact on health. Glues, paints, and sealants often emit harmful gases, so that the use of products and materials with high levels of volatile organic compounds (VOCs) can produce health problems for residents. Plywood in cabinets and flooring often contains formaldehyde that can be released into the air, while carpeting and padding containing manmade fibers often release harmful gases. Canada has developed incentive programs to minimize the use of these materials in domestic construction; the United States, however, has not followed its lead.

Macro Environments: Cities as Unique Environments for Living

Just as the house presents unique opportunities and challenges for human development and health, cities are distinct contexts with their own health implications. An underlying assumption of many urban sociologists has been that cities were unique environments for living and that the city's distinctive features shaped the experience of urban residents. The most famous articulation of this perspective was Louis Wirth's 1938 article "Urbanism as a Way of Life." Wirth defined cities as large, dense, permanent settlements of socially heterogeneous individuals. He believed that these three qualities of the urban space produced an environment with greater potential for anonymity, social isolation, and impersonalization. Urban spaces had the potential for promoting pathological behaviors and unhealthy places.

While considerable research and writing following Wirth's original article provided only mixed support for his characterization of the city as a pathological environment, the sheer immensity and diversity of urban communities was believed to have real consequences for everyday life (Fischer 1975; LaGory and Pipkin 1981; Reiss 1959). City experiences were fundamentally different from suburban or rural ones in several ways:

1. *Complex patterns of interaction.* The urbanite has the possibility of initiating an enormous number of social ties, given the high density of urban settlements (Fischer 1975; Milgram 1972).
2. *Exposure to strangers.* Because of the large number of residents and their diverse characteristics, urbanites share the community with many unknown others (Lofland 1973).
3. *Exposure to unconventional norms.* The scale and heterogeneity of urban life is also likely to foster opportunities to explore unconventional behavior patterns and ideas (Fischer 1975).

The significant scale of urban settlements can make social life more stimulating and complicated. Stanley Milgram (1972) talks about the implications of urban complexity for everyday life, arguing that it creates the potential for a unique pattern of public behavior. Urban stimuli can be overwhelming, with sights, sounds, and smells coming too fast to be processed effectively by residents—as a result *stimulus overload* is possible. Humans' ability to process information is physiologically limited. It follows, then, that the city resident's capacity to recognize the potentially large number of fellow urbanites is limited. The "overloaded" urbanite is unable to absorb all the information from this complex environment either because there are too many stimuli to process or because stimuli are coming too fast. When such overloads occur, the urban resident copes, Milgram believed, by selectively reducing stimulus inputs. This can result in a lifestyle of seeming indifference, particularly in public places where individuals may feel especially vulnerable. Coping with complexity may mean ignoring the countless unknown others who share public space.

> The blank, nearly expressionless faces of urban pedestrians provide one example of this adaptive ability. For urbanites, most of the people sharing public space with them, whether it be a subway, sidewalk or market place, are nonpersons to be maneuvered around.
>
> (LaGory and Pipkin 1981:39)

The stance of indifference may also produce a situation of *diffused responsibility* and inaction in a situation that normally would command immediate response. One often-used example of diffused responsibility is that of Kitty Genovese, a young woman who was raped and fatally stabbed outside her Kew Gardens apartment in Queens. While at least 38 people witnessed the attack, no one called police until 35 minutes after the assault began, despite the fact that many witnesses watched from the safety of their own apartments. One explanation of this pattern of non-response is that the large size characteristic of urban settings falsely reassures people they have no moral responsibility to respond to someone else's crisis because others are likely to take responsibility. In short, the scale of urban contexts, like the Kew Gardens residential complex in Queens, tends to shift responsibility from the individual to the aggregate. Darley and Latane's study of bystanders (1970) suggested that urbanites are not typically uncaring about other's troubles. However, when an incident occurs, witness behaviors appear to be a function of the size of the crowd. That is, the more witnesses, the less likely that someone will intervene. This stance of non-response is often characteristic of urban areas with heavy concentrations of poor minorities (Suttles 1968; Wilson 1996). Such evidence reinforces Wirth's view of the city as impersonal and alienating. It has been suggested, however, that these outcomes are not inevitable.

Indeed, there are circumstances in which the urban context actually serves to promote a sense of belonging, shared identity, and responsibility. Fischer (1976) argues convincingly that urban scale, instead of destroying social ties among residents, actually has the capacity to create and stimulate social bonds. He claims that large size promotes intense and varied social worlds in several ways:

1. Large communities attract migrants from a wider area than smaller communities. The wider the range of places from which migrants come, the greater the probability they will have diverse experiences and cultural backgrounds.

2. Large size produces greater structural differentiation in the form of highly specialized occupations and institutions, as well as special interest groups. Each of these special groupings has its own unique set of life experiences and interests.

3. Increased size, however, does more than simply stimulate diversity and a variety of social worlds. It provides a critical mass that actually intensifies subcultural experiences and promotes a strong sense of community identity. This critical mass transforms what would otherwise be a small group of individuals holding steadfastly to a set of beliefs and traditions into a vital, active subculture. For a culture to survive, certain minimal numbers are necessary to support the institutions that give the group its identity. In the case of an ethnic enclave this may simply mean enough people to staff the specialty shops, churches, newspapers, and clubs that service and sustain the group.

This tendency to promote diverse, small, and even unconventional social worlds is enhanced by the city's spatial structure. Contemporary cities are segregated places, and this segregation makes unconventional behavior possible by removing the smaller community from the social controls and expectations of the larger, more traditional society and its majority population.

The city's spatial organization, with its distinct pattern of sociospatial landscapes, creates a more personal world than that envisioned by Wirth and Milgram (LaGory and Pipkin 1981). Tightly segregated local communities, places with a distinct sociocultural identity, can actually reduce the possibility of social isolation and alienation if what Taylor (1988) refers to as "territorial functioning" occurs within them. At the same time, these very settings (highly segregated and densely populated areas with high territorial functioning) may promote cultural isolation and discourage the formation of ties and identities outside the local area. The very same segregation that can be liberating for those with physical, economic, and intellectual resources can be debilitating for those with limited resources (Davis 1990; Massey and Denton 1993; Mitchell and LaGory 2002). That situation of high segregation and limited personal resources can create special problems for those living in areas of concentrated poverty. Segregation places real spatial boundaries on the free flow of information and social interaction. It can actually accentuate and intensify the poverty experienced by individuals, a point we explore later in this chapter.

This structuring of diversity via segregation presents particular problems for city residents as they venture out of their private residential worlds (homes and neighborhoods) into the larger public arena. Urban public space presents its occupants with a potential crisis of knowing (Lofland 1973). To carry out our daily activity in an orderly fashion, and to feel secure in settings populated by many personally unknown others, individuals must be able to anticipate answers to two related questions: (1) What do others expect of me in this setting; and (2) What can I expect of others here? Because the urbanite has no personal knowledge of the countless others sharing public space, they rely on established rules for coding and defining these unknown persons. The rules derive from cultural stereotypes triggered by spatial and appearance-based information. How a person looks, what they are wearing, where they are located, as well as the individual's body language give cues that people use to provide information about the other's expectations, intentions, and more. Fashion becomes a key ingredient in the public behavior of metropolitan residents. Clothing colors, styles, materials, and brands, along with body markings and hairstyles, communicate volumes about the personally unknown. In addition to fashion, certain physical qualities of individuals are stigmatized (Goffman 1963), such as evident disability, disfigurement, racial differences, age, and hygiene. Taken together these become representations of the inner intentions and the personal qualities of the stranger. Hall (1966) and Lofland (1973) also note the importance of spatial cues in communicating intentions. Where persons place themselves in public space (an alley versus a square), their stance (standing, sitting, lying down), and the distance they keep from others are non-verbal communications that suggest the rules of engagement, and the expectations and intentions of others.

Besides these methods of negotiating public space, a process of privatization has occurred to some types of public spaces over the last several decades. The most notable is the privatization of concentrated retail business districts in the form of large covered malls. In these privatized spaces, access is controlled and well surveilled, providing a sense of security less available in downtowns (Davis 1990). These spaces are socially sanitized, homogenized spaces, legally capable of excluding socially stigmatized and disruptive elements. Mall shoppers will not find pathways littered with the pallets of the homeless, no beggars will accost them, no signs of political protest will be found. Because of this security, such places have drawn considerable pedestrian traffic away from traditional public districts in cities. Shopping centers now account for the majority of annual retail sales in fixed-space shopping venues, and the number of these centers has increased tenfold since the 1960s (Gottdiener 1994; Jacobs 1984). This retail restructuring further accentuates the already segregated nature of urban space, since most are located in the suburbs. Metropolitan areas are characterized by divided spaces and segregated places. These divisions often make it difficult to conceptualize a singular urban place because space is multidimensional.

The Dimensions of the Urban Mosaic

The urban space is distinctive because of the sheer scale and diversity contained within it. But because of the segregation that pervades this space, not everyone experiences urbanism equally. Obviously, residents of Village Creek do not come into contact with the same Birmingham as persons living in the metropolitan area's outlying suburbs. Indeed, while the Dursban emitted from the downtown warehouse fire flowed through both inner-city Village Creek neighborhoods and outlying suburban communities, the experiences and responses to that incident varied by place.

Social Areas

The city is a mosaic of distinctive places, and the characteristics of these places can play a vital role in the everyday life of residents and the community as a whole. In the next part of this chapter we explore the nature of this mosaic of places (its dimensions and geometry) and its potential impact on community and individual experiences.

One of the distinctive features of cities is their spatial structure. Space is what keeps everything from being in the same place, and in so doing, space greatly differentiates urban life. People's experiences in a metropolitan area are shaped by a variety of contextual factors or dimensions linked to spaces. As already suggested, the urban qualities of space can be characterized as scale (size and density) and diversity. These qualities of urbanness, however, vary by place. Different places in the mosaic afford different levels of scale and diversity; the diversity of places is a function of the social characteristics of its occupants and the uses to which the space is put. Research and theory in urban sociology suggest several social characteristics by which neighborhoods may be segregated in contemporary metropolitan areas (LaGory et al. 1980; Shevky and Bell 1955). These dimensions include socioeconomic status, race/ethnicity, and age/family status, though each is somewhat independent of the other. These independent social components of place allow for a variety of dimensional combinations, producing many unique social spaces and social experiences (e.g. high-status young White neighborhoods, high-status young African American neighborhoods, etc.).

While there is some disagreement over the factors affecting the quality of participation in different places, social area analysis contends that the neighborhood context, composed of a unique combination of neighborhood social characteristics, creates a "climate" for interacting with neighbors (Bell and Force 1962; Greer 1956, 1960; Greer and Kube 1972; Greer and Orleans 1962; LaGory and Pipkin 1981). In essence, the degree to which people are segregated according to these dimensions is evidence of the strength of a particular "social climate" in the neighborhood. It not only shapes the personality of a place, but also encourages distinctive patterns of local interaction.

Social climate, by affecting patterns of local association, influences the degree of community attachment—an indicator of the significance of local place in the person's everyday life. Greer's (1956, 1960) early work on social areas demonstrated clear differences in patterns of neighborhood interaction between places characterized by large numbers of households with a married couple and children (high-family-status areas), and places characterized by single-person households, or households consisting of a couple with no children (low-family-status areas). High-family-status area neighbors define close-knit local ties as a critical feature of neighborhood life; residents of these places participate actively in the local area. They interact with neighbors more, have more neighborhood friends, and participate more in local voluntary organizations. Those in low-family-status areas, on the other hand, see locations near amenities and work, and neighbors who keep to themselves, as critical ingredients of a good neighborhood. As might be expected, people in these areas are less likely to develop friendships with neighbors. They are more likely to see the neighborhood as a location, rather than a place of social attachment. Work by Bell and Boat (1957) and Greer (1956) further confirms the importance of these contextual characteristics. Social participation in the local area is a product of social context and not just the individual's personal characteristics (Fischer and Jackson 1976; Sampson 1988). For example, while not all neighbors in a high-family-status area will have large families or will even be married, their participation behavior will have more in common with others in the neighborhood than their family-status equals in other types of neighborhoods (Timms 1971).

Two other characteristics of neighborhoods have been shown to affect the level of place attachment—neighborhood residential stability and the neighborhood's location in the metropolitan space. Residential stability, the average length of time residents have lived in the neighborhood, appears to be important to the number of local friendships, the degree to which people feel attachment to the local area, and the extent of participation in community activities (Sampson 1988). People who have been in a neighborhood longer are likely to have more local friendships and social supports, and these place linkages, in turn, strengthen the residents' sense of community attachment and territorial functioning. Hence, areas in transition may also create a climate of "placelessness" or rootlessness.

In addition to the social characteristics of the neighborhood, its residential stability, and social climate, location is important for neighborhood interaction (Fischer and Jackson 1976). Suburban areas further from the center have higher levels of local participation. While social-area analysts look exclusively at the role of social characteristics in affecting the local experience, location has long been considered an important aspect of the social space. Local intimate ties exhibit a gradient effect. Geographers have shown that residents' potential ties are conditioned by location, with the probability of local social contact affected by the level of contact opportunities (residential densities, level of territorial functioning, extent of physical barriers to interaction, etc.). These contact opportunities often vary by location (LaGory and Pipkin 1981). Although location seems to matter less than ever before in terms of defining the social networks and supports people use in their everyday lives, place still matters. For all social classes, strong ties fall off as distance away from the individual's residence increases (Fischer and Jackson 1976). Distance is a particularly important issue in areas with limited transportation options.

Location Models

For many years urban ecologists devoted a great deal of attention to the structure of the urban mosaic and the location of social areas within the metropolis. The research concluded that metropolitan areas were organized into a collection of distinctive social and economic spaces. This segregation was multidimensional, with a predictable pattern to the location of places in the urban space. The earliest models of the industrial city portrayed urban areas as consisting of segregated residential spaces organized in distinctive zones or districts. The concentric zone model depicted a central urban area where slums were concentrated around a business and industrial district (Park et al. 1925). The quality of residential areas varied by distance from this central area of commerce, with the status of neighborhoods increasing in successive bands away from the center. According to this view, the deterioration of residential areas is a direct result of expanding economic activity at the city center. Slums emerged near prosperous business areas because land speculators allowed residential areas to deteriorate in anticipation of making higher profits on the land in the future as a non-residential property. In addition, encroaching businesses increased the hazards to residents by attracting more traffic and introducing more noise and pollution into the area. Hence, the environmental risks associated with growth tended to accrue disproportionately in the area immediately surrounding the central business district. Later models of the industrial city disputed the impact of the central business district on residential arrangements (Hoyt 1939) and suggested that the metropolis contained multiple centers of concentrated economic activity (Harris and Ullman 1945). While these models disagreed with the single-center view of urban development, all depicted a situation in which poverty concentrated around areas of economic activity associated with significant environmental hazards such as manufacturing and warehousing districts. In addition, these concentrations of poverty seemed to serve as buffer zones between certain hazardous areas and higher-status residential groups.

Metropolitan regions are no longer dominated by a single economic center. Indeed, suburban rings often display heavy concentrations of businesses, jobs, and office buildings surrounding shopping malls. These so-called "edge cities" are the high-growth areas of the contemporary metropolis, yet they bear little resemblance spatially to the central business districts that were the economic centers of past urban forms. They are not always characterized by a dense collection of high-rise buildings, they are not usually politically organized, nor do they have clearly defined centers and edges (Garreau 1991). Perhaps the most notable distinction, for our purposes, between the modern urban space and earlier structures, however, is in the social and economic processes that produce areas of concentrated poverty in the new post-industrial metropolis.

The development process is sometimes far less patterned in post-industrial cities than in the earlier industrial cities described by Chicago School sociologists. Michael Dear (2002) refers to post-industrial development as "Keno capitalism," a game of chance.

> Capital touches down as if by chance on a parcel of land ignoring the opportunities on intervening lots . . . The relationship between development of one parcel and non-development of another is a disjointed, seemingly unrelated affair. While not truly a random process, it is evident that the traditional, center-driven agglomeration economies that have guided urban development in the past no longer generally apply.
>
> (Dear 2002:24)

Just how patterned or unpatterned development is in post-industrial cities is debatable (see the inaugural edition of *City and Community*, Dear 2002, 1:5–58). What is not debatable, however, is that slums and deteriorating neighborhoods are no longer a product of center-driven economic expansion, but of a loss of work in certain areas of the city (Wilson 1996). The high-poverty areas of contemporary American cities have experienced a steady loss of the type of work that their residents are capable of performing. The global economy characterized by flexible production and the growth of producer services fuels the expansion of edge cities at the expense of the urban core (Dear 2002; Greene 1997; Sassen 2000). This flexible production also leads to areas that experience quick turns of fortune from boom to bust.

While inner-city areas in industrial societies have always featured concentrated poverty, for the last several decades there has been an increase in the concentration of African American poverty and joblessness in the inner city and some older suburbs. As Wilson notes (1996), a neighborhood containing poor employed people is a different place from one with poor and unemployed residents. This is the distinctive feature of post-industrial ghettos—high levels of poverty and unemployment. Economists began to notice a trend in this direction as early as the 1950s, when traditional urban manufacturing and retail activities began to decentralize. By the next decade they were writing about the growing mismatch between jobs and the skills present in residential areas nearest these opportunities (Kain 1968). Kain suggested that the levels of underemployment and unemployment in predominantly African American inner-city areas were growing because of this spatial mismatch. The lower-level skills of the inner-city labor force contrasted with the high skill levels required of job categories growing fastest in the center city (banking, administrative, and communication-related activities). Since the 1970s, large American metropolises have experienced a dramatic polarization of social space, with large principal cities developing dramatic concentrations of ethnic poverty and joblessness (Morenoff and Tienda 1997). Paul Jargowsky (1997, 2003) demonstrates the pervasive nature of this intensifying concentration of the poor in principal cities, ethnically segregated neighborhoods. His review of census tract data for the United States from 1970 to 2000 reveals the dimensions of this spatial polarization:

1. While the number of poor in metropolitan areas grew by 37 percent during these 20 years, the number of poor residing in high-poverty neighborhoods (tracts with 40 percent or more of total households below the poverty line) rose by 98 percent.
2. The number of poor persons living in high-poverty neighborhoods nearly doubled, from 1.9 million to 3.7 million.
3. The number of high-poverty neighborhoods more than doubled, suggesting the spread of urban blight.
4. Urban poverty concentration varied dramatically by race. The greatest concentrations of urban poverty were for African Americans.
5. One out of every three African American poor now lives in high-poverty neighborhoods, while only 6 percent of poor Whites live in highly concentrated areas of poverty.
6. By 1990, half of all high-poverty neighborhoods were Black ghettos. Almost all of the growth in high-poverty neighborhoods took place in principal cities.

7. While the concentration of minority poverty eased somewhat in the 1990s (Jargowsky 2003), recent economic and housing changes associated with the worst recession since the Great Depression have exacerbated problems for the urban poor, leading to a continuation of the trend toward ever-expanding high poverty ghettos (Kneebone and Berube 2008).

This tendency toward the growth of high-poverty neighborhoods is significant because in such places people must deal not just with their own poverty, but with the poverty of those around them. The high degree of stress associated with personal poverty is thus magnified by a contextual effect—a situation with obvious consequences for the physical and mental health of residents. Daily life for the high-poverty ghetto resident is characterized by the confluence of personal and contextual stressors associated with impoverished lifestyles and racial discrimination (Smith 1988).

Although the new urban sociology downplays the distinctive nature of the metropolis's inner-city and outer-city areas (Dear 2002), with much being made of the fact that suburbia is not a singular homogeneous place, real differences remain in the social areas of the city. The deconcentration of the metropolitan region is a reality linked directly to economic and political forces in late American capitalism (Gottdiener 1985) and the global economy (Sassen 2000). The shift of industrial jobs from the central city to the suburbs, to the Sunbelt, and to foreign countries has accentuated the divisions between inner city and outer city (Jargowsky 1997; Wilson 1996). The deconcentration of the metropolitan region stands in sharp contrast to the heavy concentration of minority poverty.

Where people live in the deconcentrated metropolitan region makes a difference in their own health and welfare. The metropolis is a highly segregated place consisting of many distinct social areas. The scale of life and the social characteristics of residents vary widely. These factors affect the social climate and ultimately the level of attachment people have to the local residential space. In turn, various places in the metropolis afford different access to resources and opportunities and different levels of exposure to hazard. Together, these differences create a mosaic of social and health experiences in the metropolitan region—a wide and very visible divide.

Capitalism and Landscapes of Hazard and Despair

The divided landscape of the contemporary city is a consequence of powerful social and economic forces. Places are social spaces transformed by users not only into areas of everyday interaction but also into commodities. That is, not only do the neighborhoods and houses of residents have intrinsic value as the home where people live and carry out their daily lives, they also have value as a commodity to be bought and sold in the real estate market. Various locations have both "use value" and "exchange value" (Lefebvre 1974; Logan and Molotch 1987). In some sense, this is one aspect of the distinction between place and space—place being a complex *phenomenon* intertwining personal, cultural, and social factors, and space being a *container* of objects and locations with measurable dimensions. Exchange value and use value, however, are not merely complementary views of the same thing; rather, they are competing ways of valuing locations. This conflict plays itself out in metropolitan areas in ways that do more than constrain the choices of friends and role models in neighborhoods. It literally shapes the urban landscape, determining the location of activities, resources, hazards, people, and ultimately the life chances attached to residents in various segments of the urban mosaic. Its consequences can be catastrophic for some.

The link between urban space and markets is ancient, but as Logan and Molotch (1987) point out, the commodification of place in the United States represents a near-idealized version of capitalism's transformation of the urban landscape. While the early industrial period promoted urban growth and linked markets to places, as capital became more portable in the global economy the idea of place has been trivialized (Zukin 1991). The use value of place yields to its exchange value in this economy, and exchange value is determined by forces in a placeless, often unregulated global realm. The same industrial product can be produced now in a variety of places throughout the world, so the jobs involved in manufacturing these products can also be quickly shifted. As Zukin

(1991) suggests, this is the basic problem confronting modern communities—capital moves, communities do not. As capital decouples from place, spaces become commodities responding to ever-shifting international economic forces. Capital shapes and controls the urban ecology. Ultimately the same forces that built an urban space can destroy it, and residents can do little about it except move.

At the heart of modern capitalism is energy of creative destruction (Schumpeter [1934] 1961). Capitalism involves recurrent innovation, innovation which leaves in its wake a pattern of destruction in which "capital creates and destroys its own landscape" (Zukin 1991:19). Thus, in addition to referring to the metropolis as a mosaic of social worlds, we can describe it as a landscape of uneven development with enormous discrepancies in the socioeconomic conditions of the city's social areas. Cities are acutely polarized places, divided up into "fortified cells of affluence and places of terror where police battle the criminalized poor" (Dear 2002). The structural reorganization of center-city economies touches most directly the lives of people already poor. As low-skill jobs decline dramatically with economic restructuring, economic deprivation accelerates in those areas that in the past may have been contiguous to development. This deprivation not only changes the opportunity structure in these areas, but also transforms their social climate. Places that have experienced a decline in low-skill jobs are eventually touched by higher crime rates and a general environment of violence (Shihadeh and Ousey 1998). In this sense, the undulations and rhythms natural to capitalism produce devastating ecological changes, creating the context for fear, hopelessness, and placelessness.

The link between the ecology of opportunity and the ecology of hazard is deeply entrenched in global capitalism, shaping landscapes of fear and despair. One of the best predictors of the location of toxic waste dumps in the United States is the geographical concentration of people of low income and color (Harvey 1997). Chicago's Southeast Side is a case in point. A predominantly African American area with more than 150,000 people, it has 50 commercially owned hazardous waste landfills and more than 100 abandoned toxic waste dumps. Not surprisingly, it also has one of the highest cancer rates in the United States (Bullard 1994).

The environmental justice movement draws direct attention to the nature of the problem. Harvey (1997) reviews the political-economic dynamics of this concentration of hazard. First, the location of toxic dumps is less costly in low-income areas and also has less impact on property values in these places. Second, a small transfer payment to cover the negative effects of location may be significant to the poor, while basically irrelevant to the better-off. This situation is particularly paradoxical because the rich are unlikely to give up an amenity at any price, and the poor, who can least endure the loss, are likely to give it up for a mere pittance. Third, the poor generally live in areas with weak political organization and hence are unable to resist the relocation of health-depriving hazards. These economic forces obviously produce environmental injustices and a vastly uneven terrain of hazard and risk in cities. Not only is the world a more hazardous place than ever before, but these dangers tend to be more spatially focused. The concentration of hazard, noted by urban ecologists since the 1920s, has increased in the last 30 years in American cities.

> The accelerating and spatially deepening uneven processes of "creative destruction" leave urban communities uprooted and displaced while propelling others on to new dizzy and commanding heights. . . . For the privileged—who are able to benefit from new technologies, new multimedia and modes of communication— movement, access and mobility have been augmented. . . . Meanwhile, there are those on the receiving end of this process—like the impoverished, the aged, the unemployed . . .—who have increasingly been imprisoned by it.
>
> (Merrifield and Swyngedouw 1997:12)

While hazard and danger have concentrated in high-poverty ghettos, fear has concomitantly intensified in middle-class areas. This divide, and the ecology of fear that it perpetuates, are precisely what Wilkinson (1996) had in mind when he talked about unhealthy postmodern societies. Understanding the shape of this uneven landscape and the processes that underlie it is essential to understanding the patterned inequality of health. Ultimately, as Wilkinson (1996) notes, it is also essential to understanding and addressing the significant health costs that accrue to wealthy social systems with such disparities.

The dramatic spatial inequality of postmodern American cities has deep consequences for the health of all metropolitan residents. The vast spatial divide between inner and outer city courses like a polluted stream through the very heart and soul of the American metropolis. The result is an "ecology of fear" that pervades urban areas from richest to poorest (Davis 1990, 1998).

> The carefully manicured lawns of Los Angeles's Westside sprout forests of ominous little signs warning "Armed Response!" Even richer neighborhoods in the canyons and hillsides isolate themselves behind walls guarded by gun toting private police and state-of-the-art electronic surveillance. . . . In the Westlake district and the San Fernando Valley the Los Angeles Police barricade streets and seal off the poor neighborhoods as part of their "war on drugs." In Watts, developer Alexander Haagen demonstrates his strategy for recolonizing inner-city retail markets: a panopticon shopping mall surrounded by staked metal fences and a substation of the LAPD in a central surveillance tower.
>
> (Davis 1990:223)

Los Angeles is just one example of the consequences of late capitalism's landscape of creative destruction, where the defense of luxurious lifestyles in the outer regions is translated into a fortressed urban ecology where "fortified cells" of affluence are separated from "places of terror" in areas of concentrated, minority poverty (Davis 1990). This is not merely a reproduction of the old ecology noted in urban sociology textbooks from the 1920s through the 1970s; it is brought about by revolutionary economic forces that ruthlessly divide society and intensify in cities the most malevolent aspects of postmodernity.

The "Second Civil War" that began in the long hot summers of the 1960s has been institutionalized into the very structure of the urban

space. The old liberal package of social control, attempting to balance repression with reform, has long been superseded by a rhetoric
of social warfare that calculates the interests of the urban poor and
the middle classes as a zero sum game.

(Davis 1990:224)

While capitalism plays a critical role in shaping the landscape of fear
and hazard in cities, the federal government has also left its imprint on
city space. Dear and Wolch (1987) argue that service-dependent inner-
city areas have arisen, in part, from the deinstitutionalization movement
in North America. Deinstitutionalization was intended to remove the
mentally disabled, physically handicapped, mentally retarded, prisoners,
and other groups from confining institutional settings and place them in
more "normal" residential settings. While well intentioned, it actually
flooded local communities with service-dependent individuals. As institutions closed, the people discharged from them gravitated toward specific areas of the city, typically inner-city areas where they found
affordable housing. "As dependent persons migrated to those urban
locations (often from considerable distances outside the city), they
attracted more services which themselves acted as a magnet for yet more
needy persons" (Dear and Wolch 1987:4). This process further reinforced the ecology of fear and despair perpetuated by economic forces.

How Spatial Structures Affect Our Choices:
A Constrained-Choice Approach

The foregoing discussions demonstrate the importance of place for the
everyday experiences of metropolitan residents. While early urban analysts such as Wirth thought that the scale and diversity of urban life
would lead to social disorder, that has not yet happened. But a fear of disorder does seem to have emerged at the same time that freedoms and
opportunities presented by postmodern economies have been publicly
touted. As we have already seen, Tuan (1982) argues that urbanization
itself has led to an interiorization of domestic space and growing possibilities for self-development. Expanding choice is often noted as a

hallmark of urbanization (Baldassare 1977), yet choices in the metropolitan area are highly constrained by spatial factors.

Ultimately, most human problem solving requires spatial problem solving. Location is a critical factor in fulfilling needs because traversing space requires the expenditure of resources (energy, time, money). Following this line of reasoning, the city can be seen as a gigantic resource machine in which access to resources is unequally distributed in the urban space. The city is not only a mosaic of social spaces, but also a mosaic of resource spaces. Social and economic resources occur in fixed locations, and thus are more or less accessible to some than to others depending on the distance of these locations from the individual's home. People living in certain places will have greater access to social ties, services, and products than others because of the travel costs, both real and imagined. This so-called "friction of distance" is an important aspect of space's role in the human experience. While the friction of distance has declined dramatically with transportation and communication improvements, space continues to be significant for everyday choices and actions. These constraints are both behavioral and cognitive in character. Space imposes bounds on both our access to resources and knowledge of the resources available. The mental maps people carry around with them represent the horizons of their choice field, which, in turn, are shaped by location. A person born and raised in one section of a metropolitan area, for example, is unlikely to be aware of, or prefer, residential options available in other sectors of the metropolis (Johnston 1972).

To understand how space constrains choice requires knowledge of (1) the spatial dimensions that affect local experiences, and (2) the dynamics of human decision making. Scale and diversity are two essential aspects of the urban space. Both vary greatly across the metropolitan area, impacting the place's social climate by determining the number and type of options available in a given location. How scale and diversity affect a place's social climate and a resident's choices within that residential place is clearer when the parameters of human decision making are considered. Choice theories typically suggest that we make decisions based on a "satisficing" rather than "optimizing" strategy (Cyert and March 1963; Simon 1957). That is, we don't search endlessly for the best option; rather, we stop when we find something satisfying within the parameters of our preferences and values. In essence, once satisfied, we stop looking for alternatives. This view of choice suggests a potentially important role for spatial arrangements in decision making. Satisficing behavior implies that moving across space requires effort and resources (time, energy, and money). Therefore, if satisfying options can be found nearby, people will make choices without seeking distant alternatives.

But choice involves more than cost considerations. Satisfaction is dependent on the options available and how they fit with our preferences. Two aspects of space, intimately tied to Wirth's notions of the city as place, affect the options available to people: (1) the number of options available in a given place (choice density), and (2) the degree to which these options have the qualities preferred by those choosing. Perhaps the most important type of options offered in a community are the social opportunities available in a place—most particularly the range of available friends. The number of available neighbors governs the number of interaction choices presented in a place. If the choice density of neighbors is high, each individual in the neighborhood will have a higher probability of finding satisfying interactions there. In effect each place has its own "carrying capacity for community ties" (Blau 1994). Sustaining these ties, however, is likely to be a function of how much persons have in common with one another. People who share a salient social identity are likely to share other things—homophily prevails in most social associations (Blau and Schwartz 1984; Lin 2001).

The significance of homophily for patterns of local association, however, is likely to be complicated. While a homophily principle may govern social associations, its effect on local patterns of neighbor interaction may vary, depending on which statuses are homophilous. If the homophilous status signifies great access to resources outside the neighborhood (e.g. high income and education), then dense, status-segregated neighborhoods could encourage extensive ties in the local area, but the ties are likely to be shallow and short term. On the other hand, if the status embodies need (e.g. low income, low education, minority status) then networks may be less extensive (because people have friends here out of necessity), but the ties may be deeper, involving more frequent contact and greater intensity. Work by Campbell and Lee (1992) on 81 neighborhoods in Nashville substantiates the view that level of need affects the operation of the homophily principle. If, however, a neighborhood is characterized by residents with high need and pervasive fear, social networks may be further truncated. In such places, need and fear reinforce one another, producing detachment and very limited ties inside and outside the neighborhood.

Whatever the permutations, local ecology is important for community dynamics, and ultimately it affects the quality of residential life. The levels of choice density and social segregation vary widely across metropolitan areas, constraining social networks in some places while freeing up social ties in others, ultimately helping to shape the character of places. While some places have characteristics that promote dense and closed networks, others encourage open and wide-ranging social ties. Space matters greatly for the individual's experience, quality of life, and overall health. The spatially constrained choices of individuals accumulate and produce the neighborhood's social climate and its ability to relate effectively with the larger metropolitan institutional structure. In turn, these two factors, *social climate* and *linkages to outside resources*, are critical determinants of a neighborhood's "viability" (Schoenberg and Rosenbaum 1980). Research has demonstrated that the spatial dimension is an essential ingredient in the persistence of African American minority group status in the United States; the heavy concentration of Blacks in high-poverty ghettos has created special disadvantages that intensify the disadvantages of class (Massey and Denton 1993). The flood-ravaged Ninth Ward of New Orleans and Birmingham's Village Creek are but two examples among hundreds nationally of such places and their consequences.

Local Friendships

Table 3.1 considers the effects of spatial structure (choice density and social segregation) on the degree of intimacy within local social networks, other things being held constant. The situation of high homogeneity and wide choice noted in Cell 1 produces a pattern of

Table 3.1 The Intensity of Local Networks as Affected by Spatial Constraints

	Choice Densities	
Segregation	*High*	*Low*
High	Communal	Sociable
Low	Cosmopolitan	Unattached

Source: LaGory 1982:73.

communalism. In its ideal form this may produce a very cohesive social space, with strong social ties and dense social networks. Under conditions of high segregation and dense population, as well as significant socioeconomic constraints, highly localized intimate ties are probable because choice of local friendships is extensive, and potential to make friends of similar background and identity is high. Need intensifies this probability, with persons unable to bear the costs of transportation and communication with outside areas having an even greater likelihood of dense localized networks.

The degree to which these individualized spheres of confidants mesh together to form a strong community bond is highly variable, particularly in communities where the transient population is high. Under such circumstances, the opportunities for interaction may be high. The number of local ties, however, may be low because of limited territorial functioning and the lack of trust in an environment characterized by transience and limited personal knowledge of other neighbors. The presence of a great many strangers increases fear and distrust, which can minimize the potential of an area to produce a strong sense of community. "Fear proves itself" (Davis 1990). On the other hand, if the community is characterized by a small number of transients, then an idealized form of communalism is likely to develop. Under these conditions, the spatial characteristics described in Cell 1 can produce a vibrant local community.

Even under the more preferable circumstance of low transience, however, communal social networks present a difficulty to local inhabitants.

In a communal setting, networks are so tightly knit that there is an absence of "weak ties" (friends of friends) outside the local area (Granovetter 1973a; Massey 1990; Shrum and Cheek 1987). Hence, linkages to outside resources are minimized. As has been demonstrated, weak ties provide essential links to the larger political and economic resources in the metropolitan area and empower communities. These reduced connections to the local and regional power structure inhibit the influence such places can have over their own fate. Thus, even vibrant neighborhoods with strong social and cultural ties face dramatic challenges from the outside unless they have significant resources to resist such efforts.

The second cell represents spatial circumstances common in some suburban and rural fringe areas, as well as in racially segregated urban neighborhoods with high vacancy rates undergoing a period of decline. Here the local community is relatively homogeneous, but the range of intimate friends available is limited by low population densities. As a result, people have the possibility of maintaining local ties, but their ties are unlikely to be either intense (i.e. frequent or intimate) or extensive in character. As stated previously, need promotes this outcome. While residents in general are likely to participate in some neighboring, for those who can afford the costs of transportation and communication, friendships will likely be scattered in many places throughout the urban area (Fischer 1982). For wealthy neighborhoods, then, limited liability (i.e. few local obligations and strong ties) characterizes the social climate of places with Cell 2 spatial characteristics. Low-income neighborhoods, however, are likely to be disadvantaged because residents there will have limited ties to the outside (due to limited access to other areas), as well as the potential for limited local intimate ties due to choice limitations. Low-income and minority-dominated neighborhoods with these spatial qualities suffer from both limited political influence and an atmosphere of limited liability. If the neighborhood is also characterized by high transience, the social climate will exhibit even more detachment.

The circumstances described in both Cell 1 and Cell 2 of Table 3.1 suggest a situation in which those with already limited influence and resources (hyper-segregated minorities) find themselves in residential contexts that exacerbate their sense of disconnectedness from the larger metropolis. While "communal" spatial conditions can promote a sense of place, residents' dense social networks potentially neutralize these benefits. Such spatial conditions intensify the already negative effects of poverty and minority status by limiting the weak ties of residents. These ties are essential to accessing personal resource networks. Residents with only a few weak ties, or none at all, lack power and the ability to garner the resources to change their circumstances.

The third and fourth cells of Table 3.1 display neighborhood social patterns that evolve under conditions of low segregation. Greater variety in friendship options allows for more freedom in the formation of social networks. Homogeneity, on the other hand, enhances the stability of local friendships by increasing the probability of satisfying choices, with people from similar backgrounds and experiences having much in common. For people with limited resources, freedom of choice may be highly desirable under circumstances of high choice density (Cell 3). In cases where choice densities are high, a cosmopolitan community form is likely. Perhaps the best-known example of this is New York's Greenwich Village, but most large cities have such places where an amalgam of ethnic, racial, and socioeconomic groups share residence, usually along with a number of urban amenities. These communities exhibit moderately strong local networks, but because of the variety of social ties they are also likely to have substantial "weak ties" to other portions of the metropolitan area. This community is capable of political action, is more open to outsiders, and is likely to garner resources effectively from the larger community. It is an outward-looking community form rather than an inward-looking one. The social climate here tolerates differences. Trust in such areas is also higher. In cultures that emphasize individuality and control, this particular set of spatial conditions promotes physical and mental health (Davis 1990).

The final cell of Table 3.1 represents a situation of "detachment" not unlike Wirth's (1938) description of urbanism. In these areas, the choice of local primary ties is arithmetically constrained, and because of the differences among neighbors, they have little in common. Such places make it difficult to find and sustain local friendships. While these areas certainly promote individuality and freedom, the degree of personal control over friendships is minimal. Trust is eroded. Such places lack social identity as well as any political control over their future. Identity and control may be further exacerbated by the fact that they also tend to be areas with high rates of transience, further intensifying detachment (Sampson 1988).

Patterns of Socialization

Because spatial circumstances affect the conditions for local interaction, they also shape socialization experiences and thus the cultural climate of residential areas. A variety of research traditions emphasize the role of space in self-development and the acquisition of roles, including: criminology (Bursik 1986; Krivo and Peterson 1996; Sampson and Wilson 1995; Taylor and Covington 1988), deviance (Crane 1991), ethnic assimilation (Lieberson 1961), and status attainment (Crane 1991; Datcher 1982).

In the criminology and deviance literatures, two health-related metaphors are used to explain role acquisition—risk exposure and contagion. Sutherland's classic theory (Sutherland and Cressey 1960) of differential association provides an idealized version of the risk exposure view. Here the likelihood of individual criminal behavior is a function of the local context and the individual's access to a diversity of roles and norms. If individuals are exposed to a predominance of deviant norms and institutions then the individual has a high likelihood of performing deviant acts. The relationship between exposure and the performance of deviant acts, however, is not linear. Crane (1991) suggests that a tipping point exists in the relationship between exposure to deviance and the likelihood of deviant behavior. In this view, a contagion effect exists when a tipping point is reached in deviance exposure, causing the levels of deviance in the area to increase at an exaggerated rate. Crane shows this effect in rates of both teenage pregnancies and high school dropouts.

These views can be set in a broader sociological context. Role theorists argue that the structure and process of human thought are affected by the social context. "Social structures differ in the extent to which they encourage or discourage . . . the use of intellectual flexibility" (Coser 1975:252). Social contexts characterized by great role diversity stimulate the development of intellectual flexibility and self-direction. If people are exposed to complex social environments, with competing expectations (role articulation), the individual is forced to evaluate and reflect upon appropriate courses of action. This situation promotes innovation (deviation from the local norms and patterns of behavior) rather than conformity. In essence, this is one of the weaknesses of strong ties suggested by Granovetter (1973a and b). In highly segregated, dense settings, peer pressure becomes intense. The communalism of Cell 1, Table 3.1, can have contagion-like effects on the behaviors of its residents. Obviously the social linkages shaped by locale have direct bearing on the behavioral repertoire available to participants. In this sense, the same forces that constrain friendship choices should also channel likely paths of behavior via learned values and norms and available role models (Wilson 1996).

Table 3.2 presents the likely consequences of various spatial contexts for socialization outcomes in neighborhoods and communities. As such, they depict another aspect of the expected relationship between space and social climate. The phrases used to describe various outcomes reflect terms used in Robert Merton's classic essay on deviance (1968). We assume that, particularly for the young with limited mobility (no access to regular transportation), commitment to a given behavioral pattern will be affected by (1) the diversity of roles and norms present in the neighborhood (degree of segregation); (2) the extent of role models available there (choice density); and (3) the youth's awareness and exposure to norms and role models outside the local context. Of course, in modern

Table 3.2 The Likely Paths of Behavior in Various Spatial Contexts

	Choice densities of possible significant others	
Diversity of norms	*High*	*Low*
Low	Conformity	Ritualism
High	Innovation	Retreat

Source: LaGory 1982:75.

societies, role models and behavioral repertoire are readily available from a variety of extraspatial sources—print media, radio, and television—so that at least awareness and exposure to alternatives may be constant. If there is reasonable consistency of awareness, then local features should play a special role in the development of local subculture for less mobile groups (youth and elders). As youths gain access to transportation this may change somewhat, although the evidence presented earlier on social areas suggests a local effect for all age groups.

The first cell of Table 3.2 portrays a situation of high choice but limited diversity in the range of role models available. This situation, common in inner-city neighborhoods, is likely to produce high levels of conformity to the prevailing local norms. In cases where the neighborhood is riddled with illicit activity and local institutions supporting deviance, young persons learn to conform to deviant expectations. This environment promotes the presence of a pervasive local deviant subculture. Under this spatial circumstance, lifestyle orientations are relatively homogeneous, but the individual is given the illusion of some choice between role models. Here local ties are intense, but role articulation is low (i.e. limited presence of conflicting roles). Thus, both private conformity to neighborhood peer standards and limited individual autonomy are the rule.

The ritualist of Cell 2, on the other hand, may be more capable of independent action because ties are less intimate and more "sociable." While individuals are likely to experience similarly low levels of role articulation, peer choices are very limited. This situation is likely to encourage public acceptance of local norms, but individuals may be more inclined to seek role models in the public arena (media) or in other areas. In essence, pressures to conform to the local social climate are less significant than in Cell 1.

The last two cells of Table 3.2 describe spatial conditions that afford individuals greater opportunities for autonomy. The choice of role models in the cosmopolitan community is wide ranging, in both number and variety. In this case, role articulation is more plausible and friendships are less spatially confined than in Cell 1. People have connections (weak ties) to other areas. Here the individual is free to be more innovative, and community tolerance is likely to be higher than in conditions of conformity or ritualism. In this case, people may be encouraged to consider alternative lifestyles, and no single subculture is promoted. The retreatist stance is most likely when role articulation is probable but the choice of available role models is constrained. This condition is potentially alienating because individual freedom is encouraged (via role articulation) but the local area does not offer the array of social networks to exert this independence, a fact which may lead to social disorganization.

Conclusion

Both interior spaces and neighborhood places have the potential to affect individuals' lives in many ways. As we demonstrate in Chapter 4, health is in part a function of human experiences and actions. To understand the experiential and behavioral factors connected to health, we should be aware of the significance of place, taking into account the role that spatial structures play in constraining or expanding the choices people have and the circumstances they are exposed to. As just seen, certain spatially structured conditions (sociocultural diversity, choice densities, levels of transience, and employment opportunities) set the social climate (friendship networks, socialization experiences, and level of violence) for various neighborhoods and thus affect residents' everyday lives. Besides this social climate, there is a physical climate shaped by forces in the global economy and the local metropolitan area which impacts everyday life. Hazards are unequally concentrated, and those with the most limited resources have the greatest exposure to hazard. In the modern high-technology, high-risk society, haves and have-nots are easily distinguished by their levels of risk exposure. This stratification of risks is deeply embedded in the urban landscape. That landscape, in turn, intensifies the risk experience. In the next chapter we show how these spatial structures may also help to shape people's health.

4

THE SOCIOLOGY OF HEALTH

America has the best doctors, the best nurses, the best hospitals, the best medical technology, the best medical breakthrough medicines in the world. There is absolutely no reason we should not have in this country the best health care in the world.

William Frist

If we aren't willing to pay a price for our values, then we should ask ourselves whether we truly believe in them at all.

Barack Obama

The story of Village Creek is not unlike those told in high-poverty neighborhoods across the country that have been threatened by exposure to environmental hazards. Residential toxic exposure is highly disruptive (Downey and Van Willigen 2005; Ellaway and Macintyre 1996, 1998; Greenberg and Schneider 1996; Kawachi and Berkman 2003). The stress experienced by contamination or even the threat of contamination is significant and underscores the importance of understanding health. Beyond the obvious physical health risks, exposed residents often report feelings of anger, frustration, aggression, and depression, and in some cases require hospitalization for mental or emotional illness. Many families experience disruption, financial difficulties, divorce or separation, and extended unemployment as a result of their exposure to hazards (e.g. Edelstein 2004). The community's social fabric is torn apart by the stress of exposure to hazards. When physical stressors collide with the stressful circumstances of individual and contextual poverty, neighborhood detachment is likely to occur (Kawachi and Berkman 2003; Woldoff 2002). These "detached communities" are more likely to be urban, high density, low income, and predominantly minority. It is estimated that there are over 400 hazardous waste sites in the United States, with 9 million people living within 2 miles of one of them. Over half of those residents are minorities, living in neighborhoods where the poverty rate is 1.5 times higher, and the population density is nearly 30 times greater (Saha 2009).

While the physical impact of environmental disasters on residents in urban areas is well documented (Bullard 1990, 2000; Edelstein 2004), the feeling of helplessness experienced in such disasters is often overlooked. As was the case in the Village Creek incident, residents often report experiencing depression-like symptoms as their home and neighborhood are threatened. In addition to affecting individual health, exposure to hazard challenges the overall well-being and quality of life in the local community. While threats to health are the immediate issue, these threats themselves initiate an extraordinary distress process with long-term implications for residents.

The Healthy Society

Anticipation and worry over threats to physical health are not surprising or necessarily community specific. There is a revitalized interest in health in American society that, in part, has been motivated by an increase in chronic diseases associated with negative health behaviors (Becker and Rosenstock 1989). In addition, the recent convergence of several social phenomena, including the graying of America, technological development leading to increased health risks, health care reform, along with a culture that increasingly promotes self-development, has encouraged Americans to rethink their health behaviors. Expenditure patterns reveal that the U.S. population spends billions of dollars each year on fitness and health-related activities and equipment (U.S. Department of

Commerce 2005). In addition, the health service industry now accounts for over 15 percent of the gross domestic product, with billions spent on health care annually (Organization for Economic Cooperation and Development 2007). Ironically, in the midst of the "health craze" and the boom in health-related spending, general health and health care remain significant social and political problems for the United States (Link 2008). Our population's health does not reflect the country's significant and growing expenditures for health care.

This motivated the Obama administration to work with legislators and health professionals to reform health care delivery in the United States. While the consequences of this effort remain uncertain, the intention is clear. Successful reform requires expanding coverage and emphasizing preventive care, while honoring patient choice, reducing inflationary pressures on costs, and holding insurance companies accountable. An effective health care system must offer universal access to basic care. Postmodern capitalism has produced not only great wealth for some, but also dramatic poverty for others. In America's current free market-driven system, the economically disadvantaged are medically disadvantaged. The quantity and quality of health services are unevenly distributed geographically, and there are clear-cut disadvantages for those living in inner cities where poverty and minority status combine and are concentrated (Collins and Schulte 2003; Wright and Fisher 2003).

Besides structural barriers to good health, the quest to become the "healthy society" often has been overshadowed by lifestyles that promote health-compromising and risk-taking behaviors. Health-compromising lifestyles continue to challenge health care professionals as they struggle to find new ways to modify old behaviors. America's comparatively poor health appears to be due in part to such risk-taking behaviors as smoking, drinking, drug use, poor eating habits, sedentary lifestyles, and risky sexual practices, among others (American Heart Association 2009; Colditz et al. 1996; Goldstein 1992). Although health-related behaviors are important for health outcomes, this individualized perspective overemphasizes genetics and behavior while ignoring the critical role that social structure plays in determining health care access, as well as physical and mental well-being (Link 2008; Wilkinson 1996). For example, obesity is a major contributing factor to the poor health of Americans. Obesity is linked in complex ways to social structure. The highest rates of obesity ironically occur in states with the lowest median income and education, and the highest rates of physical inactivity (Drewnowski and Specter 2004). Poverty encourages poor diets. Healthier foods are less available in poor neighborhoods because such foods are often considerably more expensive, and low-cost foods are higher in sugars and fats and frequently more palatable than healthier, more expensive foods (Drewnowski and Specter 2004). In effect cheap foods are often preferred because of taste and cost per calorie, even when their long-term costs to health are considerable.

It is essential to understand the complicated relationship between health, social structure, and social behavior. Attempts to disentangle that relationship have been ongoing since Hippocrates. In *On Airs, Waters, and Places*, he noted that well-being was influenced by the intersection of social and environmental factors including climate, topography, quality of natural resources, and living habits and lifestyle. Since this first "ecological" examination, scientists have struggled with identifying specific social and behavioral causes for disease.

Rooted in eighteenth-century Western European thought, modern medical practice emerged with two distinctive orientations: a "medicine of the species" and a "medicine of social spaces" (Cockerham 2009; Foucault 1973). The medicine of social spaces represented the precursor to modern-day preventive medicine. It was based on the simple notion that if a person's daily activities were regulated, health and health behaviors could be positively affected. This critical assumption represents the basis for the modern public health approach, which assumes that health and behavior are intimately connected and that improvements in health require changing people's behavior patterns. There are numerous contemporary examples (AIDS, heart disease, tuberculosis, cancer, cirrhosis, depression, anxiety, post-traumatic stress disorder) that illustrate how certain behaviors, conditioned by structural circumstances, can negatively impact an individual's physical and mental health. One of those structural circumstances is residence.

Place of residence influences an individual's mental and physical well-being and is a critical sociological variable affecting health. That relationship is central to this chapter and this book. In the last decade, research examining the link between place and health has grown exponentially, with convincing results (Corburn 2009; Kawachi 2002; Macintyre et al. 2005; Mirowsky and Ross 2003; Ross and Mirovsky 2001). In an attempt to explore this relationship we examine five theories that address the relationship between social structure, behavior, and health: health beliefs, healthy lifestyles, risk and protective factors, psychosocial resources, and neighborhood disadvantage/disorder. We then show how they can be used to develop a comprehensive place-based theory of health. To accomplish this, the ecological theory discussed in Chapter 3 is employed to explore the links between ecological characteristics, health-related aspects of social structure and behavior, and the health of urban populations.

Health Beliefs

The first of the major social science theories of health is the health beliefs model (Becker 1974; Rosenstock 1966, 1990). This theory uses attitudes to explain why certain individuals engage in health-protective behaviors while others do not. It rests on the assumption that individuals take disease-preventive action when their behavior can lead to a valued outcome, and they believe that the desirable outcome is achievable. In an attempt to explain health-related behavior, the theory shows how disease-prevention behaviors occur when four conditions are present. First, individuals must believe (susceptibility) that there is some threat (disease or condition) to their health. Second, they also must believe that contracting a particular disease or developing a particular condition will have serious consequences. Third, they must assume that taking certain actions can reduce their susceptibility to the disease or the seriousness of the condition. Fourth, modifying factors exist (demographics, psychosocial factors, media campaigns, advice from professionals and friends, etc.) that can influence a person's perception of the disease's threat and the likelihood that she will take preventive action (Becker 1974).

In short, the theory suggests that individual perceptions can be modified to increase chances that persons take a recommended preventive action to improve or maintain their health. The modifying influence of television and radio, reminders from physicians, newspaper or magazine articles, prior knowledge or contact with a particular disease, and peer pressure can work in combination to mediate the negative expectation of individuals and their perception of disease threat. The model assumes that elements of a person's belief system can be changed in order to ensure a successful treatment or prevention outcome (Becker 1974).

Over the last several decades, the health beliefs model has been used with some success in explaining health-preventive behavior. Applications of the theory have included AIDS prevention (Brown et al. 1991; Connor and Norman 1996; Montgomery et al. 1989), dengue health education (Lennon 2005), and seat belt use (Nelson and Moffit 1988). Most studies indicate that the model's real merit is in identifying the role that a person's subjective health assessment plays in the decision to seek health services. Indeed, research shows that an individual's opinions about his or her health are often a better predictor than an actual medical diagnosis as to whether individuals will seek treatment for a disease or condition. While not without criticism, this micro approach demonstrates the role of attitudes and beliefs in determining health-related behaviors. It suggests that a macro-level theory of health requires acknowledgement of the subculture's function in shaping the health of various populations.

Criticism of the theory centers on the questionable ability of attitudes and perceptions to predict health behavior. Do perceptions actually cause behaviors, or do circumstances that are either out of the individual's control or impossible to measure make the difference? Attitude-behavior approaches are often critiqued for over-rationalizing human behavior. Some argue that attitudes merely offer individuals an opportunity to provide after-the-fact explanations for personal habits that involve little rationale or calculation. In addition, critics argue that the model is difficult to quantify. Perhaps the more serious criticism, however, is that this model accounts for behavior simply by relying on attitudes and beliefs, to the exclusion of important structural and environmental factors (Bernard and Krupat 1994).

Health Lifestyles

A more recent approach to health behavior is the health lifestyles model. Lifestyles are ways of life involving preferences in food, fashion, appearance, housing, work patterns, leisure, and other forms of behavior that differentiate people. Health lifestyles are defined as collective patterns of health-related behavior based on the choices made available to people according to their life chances (Cockerham 2007; Cockerham and Ritchey 1997). Health lifestyles include nutrition and eating habits, drinking, smoking, exercise, personal hygiene, coping patterns, and other health-related patterns of behavior. Cockerham (1999) demonstrates the critical role that lifestyles play in health, showing how the widespread decline in health in former Eastern Bloc socialist countries can be attributed to lifestyle patterns.

Life chances include age, gender, race, ethnicity, and socioeconomic position. Life chances shape the choices available to people; socioeconomic standing affects the individual's ability to realize these choices. In this perspective, while people generally engage in some form of health-advancing behavior, socioeconomic position helps to determine their capacity to pursue and obtain specific health outcomes.

This model is grounded in the earlier work of Max Weber, who first proposed the idea of lifestyles in his discussion of status groups in *Economy and Society* ([1922] 1978). Weber links lifestyle to status by suggesting that the characteristics of status can be expressed in the particular lifestyles that a person chooses. Knowing that lifestyles are part of a consumption process, Weber argues that lifestyle differences between status groups are a function of their relationship to the means of consumption, rather than the means of production (Cockerham et al. 1997). Thus, consumption of goods and services is a way that social differences are expressed and actually established between status groups. So, for example, a person using a health spa at an exclusive resort is a consumer with a status and social identity clearly different from someone who cannot afford that type of health-improving activity, or someone who can but chooses other activities.

Weber views life choices (*Lebensführung*) and life chances (*Lebenschancen*) as components of a person's lifestyle (*Lebensstil*) (Abel and Cockerham 1993; Cockerham et al. 1993). Life choices reflect the preferences individuals make regarding lifestyle, which are intimately related to an individual's life chances. Life chances refer to the likelihood of achieving a particular lifestyle, based on past experiences, social status and power, and social networks. Thus, one's life chances are clearly constrained by social, political, and economic circumstances, which, in turn, affect life choices. In essence, the Weberian approach describes interplay between structure and choice, providing further elaboration of the health beliefs model.

While this model has great potential for contributing to a better understanding of health behaviors, a critical question raised by medical sociologists is: How does Weber's lifestyles concept translate into a healthy lifestyles framework? The work of Bourdieu (1984, 1990) bears directly on the contemporary version of the healthy lifestyles model. Bourdieu notes that while individuals choose their lifestyles, they do not do so freely. Rather, their *habitus* (a collection of objective social and economic conditions) predisposes them to make certain choices (Cockerham et al. 1997; Munch 1988). It provides an individual with a cognitive map of his or her social world, as well as behaviors appropriate for particular situations. Bourdieu (1990) contends that the human mind is socially bounded and limited by socialization, life experiences, and training. While most individuals understand their social circumstances, their perceptions are typically bounded by a social and economic reality. Habitus encourages development of a pattern of behavior and mind-set that appears reasonable to the individual, given their social and economic circumstances. Thus, what emerges is a lifestyle pattern, including a system of varying tastes (dress, food, and other forms of entertainment, including health and fitness) nested in a particular status group. Hence, social standing predisposes specific aspects of lifestyle, which may include eating, exercising, attitudes toward prevention, physical appearance, and a variety of risk-taking behaviors.

This relationship becomes most apparent when examining differences in health-improving behaviors between status groups. Martha Balshem (1991) illustrates the link between social status and lifestyle in a study of a working-class neighborhood where a public health program to reduce cancer risk failed. In this neighborhood, most residents believed that they could do nothing to improve their chances of preventing cancer, and so lifestyle changes were deemed futile. This finding supports Bourdieu's (1990) claim that due to habitus the usual ways of behaving prevail, and extraordinary changes in behavior are unlikely to occur (Cockerham et al. 1997).

While good health is a commonly held goal, people make a variety of choices affecting lifestyle patterns and health. Such choices usually occur for very practical reasons such as not wanting to contract specific diseases, desiring to live longer, wanting to look and feel good, or aging gracefully. In most Western cultures, a good deal of emphasis is placed on the role of life choices in effecting good health. Even as health care becomes more structured, a menu of options bombards the health consumer as they attempt to make decisions regarding who, how, when, and where they are cared for. With this overemphasis on choice, the relationship between chances and choices is often ignored. What predetermined factors influence choices? How does place affect choices? Is place a critical aspect of habitus?

Research continues to demonstrate the link between life chances and choices and their role in effecting health outcomes. Though socioeconomic status is important, it is not the only life-chance factor influencing health. In fact, certain health behaviors such as diet, exercise, smoking, and drinking patterns have been shown to be characteristic of particular groups of persons irrespective of their social standing (e.g. George and Johnson 2001; Grzywacz and Marks 2001). Beyond class, factors such as gender, residential location, and age also influence health behaviors. Researchers note that when controlling for socioeconomic status, men generally engage in more health-compromising behaviors than women (Cockerham 2005, 2007). The social area approach, reviewed previously in Chapter 3, suggests that places vary in lifestyle. The research generated from this perspective indicates that a place's social climate, independent of the individual's gender, age, and socioeconomic status, will affect the individual's style of life. No research has directly explored the impact of the social area on health behaviors. Research has been done, however, on age's implications for health lifestyles. Aging persons take better care of themselves—watching what they eat, taking more time to relax, and reducing their intake of alcohol and tobacco (Cockerham et al. 1988; Lueschen et al. 1995). The one exception is exercise, which declines with age, creating a major lifestyle change with the potential for significant impact on health (Grzywacz and Marks 2001).

Aspects of the healthy lifestyle viewpoint have been incorporated into the very consciousness of mainstream society. An overwhelming desire to look good and live longer and a conviction that these desires can be accomplished through wellness programs, exercise centers, and commercial products dominate a middle-class way of thinking that may be helping to set the health agenda in the twenty-first century. Unfortunately, this viewpoint often glosses over the critical role life chances play in determining lifestyles, creating the impression of a dialectic between life chances and choices rather than a causal or interactive process.

Risk and Protective Factors

A third framework, originally designed to explain health-compromising behaviors (drug and alcohol use) among youth, is the risk and protective factors model. Instead of conceptualizing health behavior as a function of both socially determined chances and individual choices, this distinctively public health approach concentrates on the factors promoting or discouraging health-compromising behaviors. These factors are seen as complex, multilevel forces operating at both individual and contextual levels.

The salience of certain risk and protective factors varies across individuals, families, schools, and communities. Thus, a multilevel prevention approach becomes critical to developing effective strategies for reducing health-compromising behavior. This systems approach to understanding health-compromising behaviors among youth is compatible with

Bronfenbrenner's ecological theory (1979, 1986). Here, a child's development is strongly influenced by family, schools, peers, and neighborhood, which, as the main "spheres of influence," act as interdependent, nested parts or systems. Each system contains an "organized collection of activities and resources that exists within definable social and physical boundaries" (Berger et al. 1996), and each one exerts its own influence on the individual. This systems approach to development recognizes both the child's capacities to change, as well as the social environment's power to induce such change. While genetic code is important in determining cognitive, social, and psychological outcomes, the social ecology of a community creates a powerful context of influence, significantly affecting the path of development (Bronfenbrenner 1986; Garbarino et al. 1992). These ever-widening "spheres of influence" are precisely why the risk and protective factors perspective is important for developing a place-based approach to health.

The general model proposes that the relationship between risk and health-compromising behaviors is buffered or mediated by protective factors. While the specifics of the risk and protective factors model have gone through significant theoretical revisions, the general perspective has produced a great deal of research over the past 30 years. This research has allowed generalizations to be made regarding the role of risk and protection in understanding negative health outcomes (Dekovic 1999; Fitzpatrick 1997; Fitzpatrick et al. 2008; Fitzpatrick et al. 2009; Piko and Fitzpatrick 2003; Piko et al. 2005; Sameroff et al. 1993; Stevens 2006). These generalizations include the following:

1. Risk factors exist in multiple domains. Risk occurs at various levels in the individual's environment—the family, school, social networks, and neighborhood.

2. The more risk factors present in the environment, the greater the risk and the greater the likelihood that a negative health outcome will result. Many persons are at risk for negative health outcomes. Some, however, are exposed to such a large number that their "risk quotient" is exponentially greater than others. For example, all children living in poverty are at risk for poor negative health outcomes simply

because they are poor, yet not all of these children follow similar health trajectories. If a child lives in poverty, has a low IQ, lives with a single parent, has no health insurance, has low self-esteem, and is constantly exposed to community violence, that child's risk quotient is significantly greater than for a child who lives in poverty without any other risk factors present.

3. Common risk factors predict a diverse set of health outcomes. This finding suggests that when certain risk factors are identified and interventions prove successful, additional benefits may accrue. Thus, for example, a program that successfully reduces violence exposure and improves mental and physical health may also reduce feelings of vulnerability, while increasing school performance and social competence.

4. The effects of risk factors show some consistency across race, ethnicity, and social class. Thus, while risk varies from group to group, the effects of risk do not, suggesting that community prevention efforts targeting specific risk factors should be adaptable to a variety of subpopulations.

5. Protective factors may buffer the negative effects of exposure to risk. Research has demonstrated that certain protective factors moderate the negative consequences of exposure to risk, improving health outcomes. Protective factors are both passive and active; some actually reduce risk simply by their presence, while others change the way a person responds to risk. Armed with knowledge about these multi-level protective factors, communities can develop programs that more effectively minimize or eliminate risk.

6. As is the case with risk factors, protective factors occur at multiple levels. Individual, family, school, and community-level characteristics are important in helping individuals establish a "blanket of protection." Protective factors include individual characteristics such as gender, IQ, and temperament; family and school characteristics such as bonding with parents and teachers, parental supervision and interest in child's activities; and community characteristics such as healthy beliefs and well-defined standards in a community that provides support and access to resources.

The risk and protective factors framework has been particularly useful in developing comprehensive prevention programs for spatially concentrated health problems. Developing and implementing strategies that comprehensively attend to the multidimensional physical and mental health needs of children and families is a formidable task. Unfortunately, most of the efforts have concentrated on treating the illness rather than dealing with the risks associated with the illness, such as place of residence, and the socioeconomic and general life circumstances of the individual.

As suggested, a risk-based approach to prevention can be used as a comprehensive strategy to address the health problems emerging in a diverse society with significant demographic differences in morbidity and mortality. Following theories of health discussed earlier in this chapter, health lifestyles and beliefs should be included in this framework as aspects of risk and protection targeted for the prevention of health-compromising behavior.

Psychosocial Resources

Another framework used to explain health behavior is the psychosocial resources model, a model that originated from the earlier work of stress researchers (Dohrenwend and Dohrenwend 1981; Holmes and Rahe 1967; Tausig 1986a and b; Thoits 1985). The model attempts to understand the intricate relationships among stressors, social and psychological resources, and the individual's mental health (Cobb 1976; Dean and Lin 1977; Ensel and Lin 1991; Lazarus and Folkman 1984; Lin et al. 1986; Mirowsky and Ross 1989; Pearlin 1989; Turner 1983; Turner et al. 1995; Wheaton 1983).

Stressors refer to environmental, social, or individual circumstances that give rise to stress, force people to adjust or readjust their behavior, and eventually influence the mental and/or the physical health of the individual (Thoits 1995). Pearlin (1989) suggests that two major types of stressors should be considered: *life events* and *chronic strains*. Life events are undesired, unscheduled, and uncontrollable acute events in a person's life, such as divorce, death, loss of a job, or in the case of Village Creek, an environmental accident. Extensive empirical research has shown that one or more negative events experienced in a year can have a negative impact on a person's mental health (Cohen and Williamson 1991; Tausig 1986a and b; Thoits 1983).

Chronic strains, on the other hand, are more enduring problems faced on a daily or ongoing basis. These circumstances, like life events, also have negative effects on physical and mental health (Avison and Turner 1988; Pearlin 1989; Verbrugge 1989). Chronic strains have been linked to the social roles and places that are byproducts of the stratification system. Thus, gender, race/ethnicity, and class become particularly relevant to a discussion of the association between social position and individual health outcomes (Mirowsky and Ross 1989; Pearlin 1989).

Perhaps the most obvious example of the link between social position and health is that of income inequality (Lundberg 1993; Wilkinson 1996). Poverty represents a chronic strain with significant consequences for health. Both absolute and relative deprivation cause stress; empirical evidence shows that adverse socioeconomic circumstances have the potential for long-lasting psychological and emotional damage, particularly for children living in high-stress environments (Bolland 2003). General comparisons with children not living in poverty indicate that at-risk youth are more likely to fail in school, have disciplinary problems, have low achievement scores, repeat grades, drop out of school, exhibit delinquent behavior, and experience long periods of unemployment. These same youth are also likely to encounter significant physical and mental health problems.

To further illustrate the important role that socioeconomic disadvantage plays in determining health outcomes, Wilkinson (1996), using cross-national data, demonstrates that at similar levels of development, nations with greater income inequality generally have populations with poorer overall health. Hence, in those countries where inequality is modest and social cohesiveness high, life expectancy is higher. Among developed countries, it is not the wealthiest societies that have the best health, rather the most egalitarian do. Societies with a narrower gap between rich and poor have a stronger community life, less family dissension, and higher levels of formal and informal social support. These resources, in turn, play an important role in promoting health.

In general, researchers conclude that these types of resources intervene in the stress process. Resources modify or at least mediate negative conditions (life events or chronic strains such as poverty) that may lead to the development of mental health problems. Thus, they are conceptualized as reactive elements in the stress process, which are drawn upon as either mediators or buffers against negative external stimuli (Ensel and Lin 1991).

Two major types of resources are considered critical to understanding the overall stress reduction process. *Psychological resources* are personality characteristics that enable individuals to cope with challenging circumstances. Traits such as mastery (Pearlin and Schooler 1978), self-esteem (Rosenberg 1965), and social competence (Cairns and Cairns 1994) are resources capable of moderating life stressors. *Social resources* are the resources embedded within a person's social networks that serve specific instrumental and expressive needs. One way of thinking of these networks is to see them as *social supports* that persons in distress rely upon, including family, friends, and neighbors. These supports are critical to an individual's ability to cope with challenging, undesirable circumstances and events.

In describing the various aspects and sources of support, Lin and colleagues (1986) point to the "perceived or actual instrumental and/or expressive provisions supplied by the community, social networks, and confiding partners" (p. 18). There are several noteworthy aspects to this particular definition. One is a clear distinction between actual and perceived support. Both types of support have received a great deal of attention in the literature, and in a majority of research; both perceived and actual supports have been shown to reduce the negative consequences of stressors on an individual's mental health (Lin et al. 1986; Thoits 1995). The definition also highlights the multiple sources of social support for individuals. These include the characteristics of an individual's formal and informal networks, as well as the nature of the community in which those networks are embedded.

Considerable empirical evidence shows that social support at all these levels plays an important role in the stress process (see Thoits 1995 for a comprehensive review of social stress research and its major findings);

the exact nature of this relationship has been a subject of some debate (Ensel and Lin 1991). The suggested roles that resources play include deterrence and coping. Models proposing deterrence show resources directly reducing distress. Coping models, on the other hand, argue that stressors trigger a response from the individual's social resources that, in turn, have some impact on distress. Additionally, they point out that resources generally intervene in the relationship between stressors (events and circumstances) and levels of distress. Social science research most strongly supports the coping perspective (Ensel and Lin 1991; Thoits 1995). This perspective is also compatible with ideas contained in the risk and protective factors approach. Both models propose that social resources act as protection against the risks contained in a stress-filled environment.

But social ties are more than simply a coping mechanism or a vehicle for protection. They are assets that individuals can draw on both to get by as well as get ahead (Putnam 2000; Irwin et al. 2008; LaGory 2009). They are a form of capital as valuable to the well-being of individuals and communities as their financial assets, their education and training. Like financial capital and human capital, *social capital* is a resource that can be used not just to alleviate distress, but to actually promote health and well-being.

Just like financial and human capital, in order for them to be beneficial they must be spent from time to time. At a personal level such ties offer access to information, opportunities, and resources available only to the friends and acquaintances in those networks. With a little effort they can help the individual solve a range of personal challenges from finding work or a loan, to getting help when they are sick. The community can benefit from social capital as well. A multiplier effect is realized when groups share their talents and resources. Partnerships have the potential of being stronger, more resilient, and more creative than their partners.

Social capital benefits individuals and groups in two ways. It *bonds* similar individuals together, producing "strong ties" between them. A strongly bonded group offers entrée to a community of persons with similar characteristics, influence, and resources. On the other hand, social ties *bridge* or link differing groups of people, unlocking a wider array of resources and a wider span of influence. Bonding social capital allows people with limited resources to maintain their current circumstances and lifestyles better than they might on their own; a protective function (Putnam 2000). Bridging social capital, on the other hand, allows these same people to achieve a better life by providing admission into groups with a greater variety of resources and power. These ties are sometimes referred to as "weak ties" because they extend beyond the immediate support system of family and friends and include the individual's larger acquaintance structure. Weak ties can help people and communities overcome structural barriers to advancement. One critical problem, however, is that high-poverty ghettos, because of significant segregation, tend to have little bridging social capital, leading to circumstances in which residents have few social resources to overcome the structural disadvantages of poverty (Mitchell and LaGory 2002).

Neighborhood Disadvantage and the Ecology of Health

Ecological factors constrain the choices and actions of individuals in neighborhoods, and these actions and choices affect the health of residents and their communities. In addition, the ecology of a metropolitan area can directly affect health because of the differential risks distributed across the urban landscape. The nature of the relationship between ecology and health is obviously complex, involving more than just the physical and psychological risks inherent in a place. The ecology of an area has an impact on the health beliefs and practices of residents, their health lifestyles, their access to various health resources, and the social network of friends and supports that help people cope with stressful circumstances and events. Certain ecological conditions can intensify the health disadvantages of some groups, promoting the emergence of unhealthy lifestyles mired in risky and dangerous behaviors. They can concentrate persons with already limited options into areas that, because of their ecology, further restrict the lifestyle options, social supports, and health resources available to them. There are clearly unhealthy places.

Risk and *life chances* are spatially structured in the urban landscape. Because housing is delivered in the marketplace, residential location is a function of a group's ability to pay for housing and transportation, as well as their ability to gain advantage and control over the market. Hence, the urban space is home to a mosaic of groups sorted and sifted according to their political and economic resources (life chances). Those with greatest resources generally reside in areas containing low levels of risk, while those with limited resources find access restricted to undesirable areas with the greatest amount of risk. Thus, the ecology of risk follows fairly straightforward patterns in which people are segregated according to their abilities to gain housing. Risk, in other words, typically is segregated by those factors associated with life chances (race/ethnicity and class). Communities with the greatest concentration of risk contain large numbers of minorities and low-income persons living in aging residential areas—the low-resource populations and places of the high-poverty ghetto (Logan and Molotch 1987). These also happen to be groups whose lifestyle choices are constrained by their life chances or habitus.

The final health model included in this review of health theories, *neighborhood disadvantage*, examines these ecological aspects of health by exploring the role of neighborhood poverty in determining health and well-being (Cohen et al. 2003; Hill et al. 2005; Latkin and Curry 2003; Mirowsky and Ross 2003; Ross and Mirowsky 2001; Sampson et al. 2002). Neighborhood disadvantage theory offers a road map for a place-based approach to health, and has its roots in Wilson and Kelling's (1982) "broken-window" hypothesis. The urban disadvantage theory examines the complex interplay between neighborhood disadvantages (poverty, minority residents), personal disadvantages (low socioeconomic status, unemployment, low education), and neighborhood disorder (vacant housing, limited social capital), and these factors' impact on residents' physical and mental health (Browning and Cagney 2003; Ross and Mirowsky 2001; Sampson 2003; Sampson et al. 2002). Negative neighborhood conditions promote social disorder. Whether incivility or crime, fewer jobs or opportunities for success, residential disadvantage weakens the social fabric of places, creating an environment of fear, anxiety, depression, hopelessness, and poor physical health (e.g. Mirowsky and Ross 2003).

Perhaps no better example of this is Eric Klinenberg's (2002) study of heat-related deaths in Chicago during the unusually long and severe heat wave of 1995. In six days, 740 people died from heat-related causes (twice as many as during the Great Chicago Fire of 1871). The incident was more than a natural disaster, according to Klinenberg, it was "a catalogue of urban horrors" and a "biological reflection of social fault lines." While many elderly died, this wasn't just a manifestation of age-related health risks, but the lethal combination of a concentration of elderly living in socially isolated, deteriorating neighborhoods with limited social capital/support and declining commercial activity (Browning et al. 2006).

This incident is far from unusual—neighborhood conditions shape health outcomes across all age, gender, class, and racial groups. While separating individual from place effects is difficult, studies continue to show that neighborhoods with concentrated poverty and minorities, poor housing stock, and social disorder have poorer health outcomes (e.g. Baumer and South 2001; Elliot 2000; Ross 2000; Sampson et al. 2002). These places lack the resources necessary to promote good health and healthy lifestyles. High-poverty ghettos cannot keep or attract the supermarket chains or drugstores that offer healthy foods or the bare medical necessities to sustain a healthy way of life. The absence of health-promoting places such as parks, doctor and dentist offices, drugstores or chain grocery stores is complemented only by the prevalence of liquor stores, pawn shops, pay-day loan offices, and drug dealers.

In such places social capital is also limited, and even when it exists, it often functions in unhealthy ways. In neighborhoods where everyone is poor, bonding social capital may actually operate as an obligation network rather than a support system, where well-connected people are more frequently tapped for help, than provided support (Mitchell and LaGory 2002). In addition, since disadvantaged communities are also highly segregated places, their residents tend to lack the bridging capital that ties people to diverse resources. This makes it difficult for residents to escape the poverty dominating their personal lives and the lives of neighbors living around them.

These are places where trust is a scarce commodity. Those living and those coming into the community often cannot be trusted. Such places lack *collective efficacy*, defined as "the willingness and ability to intervene on behalf of the common good" (Sampson et al. 1997). They are unable to respond effectively to threats from inside and outside the community. In such places, crime accelerates and fear grows, keeping residents from using sidewalks and parks for physical exercise.

If, on the other hand, people feel strongly attached to a place and trust their neighbors, they are more likely to function territorially, and collective efficacy will be high. Collective efficacy may be exhibited in behaviors ranging from increased maintenance of their surroundings to assisting their neighbors. Territorial functioning spills over into strong neighborhood ties. In communities where the neighborhood becomes a central behavioral space, community ties strengthen and the area becomes more capable of defending itself against outside threats. Certain ecological conditions promote or reduce territorial functioning. These include spatial conditions that make neighborhoods defensible, such as opportunities for residential surveillance; attractive exteriors; real barriers that separate the residential area into manageable sectors; the absence of "spatial incivilities" such as litter, dilapidation, and graffiti; and the presence of shrubs, trees, and gardens (Perkins et al. 1996).

Disadvantaged neighborhoods with limited collective efficacy, on the other hand, are places where access to health-promoting resources are limited. The poor diets of disadvantaged residents, due to limited access to healthy foods and the costs of these foods, couple with the lack of exercise to promote obesity. Obesity is linked to an urban ecology that concentrates poverty and hazards, limits trust, and promotes unhealthy lifestyles (Drewnowski 2004). It is almost as if some communities were designed to make people sick. Not surprisingly, this link between neighborhood conditions and residents' health seems true for cities throughout the world (Cummins and Macintyre 2006; Macintyre et al. 2002, 2005; Mirowsky and Ross 2003), and for a range of U.S. cities (Boston, Chicago, New York, San Antonio, Birmingham, St. Louis, Raleigh, New Haven, Los Angeles, etc.) where researchers consistently find that high-poverty ghetto residents are at greater risk of experiencing physical and mental health problems than those living in other parts of the metropolis (Cockerham 2007; Kubzansky et al. 2005; Laraia et al. 2006; Sampson et al. 2008).

Another factor at work in the link between urban ecology and health is *health-related subcultures* (LaGory 1983). Disadvantaged neighborhoods characterized by residents with limited life chances and high levels of segregation have spatial structures that encourage the development of subcultures. Individuals in such areas develop significant bonding social capital but have few links outside the social area—creating what Fischer (1976, 1982) describes as a "critical mass" for subculture formation. For a subculture to emerge, certain minimal numbers are necessary to support the institutions that give the group a unique identity. Individuals learn cultural norms and values from role models. If the number of role models is high, but their social diversity low, then a situation of high conformity to the local subculture is likely. This conformity will be further intensified if people in the community also have limited resources to seek contacts outside the area, a condition occurring in inner-city areas where transportation is limited by low income and high rates of unemployment. Under these circumstances of limited life chances and highly concentrated social networks, conformity to the norms and values of the local area and limited individual autonomy will be the rule.

The degree to which the subculture deviates from the traditional culture will depend partially on how isolated the local group is, how big it is, as well as whether or not the resources and institutions in the community promote traditional values and norms. Whether risky behaviors become part of the local subculture will depend on the presence of "illegitimate institutions" and "deviant role models" (Cloward and Ohlin 1960). These institutions and models are most likely to emerge in places where the dominant culture's goals (such as achievement, material acquisition, etc.) are difficult for the local group to attain—a situation most common in areas with limited life chances (Merton 1968). These ecological circumstances (high density, high segregation, low access to health-promoting resources, presence of illegitimate institutions, presence of deviant role models) represent the spatial conditions that nurture high probabilities of health-compromising behaviors and health beliefs. This health-compromising subculture will further exacerbate the high risks

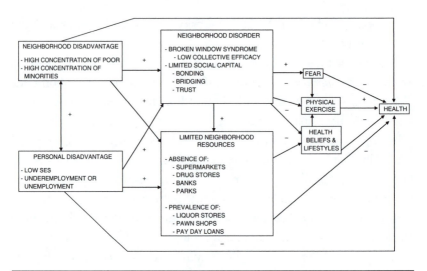

Figure 4.1 A synthetic model of the role of place on health

concentrated in such communities. Hence, local ecology often promotes a mosaic of distinct health challenges, combining unique subcultures with high amounts of hazard and risk, reduced social capital and collective efficacy, and limited health-promoting resources. The most obvious and discussed of these subcultures are high-poverty ghetto areas where the "urban health penalty" is the highest.

The urban disadvantage theory is currently the most effective way to organize and describe the ecological forces contributing to health and disease. Figure 4.1 summarizes this perspective on health and underscores the health disadvantages attached to living in high-poverty ghetto areas.

Conclusion

Until recently social science theories have not adequately integrated place into an understanding of the social forces that impinge on the general health and well-being of individuals and populations. A review of the five social theories of health provides a necessary backdrop for integrating basic ecological concepts into a more comprehensive approach to health and health behavior. This approach is particularly relevant to understanding the etiology and dynamics of the "urban health penalty." Certain neighborhoods within the United States clearly have distinct spatial qualities that shape residents' health risks, health beliefs, and behaviors, as well as the formal and informal networks of protection and support. Identifying these ecological characteristics is an essential first step to developing comprehensive programs that minimize or eliminate the urban health penalty. The value of this spatial approach derives not only from the ability to identify critical, yet often underexplored aspects of health, but also from the fact that spatial structures are more easily manipulated than social structures. Thus ecology of health becomes both a useful and an essential ingredient in a comprehensive health policy attending to the extraordinary needs of the high-poverty ghetto and its residents.

5

CITIES AS MOSAICS OF RISK AND PROTECTION

City life is millions of people being lonesome together.

Ralph Waldo Emerson

When you look at a city, it is like reading the hopes, aspirations and pride of everyone who built it.

Hugh Newell Jacobsen

As noted in Chapter 3, inner-city neighborhoods have undergone dramatic transformation in the last several decades (Massey and Denton 1993; Sampson and Wilson 2005; Wilson 1996; Wilson and Taub 2007). The concentration of poverty and the segregation of neighborhoods by race and class are powerful forces in the reshaping of metropolitan areas and their principal cities. Poverty-stricken neighborhoods have become an all too common feature of the modern metropolis; by the twenty-first century nearly 3.5 million people were living in census tracts where at least 40 percent of residents had poverty-level incomes (U.S. Department of Housing and Urban Development 2003). These same neighborhoods tended to be racially stratified, with the average Black family, for example, living in census tracts where 30 percent of residents were poor. While the percentages vary for different racial and ethnic groups, there is a shared reality—nearly 90 percent of all residents in poor neighborhoods are members of a racial or ethnic minority.

With this high concentration of minority persons, underclass neighborhoods have become characteristic of the inner city and aging suburbs. These neighborhoods typically have relatively high average values on several poverty indicators: (1) working-age males without jobs; (2) households headed by women with children; (3) households receiving welfare; and (4) dropouts among the school-age population (Jargowsky and Park 2009; Kawachi and Berkman 2003; Ricketts and Mincy 1990). The multidimensional character of poor neighborhoods implies potentially profound effects on the health and well-being of residents (Evans 2004; Fauth et al. 2007; LeClere et al. 1997, 1998; Rabito et al. 2003; Riva et al. 2007; Sims et al. 2007). With their youngest residents at greatest risk, inner-city communities have experienced a steady increase in the number of parents and young children living in poverty, an escalation in the number of female-headed households, expanding unemployment, growing welfare dependency, and a continual battle with rising crime and rampant drug abuse (Bolland 2003; Evans 2004; Hanson and Chen 2007; Wilson 1996; Winslow and Shaw 2007).

The present chapter focuses specifically on the unevenly distributed hazards and risks confronting residents of high-poverty ghettos, as well as the layers of protection available to assist them in mediating the negative impact of these risks. As discussed in Chapter 1, hazards represent the circumstances and physical conditions that can produce harm in a population. On the other hand, risks represent the probability that certain individuals or groups will be harmed in their environment. Both hazard and risk are differentially distributed across neighborhoods in principal cities (formerly referred to as central cities), suggesting that levels of harm have a spatial component. The role that space plays in affecting exposure to hazards and risks is complicated by the fact that place is socially and culturally structured. Hence, the roles of salient social identities such as age, race, ethnicity, and socioeconomic status are confounded by hazards and risks inherent in certain places.

Uncertainty is characteristic of life in the high-poverty ghetto. Understanding this uncertainty, its effects on health and well-being, and the availability of services and programs designed to protect persons from the consequences of this pervasive uncertainty is critical to addressing the health–place relationship.

Physical Hazards and Risks in the Residential Environment

There is a growing recognition that disadvantaged populations are disproportionately exposed to a wide range of environmental health hazards threatening their general physical health and well-being (American Heart Association 2009; Cohen et al. 2003; Downey and Van Willigen 2005; Kawachi and Berkman 2003). Minority populations, particularly African American and Hispanic, are at risk for exposure to high levels of environmental contaminants not because of inherent genetic characteristics or behavioral patterns, but rather because of the places where they live and work. More so than other racial or ethnic groups, they disproportionately live in areas that are non-compliant with national air-quality standards. For example, an estimated 27 million children under the age of 13, and nearly 2 million children with asthma were living in areas that did not meet current national ozone standards; almost 70 percent of those children were either African American or Hispanic (American Lung Association 2009; Mortimer et al. 2002; Peters et al. 1999).

Of course the problem is not limited to air quality. When considering other forms of pollution (water, noise, toxic and hazardous waste), the statistical and practical realities are similar—socioeconomic conditions coupled with race appear to be major factors in determining exposure to multiple environmental hazards (Do et al. 2008; Pickett and Pearl 2001; Robert 1999; Schulz et al. 2002; Williams 1996). Many of these environmental hazards are directly related to population density, which is of course at its highest levels in the nation's urban centers: More than 83 percent of the U.S. population now live in 283 census-designated metropolitan areas and nearly one-third (32.3 percent) live in the principal city component of these major metropolitan areas (U.S. Office of Management and Budget 2007).

Health-related problems tied to a variety of pollution forms are particularly problematic for persons living in principal city neighborhoods. Toxic waste dumping, water pollution, and runoff are examples of hazards with significant physical and mental health consequences, particularly for the disadvantaged and underserved subpopulations in inner cities. Research findings underscore the importance of examining the connection between physical risk and the residential location of low-income and minority subpopulations. The tendency for low-income, minority communities to serve as sites for hazardous waste facilities suggests that the more economically depressed and desperate an area, the less capable it is of recognizing and rejecting such hazards (Downey and Van Willigen 2005; Gould 1998; Kawachi and Berkman 2003). Industry is likely to search out areas where resistance to placement of hazards is lowest. Communities with reduced access to economic opportunities are vulnerable to, and more accepting of, the health and environmental costs of hazard placement (Krieg 1998). In such areas, private industries manage to frame hazard placement as a benefit rather than a health risk, reducing the chances of consciousness-raising and local political mobilization. Besides these communities' economic disadvantages, however, places with concentrated minority poverty are disadvantaged by their limited social capital, particularly bridging capital, where ties outside the local community/neighborhood are severely limited. The absence of bridging social capital often prevents successful mobilization. Communities that can mobilize local institutions and grassroots support are more capable of preventing the placement of hazardous activities and sites in their area (Gould 1998).

Indeed, significant changes can occur in communities when the relationship between place and health becomes highlighted and communities become involved in mobilizing against external threats. The first environmental discrimination lawsuit was filed in Houston in 1979, charging that Browning-Ferris Industries had targeted an African American neighborhood for the placement of a municipal solid-waste landfill. The argument was that this represented only one example of a long-term pattern of environmental racism in the city of Houston. Since the early 1920s, five Houston landfills and six of its eight incinerators had been placed in predominantly African American neighborhoods. While the lawsuit failed, it represented a significant first step in the development of an environmental justice movement (Bullard 1990, 1993).

The existence of a newly emergent environmental justice movement organized and controlled by communities of color, with support of local churches networked regionally and nationally and with a history of effective consciousness-raising and political conflict with more structurally powerful social actors may indeed have the capacity to repel private capital interests seeking to externalize hazards in minority communities. This may in fact be sending capital to look at less politically conscious and mobilized communities where local access to economic options may be slightly greater but potential resistance slightly lower.

(Gould 1998:23)

The experiences of residents living along Village Creek have been very similar to the experiences of persons living in hundreds of other American inner cities. The health of these residents continues to be challenged by the environmental hazards produced by under-regulated polluting industries. Yet evidence continues to accumulate establishing the role of environmental hazards in the physical and mental health of those at greatest risk (Downey and Van Willigen 2005; Kawachi and Berkman 2003; LeClere et al. 1997, 1998). While recognition of the unequal distribution of risk is not new, the environmental justice movement has provided a framework for more effective advocacy. This framework allows local neighborhoods and action committees to organize and establish a voice, while at the same time forcing corporations to be more responsible for their actions and location decisions (Taylor 2009). By placing the local experiences of the impoverished into the context of this larger social problem, high-poverty ghetto residents with limited social capital have the opportunity to link to larger interest groups. This creates the bridging social capital that is so often lacking in these areas.

Sociocultural Hazards and Risks in the Residential Environment

A rich tradition of research, pioneered by the Chicago School of urban sociology (Park et al. 1925), has established the existence of a relationship between community structure and various aspects of quality of life. The classic work of Shaw and McKay (1942) on the ecology of crime and delinquency led to the conclusion that the combination of three structural factors—low socioeconomic status, ethnic heterogeneity, and residential mobility—created residential environments characterized by community disorganization and high levels of crime and delinquency. Since then, researchers have continued to work on isolating the environmental characteristics that contribute to high levels of deviance and their consequences for the community and its residents (e.g. Kingston et al. 2009; Peterson and Krivo 2005; Sampson et al. 2002; Sampson and Lauritsen 1994; Sampson and Wilson 2005; Wilson and Taub 2007). There is some disagreement over the existence of independent community subcultures and their role in propagating systems of norms and values that promote deviant behavior. Nevertheless, researchers generally conclude that even though conventional norms dominate most communities, subcultural differences do exist with a tolerance of crime and deviant behavior clearly varying across structural and situational contexts (Sampson 1997; Sampson et al. 2002).

Perhaps the best evidence to support the assumptions of a subcultural explanation originates from early research on juvenile delinquency, specifically juvenile gang violence (Cloward and Ohlin 1960; Cohen 1955, 1972; Miller 1958). This early work posited that gang behavior was, in part, a manifestation of the general cultural patterns of behavior embodied in the class structure. Certain areas of the city became breeding grounds for delinquency and gang behavior because of the underlying values of violence reinforced and maintained among adults and youth residing in those communities.

In addition to the cultural determinants of risky behavior, researchers have identified physical characteristics that are key markers for hazardous, high-risk environments (Aalbers 2006; Galea et al. 2005; Sampson and Lauritsen 1994). Studies suggest that these places can include public spaces near apartments or other multifamily dwellings, vacant lots and buildings, areas with high rates of geographic mobility and family instability, and street designs that allow for "open-air" drug markets to develop. These markets have the physical characteristics of narrow one-way streets with physical cover, easy and multiple escape routes, vacant buildings and lots, and landscape shapes that enable smooth-flowing drug traffic as well as a careful surveillance of police activity (Aitken et al. 2002; McEwen 2007). Public areas near multifamily dwellings are notoriously difficult areas to monitor, posing significant threats to adults and young children alike. Keeping safe in such high-hazard areas is a task not unlike that of the soldier trying to survive on the open battlefield.

While alterations in the physical environment make some difference, perhaps a more critical factor in assessing risk exposure is behavioral—people taking unnecessary risks and engaging in health-compromising behavior. For example, "lifestyle" and "routine activities" theories both propose that an individual's activities affect their level of risk. Thus, the more likely people are to come into contact with potential perpetrators in physical spaces where no one can intervene, the greater the likelihood of victimization (Cohen and Felson 1979; Hindelang et al. 1978). Empirical evidence in support of this general hypothesis is indirect; nevertheless, there appears to be a statistical relationship between location, specific behaviors/personal characteristics, and violent victimization. Teenagers or young adults who are unemployed, from low-income households, and who spend considerable time outdoors in high-risk settings (parks, abandoned buildings, vacant lots, etc.) during the evening, are at greater risk of becoming victims of violence.

Blankets of Protection

Though the physical and psychological risks associated with certain urban spaces and places are substantial, layers of formal and informal protection attached to place help to insulate residents from myriad environmental challenges. These layers of protection moderate the negative effects of environmental stressors and risks on a variety of health-related outcomes. On the basis of this relationship, we can pose several questions concerning the role of protection in understanding the place–health relationship. Are levels of protection similar for all residents, or do they vary by sociodemographic characteristics? Do they vary by place? Are formal and informal sources of protection more important for some populations living in some places compared to others? What role does the health care system play in moderating risk's impact on particular populations living in certain places?

Over the years, considerable research has developed pointing to the critical role of the family in child development (e.g. Bandura 1986; Baumrind and Black 1967; Bronfenbrenner 1986; Escalona 1982; Rankin and Quane 2002; Repetti et al. 2002). Family and the home provide models for learning, as well as protective environments during development. However, they may also create significant problems for the child in both early and later life. In fact, research shows that one important predictor of health-compromising behavior among young persons is an unstable family structure with moderately high levels of family discord (Cummings et al. 2004). In addition, children from unstable family units are more likely to drop out of high school, become pregnant as teenagers, abuse drugs, and have criminal records either as juveniles or adults (McNeil et al. 2008; Substance Abuse and Mental Health Services Administration 2008).

With health risks high in high-poverty environments, the role of the family as a protector becomes even more crucial. While family structure is clearly important, other characteristics and dynamics of the family are equally critical in moderating health outcomes. "Family protection" comprises a nurturing family environment, parental promotion of learning, a multigenerational kin network, dependable child care in the absence of parents, warm, close relationships with parents, absence of marital and family conflict, significant attention and stimulation during the first year of life, and clear behavioral guidelines and expectations. Hawkins and his colleagues defined the importance of family as a protective factor in preventing or moderating health-compromising, risk-taking behaviors such as drug and alcohol abuse (Hawkins 1995; Hawkins et al. 1992; Hawkins and Weis 1985). Their work indicates that even in the face of overwhelming odds, some children exhibit a remarkable degree of resilience when they have the protection of family, friends, and the larger community. These environmental safeguards enhance youths' ability to resist stressful life events and help promote social adaptation and competence necessary for survival and success

(Garmezy 1983; Jessor 1993; Werner 1990). Thus, at least one parent or reference person, a strong social network outside the family, a supportive educational climate, and a community that provides opportunities and resources for parents and children are necessary assets creating an "environment of support" conducive to adaptation.

Unfortunately, many of these protective factors are not typically present in families, particularly those families facing the challenges of raising children in poverty, with a single parent (usually a mother who works outside the home), displaced networks of support, and inadequate formal support services. In these cases, the child's mental and physical health risks are elevated and the life of the community as a whole becomes threatened. As the architect of the "War on Poverty," President Lyndon Johnson, reminded us:

> The family is the cornerstone of our society. More than any other force it shapes the attitude, the hopes, the ambitions, and the values of the child. And when the family is threatened or collapses, it is the children that are usually damaged. When it happens on a massive scale the community itself is crippled.
>
> (Lyndon Baines Johnson Library and Museum 1965)

Beyond the risk and protective factors literature, a substantial literature in the sociology of mental health convincingly argues for the role of social support and/or social capital in mediating the negative effects of stressors on individuals' mental and physical health (Ensel and Lin 1991; Kawachi and Berkman 2003; Lin 2001; Lin et al. 1986; Lochner et al. 2003; Veenstra et al. 2005). Informal networks of support including family, friends, relatives, co-workers, and neighbors provide instrumental, informational, and emotional assistance that can combat the negative effects of stress. The character and overall impact of this support as a stress moderator varies by place of residence as well as the person's attachment to that community.

Extensive research on social support leads to three major conclusions regarding its role in promoting health and well-being. First, support is directly and positively related to health, but it does not buffer the negative impact of stressful life events or chronic strains on health. Thus, while support clearly influences health, its role as a stress buffer is debatable (e.g. Ensel and Lin 1991). A substantial body of research suggests that support mediates, rather than buffers, the negative effect of stress on health outcomes. The distinction appears minor, but it is an important one, with very different implications for health outcomes (Ensel and Lin 1991; Thoits 1995; Wheaton 1985). Second, perceived support, even more than actual support, is directly related to better physical and mental health. A perception of strong support from others moderates the negative effects of life events and chronic strains on one's physical and mental health. Third, the most powerful aspect of support appears to be whether or not a person has an intimate, confiding relationship with another person (spouse, lover, friend, etc.). Having a confidant is extremely important for stress reduction, particularly among persons such as the urban elderly, spatially segregated minorities, the homeless, and others who may not have an extensive social network. Recently, the literature on social capital suggests that broader community ties in the form of bonding and bridging social capital also play an important role in stress reduction and overall health (Irwin et al. 2008; Kawachi et al. 2008; Putnam 2000). As noted previously, ties with socially similar others often help people get by, reducing the stress of daily living in challenging circumstances or periods of time in a person's life. Individuals share much in common with such people, and thus having them around in times of need can be beneficial. But people just like the other are also limited in what they can offer. Bridging social capital, social networks that offer access to different people and resources, offer more than the ability to cope with difficult circumstances—they offer the leverage that can actually get people ahead. But is this true for people in every place, or does social capital spend differently in different residential contexts?

General social support and social capital research is informative, providing a good deal of insight into the psychosocial dynamics of health outcomes. However, it doesn't provide much information about the role of place in the provision of social support and social capital and its subsequent impact on health. A spatial analysis focusing on the neighborhood and the neighbor's role seems particularly relevant for articulating an "ecology of health" approach.

Throughout history the neighborhood has functioned as a place for exchange and mutual aid, meeting both the psychological and material needs of residents. At the same time, industrialization and subsequent community development profoundly changed the ways in which individuals communicate and associate with one another, and as a result, neighboring itself was transformed (LaGory and Pipkin 1981). Over time, the rules of neighboring shifted. The often "taken for granted" expectation of neighbors watching over one another, moving freely from one front porch to another, and sometimes relying on informal neighbor networks for information and assistance was no longer present. The neighborhood appeared to be dissolving, as Tönnies ([1887] 1957) and Wirth (1938) had predicted. Their *urbanism* tradition argued that the changes produced by industrialization caused close community ties to be substituted with secondary ones. More contemporary research seems to support this general notion, and while close interaction among neighbors is not a lost art, it has been supplemented for many by intimacy that stretches beyond the physical boundary of the neighborhood (Granovetter 1973a, b; LaGory and Pipkin 1981; Wellman 1999).

In addition to neighborhood dynamics, we also should recognize that the content of informal support, and how it gets delivered, is not constant across all communities but determined in part by the characteristics of place. Thus, some high-poverty neighborhoods create an "atmosphere of learning" unlike that found in other areas of the metropolis. Typically, individuals are exposed to a range of recurring ghetto-related behaviors that, while viewed as adaptive, may have negative consequences. Displays of violence, public drinking, and idleness are present in many underclass high-poverty neighborhoods, and while denounced by many, the behaviors are allowed to occur. Their occurrence is a function of the larger social organization's failure to control the behaviors, and of a cultural milieu that enables it. Purposeful or accidental, cultural transmission creates a set of values and beliefs that are damaging to the future of any place.

Formal Support Services

The city can be characterized "as a gigantic man-made resource system which contains an abundance of resources for individuals and families to exploit for their own benefit" (Harvey 1972:3). While the city is a resource machine, it is important to remember that access to this machine is spatially constrained. Resources are not equally distributed across the urban landscape; critical resources are more accessible to some than to others. Segregation's impact on the delivery of services is an important illustration of the role of places in determining access to goods and services, and in turn, influencing health outcomes.

The costs incurred by the "urban health penalty" are significant. The most dramatic illustration of its costs can be seen in how health care services are distributed across the metropolitan area. Inner cities are characterized as islands of illness and premature death. Beyond the risks related to specific health conditions in core urban communities, weakening urban social and economic structures further contribute to the health penalty, and place the poor, minorities, homeless, and other core residents at greater risk. Relying on the hospital emergency room as their primary care provider, many residents encounter major problems with health care, and access is threatened when local urban hospitals have difficulty competing with suburban complexes and sometimes must close their doors. Since the late 1970s and early 1980s, large urban areas have lost many of their local hospitals (Sager 1983; Whiteis 1992, 1997). The irony of this trend points to a major problem facing the inner cities. On the one hand, these communities are the very places where preventive and primary care is needed most. Patients here tend to be sicker and are often without health insurance. Yet, on the other hand, hospitals and health care facilities are overburdened in these communities and have a much lower profit margin than those located in the suburbs. Thus access becomes a critical issue for many, and the withdrawal of services is another instance of the penalty that low-income minority residents pay for their residential location.

Nevertheless, protection and support is available from a variety of non-profits, schools, churches, as well as community and neighborhood initiatives. This safety net further defines the nature of available "formal support" in the urban area. One excellent example of a non-profit making the difference in the fight against the "urban penalty" is Habitat for Humanity. This organization, founded by Millard Fuller in the early 1980s, has as part of its mission a proposal "to eliminate poverty and sub-standard housing in the United States" (Fuller 1995). Perhaps better than any other organization, operating in all 50 states and worldwide in nearly 50 countries, Habitat understands the connection between place and health. Whether it is a community with a weakened infrastructure or a blighted neighborhood with no decent housing, Habitat stresses the importance of place in countering the impact of poverty on health and well-being. Fuller not only saw the critical links between concentrated poverty and health, but fervently believed that unhealthy places could be transformed. They can be transformed physically, socially, and spiritually into areas where people can thrive. Providing decent, affordable housing, he argues, can be a prescription for a healthier society. Habitat, more so than any other non-profit organization, has responded to this need and continues to build affordable, decent housing around the world. By 2008, Habitat had built over 300,000 houses around the world, providing more than 1.5 million people in more than 3,000 communities a safe, decent, affordable place to live. In 2009, Habitat for Humanity built more than 5,500 homes for new homeowners in the United States (Habitat for Humanity 2009a, b). It is a powerful example of how a single organization can make a difference in creating and revitalizing places within inner cities around the world.

Thousands of other non-profit groups continue to carve out niches in the local support system, meeting the needs of special populations. Homeless shelters for men, women, and children have increased significantly over the two decades since 1990. In a comprehensive study of homelessness during the 1980s, Burt (1992a, b) gathered data that showed an impressive growth in the number of shelters and shelter beds during the period between 1981 and 1989. In cities with populations of more than 100,000 in every region of the country, both the numbers and rates of homelessness, shelters, and shelter beds increased nearly three-fold over this period of time. By the end of the decade, there were nearly

1,500 shelters serving almost 200,000 persons (Burt 1992a, b). The piecemeal programs offered there, however, cannot begin to meet the complex needs of the urban dispossessed. A 2008 national survey of residential programs serving homeless and near-homeless estimated nearly 20,000 programs serving (with beds) over 600,000 residents (U.S. Department of Housing and Urban Development 2009).

United Way agencies supporting the homeless and hundreds of other causes continue to struggle to meet the needs of those challenged by residing in declining urban environments. Non-profit agencies find their budgets stretched to the limit each year as urban crises expand and new problems develop. In an effort to help fill the gap, churches have responded by developing comprehensive programs addressing a myriad of problems endemic to high-poverty ghetto populations. With more than 353,000 churches and synagogues and a membership of nearly 200 million people, these organizations represent a powerful network of social-service delivery (American Jewish Committee 2003; Early 2006; U.S. Bureau of the Census 2002). Non-profit and government agencies are largely responsible for the bulk of service delivery to those in greatest need. Their resources, however, are limited, and the needs of some populations often go beyond what is available. Outreach is a natural extension of the church and the development of a faith community. Thus, churches have provided a vision of assistance that sometimes supersedes even the most visionary non-profit agency or government leader.

Traditionally, churches have provided care and assistance to the elderly; food, clothing and shelter to the homeless and poor; health care to the elderly and poor; educational programs for youths; jobs and income assistance to the poor; housing and housing rehabilitation to neighborhoods; and infrastructural assistance to communities in need around the world. Exemplary programs abound in the community of faith. One example of a successful, long-standing program is the Central Health Center in Atlanta, Georgia. Started in 1922 by the Central Presbyterian Church, the health clinic now serves more than 10,000 patients a year. It provides basic treatment, physical exams, family planning, dental care, counseling, and a pharmacy. Another example can be found in

Birmingham, Alabama, where the Cooperative Downtown Ministries, a collection of inner-city churches, has provided dental services, shelter, physician access, transportation, job training, and access to comprehensive drug and alcohol treatment programs for thousands of homeless since the early 1980s. Hundreds of other examples around the country illustrate the important "safety net role" that churches can play in meeting the needs of special populations who fall through the formal service-delivery net.

In addition to the church, government intervention has addressed problems plaguing the inner city. Government-sponsored housing, community development programs, Job Corps, Healthy Start, Head Start, and VISTA all have played a role in problem management and assistance for special populations. Government, however, also has been responsible for the production of concentrated poverty and the divided city. Dating back to the Great Depression and the New Deal, governments shaped the direction and evolution of urban space. Generally, the purpose was twofold: (1) to encourage home ownership and (2) to improve living conditions for low-income groups (through, for example, rent control, public housing, and urban renewal). The first goal was largely successful as middle- to upper-class residents found refuge in newly developed suburban areas on the fringe of the city. Unfortunately, homeowners moved from a declining principal-city housing market and infrastructure, leaving the lower class behind and promoting income segregation across the metropolitan area. In effect, successful home ownership programs for the middle class eventually made living conditions for some segments of the poor worse rather than better. For example, though urban renewal was designed to greatly improve the quality of low-income neighborhoods, it eventually promoted an urban spatial structure that gave way to social injustice and segregation (LaGory and Pipkin 1981). Thus while some effort was made to attract the middle class back to the central city and reconstruct the tax base, large areas of dilapidated housing were cleared and thousands of residents displaced. By attacking the physical expressions of poverty in the city and not the underlying issues themselves, urban renewal became a tool of the federal government for maintaining the status quo of poverty in the city. Too often spatial changes are used to reproduce existing conditions of injustice, rather than to promote change (Lefebvre 1991).

One important agent of protection that has been very successful in aiding and supporting the population of the high-poverty ghetto has been the school. While inner-city schools continue to struggle with low achievement scores, high dropout rates, high personnel turnover, administrative overhead, declining facilities, and a shrinking tax base, they remain one of the most durable and available forms of local protection. Schools traditionally have sought to protect youths, yet in recent years many school systems have expanded their "programs of protection" to include young adult education and, more recently, the "command center" for community-wide prevention and intervention programs. One example of the change that has taken place in the last few decades is the establishment of hospital satellite clinics and hospital-based adolescent clinics that make health care more accessible to youths (Walter et al. 1995).

The growth of the school-based health clinic has been a natural extension of this recent outreach trend; currently there are more than 2,000 clinics serving students in 45 states (National Assembly of School-Based Health Care 2008). With a specific design for reaching underserved youths, school clinics serve as an important medical catchall in high-poverty ghetto areas that are often unable to furnish comprehensive medical services to this difficult-to-reach population. The school clinic provides acute care for minor illnesses, reproductive care, screening for and treatment of chronic illnesses, mental health counseling, immunizations, and health promotion. While parents and community leaders continue to be concerned about the clinic as a distribution point for birth control devices and the implicit promotion of adolescent sexuality, these clinics have proved to be a critical point in the delivery of medical services to youth.

Beyond medical care, schools also attempt to help low-achieving students by providing specific programs to address student motivation, dropout prevention, grade failure, drug and/or alcohol use, and violence. Title 1 has existed since 1965, when the federal government made a substantial financial and organizational commitment to combat the problem of school dropouts. Nationally, the program serves more than 20 million students in nearly 20,000 schools, with a funding level in excess of $10 billion (U.S. Department of Education 2009). Its primary focus is on low-income students. The evaluations of Title 1, however, have been mixed; while those schools and students touched by Title 1 programs have clearly improved, improvements appear modest compared to students enrolled in regular curricula (Kennedy et al. 1986). As a natural extension of Title 1, dropout prevention programs sprang up all over the country. By the end of the 1980s, there were nearly 1,000 dropout prevention programs operating in thousands of schools around the country. The majority of these were designed to target high-risk students for special services aimed at improving their academic perform- ance, attitudes, and rates of absenteeism and tardiness (U.S. General Accounting Office 1987).

While schools represent an important component of protection, com- prehensive community-based prevention and intervention programs exemplify cutting-edge service provision. Although a more detailed examination of these place-based delivery systems will be presented in Chapter 7, it is important to recognize their significance in providing protection in high-risk, and high-poverty urban settings. One example is the Safe Block Project in Philadelphia, Pennsylvania (Schwarz et al. 1993). The program designed a comprehensive injury-prevention trial focusing on home health hazards and injury knowledge in several poor, urban African American neighborhoods. This injury-prevention effort was one of the first to successfully provide comprehensive prevention programs in extremely poor inner-city neighborhoods. With growing public outcries demanding community-level strategies for transforming the health risks in minority populations (Braithwaite et al. 1989; Hammond and Yung 1991), new place-based efforts must be developed.

Success stories abound for risk reduction programs addressing a vari- ety of other problems. General prevention and demonstration studies show, for example, that the most promising approach to preventing alco- hol and drug problems lies in coordinated prevention efforts that offer multiple strategies and multiple points of program access that promote participation by the full community (Office of Substance Abuse Prevention 1991) (OSAP). One of the underlying philosophical assumptions of the OSAP is that "the community is the best vehicle through which to develop and implement comprehensive prevention efforts." While this philosophy is important, its execution remains hampered by social, political, economic, psychological, and cultural barriers present in many low-income, minority, underserved communities across the country. The strategy that should be introduced to overcome these barriers, and to effectively address populations at risk and in need, is of critical import to the overall framework of this book and is addressed in Chapter 7.

Physical and Mental Health Consequences for the Urban Dweller

As seen in Chapters 3 and 4, health is intimately tied to place and the circumstances and conditions of place. Places are composed of unique combinations of risks and protection that, depending on their interaction with one another, create significant health consequences. Health risk subcultures can emerge from the combination of unique demographic factors in the urban space (density and heterogeneity), along with the hazards associated with poverty and unemployment. Some populations may also be more at risk than others; Chapter 6 spotlights some of those high-risk populations. The remainder of this chapter presents a brief overview of health consequences for the general city dweller.

Low-income persons, minorities, and urban residents have more health risk factors, including sedentary lifestyles, cigarette smoking, less health insurance coverage, and less preventive care than their counterparts (U.S. Department of Health and Human Services 2009b; Centers for Disease Control and Prevention 2008b; Cockerham 2007; Moy et al. 2005) Thus, while some parts of the population have experienced improving health, the penalty for those unable to afford quality health care, or for those living in areas where access to health care services is restricted, continues to grow. This "urban health penalty" highlights the importance of addressing the multidimensional health problems endemic to high-poverty ghetto residents.

While many factors contribute to the health status of urban ghetto residents, poverty is primary among them. Lack of good nutrition, homelessness, exposure to violence, substance abuse, inadequate housing, and limited access to health care are all indicators of an area under stress. For many, poverty increases the risk of contracting disease and facing an early death. Unfortunately, adverse physical health conditions have become a fact of life for many high-poverty ghetto residents. Exposure to environmental hazards such as lead, toxic waste, and a variety of pollutants is extremely high in central cities. Children between one and five years of age living in low-income, inner-city families were more likely to have elevated lead levels in their blood compared to children in other, less-threatening environments (Centers for Disease Control and Prevention 2005). Poor, non-Hispanic African American children are at greatest risk compared to low-income Caucasian children. While lead levels have been significantly reduced (72 percent since the early 1990s), approximately 310,000 children younger than five remain at risk for exposure to harmful lead levels in their neighborhoods (Centers for Disease Control and Prevention 2005). Inadequate housing is a significant contributor to lead poisoning, and according to a recent study, lead levels are highest among children living in housing more than 50 years old (Centers for Disease Control and Prevention 2005). These pre-World War II buildings and houses are common in many older central cities in the Northeast and Midwest.

While the structural circumstances of high-poverty ghettos produce risks for some residents, residents' social and behavioral characteristics also contribute to the negative health consequences of places. HIV is becoming more common in the inner city. In 2004, HIV was the leading cause of death for African American women between the ages of 25 and 34 (Centers for Disease Control and Prevention 2008a). Some of the highest reported concentrations of new cases of HIV/AIDS were in the principal cities of New Orleans, Miami, Washington DC, and several other large metropolitan areas with large concentrations of minorities living in the principal cities (Centers for Disease Control and Prevention 2007a). Alcohol and drug use continues to be a major health problem in the United States, with urban areas being particularly hard hit by an increasing concentration of addiction. In 2007, more than 20 million people reported using illegal drugs, which was higher in metropolitan areas compared to non-metropolitan areas, and likely much of that drug abuse was concentrated in high-poverty ghetto neighborhoods (Substance Abuse and Mental Health Services Administration 2008).

Another significant health risk for city residents is exposure to violence. City dwellers are twice as likely to be victims of violence, and murder rates are more than three times greater in central cities than other parts of the metropolitan area (U.S. Department of Health and Human Services 1998). Gang activity, drug traffic, weapon availability, unemployment, poverty, and a host of other social circumstances contribute to a violence epidemic, which is clearly in need of control. It is essential to understand the role communities play in violence exposure. Communities can either insulate residents from the harmful effects of violence or exacerbate the risk of residents' exposure to violence (Levine and Rosich 1996). As discussed earlier, the physical and sociocultural characteristics of some places can be important predictors of health. Thus, regardless of their general sociodemographic makeup, structural attributes of communities can be important predictors of health-compromising behavior.

Youths are more susceptible to the adverse effects of urban violence exposure. Homicide rates among children have increased more than 300 percent in the last 50 years; these increases are particularly pronounced among high-poverty ghetto residents, especially males and African Americans (Center for Disease Control and Prevention 2009c). For persons between the ages of 10 and 24, homicide remains the number one leading cause of death among African Americans, number two among Hispanics, and number three among Asians and Pacific Islanders. This statistical reality is clearly a consequence of living in risky environments, some of which have become loci of criminal activities. Whether children are perpetrators or victims of violence, it is important to recognize that environmental circumstances can affect their developmental trajectories. A more detailed discussion of youth as ecological actors, and the role that context plays in their development, follows in Chapter 6.

Since the pioneering work of Chicago School sociologists (e.g. Faris and Dunham 1939), research has focused on the critical relationship between mental health problems and socioeconomic status (Dohrenwend and Dohrenwend 1969; Dohrenwend et al. 1992; Eaton 1986; Kessler and Neighbors 1986; Turner et al. 1995). This early research made us aware of the importance of the urban context in determining the mental and physical health status of residents. By examining the areal distribution of functional psychoses such as schizophrenia, they discovered a relationship between urban residential location and rates of mental illness (Faris and Dunham 1939). The highest rates of illness occurred near the central business district, with rates declining as distance from the urban core increased. This led researchers to conclude that there was in fact a pattern of illness directly related to place. Place and mental health were inextricably linked. As expected, areas with a high prevalence of disease were urban slums where concentrations of poverty, poor housing, crime, and homelessness were the greatest.

Some years later, Srole and associates (1962) conducted a mental disorder-prevalence study in midtown Manhattan. They found significant differences in patterns of disorder distributed across varying socioeconomic groups living in different areas of the city. More recent research, while not as ambitious as these larger epidemiological surveys, is beginning to identify core relationships between mental health and social structure. Variation in individual exposure to stress has been documented by marital status, gender, race, and socioeconomic status (Turner et al. 1995). Social variation in mental health is, in part, a function of systematic differences in the quantity and nature of stress that individuals experience by being located in a variety of social situations and positions. Thus, stress is not just an individual risk factor; stress is seen as a link in a causal chain that starts with social conditions and ends with differences in risk for mental health problems (Aneshensel 1992). As Aneshensel argues, "Stress can be systemic—it may be tied to specific locations or social group experiences and not distributed randomly but rather predetermined by location or social position." Thus, just as the Chicago School anticipated, mental illness is distributed differentially across the urban landscape.

In fact, varying patterns of illness related to community/neighborhood contexts have been documented recently, opening the door for a more careful and thorough spatial analysis of illness and disease (Aneshensel and Sucoff 1996; Brooks-Gunn et al. 1993; Cockerham 2007; Corburn 2009; Kawachi and Berkman 2003). Researchers have started cataloging aspects of life in the urban area, attempting to find out how they contribute to mental health problems. As discussed in Chapter 2, overcrowding is one aspect of the urban environment identified as contributing to mental illness among urban dwellers, but studies of overcrowding have generated mixed results. Some research found modest relationships between neighborhood density and various aspects of mental illness. A number of studies concluded that overcrowding had its greatest impact within the home (Galle and Gove 1978; Gove et al. 1979), exacerbating negative circumstances already present there and contributing to a higher prevalence of mental disorders in areas with high household density (Cockerham 2007).

Conclusion

Inner cities are facing significant health challenges promoted by the dramatic divide characteristic of the late-twentieth century urban landscape. Health status and access to services for low-income minority urban populations are significantly lower than for the rest of the country. In some cases, the health of inner cities most closely resembles that of developing countries and shows little sign of improvement. The negative health image of the city is difficult to overcome. Addressing it requires the concerted efforts of local, regional, and national governments, private agencies, and health care organizations, which pool their resources to change the current status of "health in the city."

This chapter has attempted to provide an overview of the risks and protections that are products of places. Focusing on the unhealthy aspects of high-poverty ghettos, a review of physical and sociocultural risks highlights the potential impact of these environmental irritants on physical and mental health. While risk and protection vary across the urban landscape, class, race, age, and other sociodemographic

6

HEALTH RISKS AMONG SPECIAL
POPULATIONS IN THE CITY

Conservatives argue that the United States "won" the Cold War . . . But the economy that won this victory cannot house its own people and condemns a significant
percentage of them to a life of poverty and struggle. If this is victory, it is hollow
indeed.

Joel Blau

Something that might at first seem a superficial matter, a mere question of where one
lives, can in some cases have a surprisingly deep effect on the shape and feel of the old
person's social world.

Arlie Russell Hochschild

A majority of Americans live in an age of instant access to everything
and every place; the Internet, texting, tweeting, and facebooking
make the world appear to be at our fingertips. In this "information
society," where communication technologies expand the capacity for
exchange exponentially, we seem to be approximating a situation in
which, as some media campaigns have suggested, there will soon be
"no there, there." But this world of immediate accessibility is illusory.
Indeed, as the information highway gives us the capacity for a truly
global village, a new version of the divided society is emerging, with
inequalities as dramatic and debilitating as any that have existed in
human history.

We have demonstrated throughout this book that place continues to matter for everyone. Despite the emergence of the spaceless realm in the information-based society, some groups remain very spatially dependent. In this chapter, we explore the special problems and needs of four groups, showing how spatial contexts interact with limited personal and social capital to constrain the opportunities and experiences of each group. We discuss some of the spatial challenges faced by the homeless, low-income racial and ethnic minorities, as well as the unique person–environment challenges confronted by those at the beginning and the end of the life cycle. Each of these groups represents a set of unique ecological actors who face special challenges living in the urban environment.

The first part of the chapter deals with the significance of space and place for the health of the socially disadvantaged. Overwhelming evidence suggests that the already health-compromising circumstances of personal poverty are further exacerbated by the fact that the very poor often find that they are unavoidably "in the wrong place at the wrong time." Such is the story of the impoverished, predominantly African American residents of Village Creek. It is also the picture presented in research on homeless persons where the stressful circumstances of placelessness are clearly demonstrated (Fitzpatrick et al. 2007a; Fitzpatrick et al. 2009; LaGory et al. 2005).

The Homeless

As the economy has globalized, large sectors of the urban poor have become increasingly underemployed and the poorest have gotten even poorer. Since the financial collapse of Wall Street in 2008–09, an even greater marginalization of the poor has taken place. Stagnation and decline in the nation's housing market, coupled with record levels of unemployment and underemployment have meant increasing numbers of urban poor risking homelessness. Among the most susceptible to these risks are the poor who suffer from some form of health problem— addictions, chronic physical health problems, or mental illness.

The spatial deprivation of homelessness represents an extreme form of poverty. It is an unhealthy state—an inhuman condition because we are place-oriented by nature. The homeless can make no claims to the spaces they occupy. Homelessness leaves critical place-based needs such as privacy and minimal personal space, access to places for social interaction, and safe and defensible spaces unmet. While place matters, being without place matters to human beings. We spend our entire lives struggling to find "our place" in society, in history, and in the cosmic order; the link between place and identity is basic. It is not surprising, then, that when homeless persons are asked about their single most important possession, the majority list things connected directly with their identity—identification cards, official papers, or personal and family photographs—rather than more instrumental objects such as money, clothing, travel bags, or weapons (LaGory et al. 2005). In a personal world without territory, nothing becomes more critical or basic than establishing one's place in society.

Risk and Hazard among the Homeless

The mixture of dangerous circumstances, psychologically debilitating experiences, and a high propensity for risk-taking behavior has dramatic health consequences for the homeless. These risks and hazards result in a significantly higher rate of infectious diseases, chronically debilitating illnesses, and criminal victimization than for the general population.

The hazards of living in public space's interstices are many. Homeless environments are less predictable and controllable. Among the everyday hassles confronted by the homeless are problems with noise, privacy, overcrowding, theft, safety, and access to basic resources such as food, toilets, and clothing. Not only do the homeless live on the margins where space can be easily reclaimed by force or threat of force, but also the spaces they occupy tend to be non-residential in character, posing unique dangers to those in residence there. Living in these marginal spaces increases exposure to the hazards of weather, chemical and noise pollution, unsafe building materials, dilapidated structures, combustible materials, poor ventilation, vehicular and pedestrian traffic, and vermin. Indeed, the so-called "street homeless" are officially defined as residing in spaces not meant for human habitation, such as "streets, parks, alleys, parking ramps, parts of the highway system, transportation depots and other parts of the transportation systems (e.g. subway tunnels, railway cars), all-night commercial establishments (e.g. movie theaters, laundromats, restaurants), abandoned buildings, squatter situations, building roofs or stairwells, chicken coops and other farm out-buildings, caves, campgrounds, vehicles and other similar places" (Burt 1992b:3).

Homeless people dwell in a socially predatory environment, where security and defense is a constant concern. Living in public spaces, even on the margin, exposes people to the risks of intrusion, creating a sense of defenselessness and insecurity. Those living on the street often compensate for this lack of security by adopting a military-like strategy in which individuals take shifts watching for intruders during sleeping hours. It is hard to feel at home when, during sleeping hours, circumstances are more like a battlefield than a home. Almost all homeless persons characterize the streets as dangerous, particularly at night (Fitzpatrick et al. 1993). Criminologists argue that the convergence in time and space of *suitable targets, motivated offenders*, and the *absence of capable guardians* increases the probability of predatory offenses such as robbery and assault (Cohen and Felson 1979). These three conditions are present on the street. Not surprisingly then, victimization rates are unusually high among the homeless (Fitzpatrick et al. 1993; Institute for the Prevention of Crime 2008; Kushel et al. 2002; Wachholz 2005; Wenzel et al. 2001).

In a 2005 study of homeless in Birmingham, Alabama, 17 percent of respondents said they had been robbed in the six months prior to being interviewed. Twenty-three percent of those victims had been mugged or beaten up during the robbery (LaGory et al. 2005). When robberies were excluded from victimization episodes, 12 percent said they had been attacked with a knife, and 51 percent said they were attacked with a gun. These rates of victimization are dramatically higher than those in the general population (LaGory et al. 2005). Additionally, there were ten times more rapes and nearly eight times more assaults among the homeless over those previous six months compared to the general population over the course of a year. A majority of homeless crime victims were victims of violent crimes. While some of the victimization rates could be attributable to poverty, research shows that rates of all types of victimization are considerably higher among homeless than other low-income groups (Fitzpatrick et al. 1993; Institute for the Prevention of Crime 2008).

The risky circumstances of the homeless include exposure to violence, unsafe work conditions, marginal spaces, unpredictable environments, harmful chemicals and pollutants, and contagion. In addition, health risks are further exacerbated by the stress of a life situation which by its very nature frustrates basic physical, psychological, and social needs. These unsafe and stressful circumstances are sometimes accompanied by risk-taking behaviors, which may be an additional factor in the health of the homeless. Homelessness appears to be associated with risk-taking behaviors such as binge drinking, drug abuse, risky sexual practices, and weapons possession (Fitzpatrick et al. 2007a; Institute for the Prevention of Crime 2008; LaGory et al. 2005; Novac et al. 2006). Whatever the reasons, those engaging in risk-taking behavior further exacerbate their health-compromising circumstances.

Health among the Homeless

Placelessness is a fundamentally distressing circumstance—a chronic stressor. Much research demonstrates that severe stress can trigger significant mental health problems as well as genetic predispositions to certain physical disorders such as hypertension (Esch et al. 2002; Furumoto-Dawson et al. 2007; Krueger and Chang 2008). The physical circumstances of homelessness (crowding, dangerous sleeping sites, poor diets) also increase the chances of contracting chronic and infectious disorders. The high prevalence of disease is attributable to the spatial circumstances of the homeless lifestyle (constant forced walking, exposure to the elements, cramped sleeping arrangements, and poor hygiene).

National estimates suggest that approximately 20–25 percent of the homeless suffer from severe chronic mental illness (Substance Abuse and Mental Health Services Administration 2008), compared to approximately 6 percent of the U.S. general population. In many cases, mental illness is one component of a dual diagnosis of substance abuse and mental disorder. This co-morbidity indicates a complexity of health and behavioral problems that makes treatment exceptionally difficult. Nevertheless, all major studies seem to agree that while mental illness is a significant problem for the homeless, the majority among this group does not have a severe mental health condition (Fitzpatrick and Myrstol 2008; Fitzpatrick et al. 2007a; LaGory et al. 2005; Snow and Anderson 1993; Wright et al. 1998).

Perhaps the most prevalent mental health problem faced by the homeless is depression. It is estimated that as many as 80 percent of the homeless population show symptoms of clinical depression (Fitzpatrick et al. 2007a; LaGory et al. 1990, 2005). Prevalence rates for depression are approximately seven times higher than among the domiciled population. Yet in most cases it would be inappropriate to designate this depressive symptomatology as mental illness. Indeed, it is more likely a normal psychological reaction to abnormal circumstances. Whatever its etiology (exogenous or endogenous), its prevalence suggests the level of suffering endemic to the condition of placelessness. Thirty-six percent of the homeless have had suicidal thoughts since becoming homeless, and approximately 45 percent of those persons have actually attempted suicide during their homelessness (Fitzpatrick et al. 2007a, 2007b; LaGory et al. 2005).

Racial and Ethnic Minorities

While some people are literally deprived of place, others find their place in society affected by an ecology largely out of their control. Segregation is a powerful force that reproduces inequalities over time by limiting access to the resources necessary to get by and to get ahead. Nearly 50 years after the civil rights movement, America remains a nation divided as it continues to confront disturbing inequities between Whites and non-Whites. At the heart of this division is a segregated society that perpetuates the barriers between rich and poor, White and non-White. Thus where we live in the metropolis is a function of the interrelationship between race and class, with residential location accentuating just how disparate some groups are. For example, we know that Blacks are more likely to get sick, stay sick longer, and die prematurely compared to

Whites (Do et al. 2008; Subramanian et al. 2005; Williams and Collins 2001). While other racial and ethnic minorities face similar disparities, empirical evidence suggests that health risks, mortality, perinatal health, disease and illness, and access to health care are of particular concern for African Americans (Bell et al. 2006; Collins and Williams 1999; Do et al. 2008; Kawachi and Berkman 2003; Lopez 2002). More than 40 years ago, the Kerner Commission warned that America was heading toward the creation of "two societies—one black, one White—separate and unequal" (U.S. National Advisory Commission on Civil Disorders 1968). This vision of the future has become a nightmarish reality for some as we arrive at the second decade in the new millennium.

As suggested in earlier parts of the book, health outcomes are a function of the complicated interrelationship between place, status, behavior, and social structure. While our intention has been to try to isolate this "place effect," other aspects of the relationship need to be considered. In particular, this part of the chapter focuses on the interaction between status and place and its commanding role in determining negative health outcomes for at-risk populations such as low-income minorities. Indeed, the most compelling explanation for the severity of their experiences relative to other groups is their high concentration in areas undergoing the most severe economic and social decline—the inner cities. This concentration of poverty not only affects the social and economic health of America's principal cities but also creates an underclass that slips further and further from the American dream. With more than 3,000 high-poverty neighborhoods in the United States containing more than 9 million residents, these places and their potential negative effects on residents' physical and mental health are much too common an occurrence for such a wealthy nation as the United States.

Theories of the Underclass

Urban scholars have argued for some time now that an urban underclass, consisting largely of poor African Americans and other minority groups, has become a prominent feature of the American urban landscape (Jargowsky and Young 2005; Massey and Denton 1993; Sampson and

Wilson 2005; Wilson 1987, 1996). This group has generally been cut off from social and economic opportunities for growth and success. They are isolated within specific neighborhoods in the metropolitan area—powerless, marginalized, and unable to escape from poverty given their economic and educational deficiencies. How this underclass originated is of some debate, yet its role in helping shape the character of high-poverty ghetto areas seems clear. As low-income minorities have become increasingly concentrated in well-defined geographic areas, the level of poverty has been compounded and reinforced by a host of other problems, including high rates of crime, drug use, delinquency, teenage pregnancy, and welfare dependency. This cyclical process has further contributed to the demise of many urban neighborhoods, leaving their residents disconnected and underserved by the urban resource machine.

The truth of this characterization is confirmed in the neighborhoods bordering Village Creek. As we discussed earlier, many residents continue to struggle with the environmental threats (pollution and flooding) posed by the creek as well as the weakened economic and social structure of the neighborhoods they live in. From the eastern side of Birmingham originating in the Airport Hills neighborhood, Village Creek winds through or passes under 26 census tracts. Not all of these neighborhoods are exposed to the hazards and risks equally by the creek. Rather, three neighborhoods are exposed to flooding and its concomitant health risks. These places typify what contemporary urban scholars refer to as "underclass" neighborhoods that have become home to the new urban poor (Jargowsky 1997; Massey and Denton 1993; Wilson 1987, 1996). Jargowsky (1997), through a combination of fieldwork and review of prior community classifications (e.g. Wilson 1987), operationalizes the underclass (ghetto) neighborhood as predominantly Black with at least 40 percent of the total households living below the poverty level. Interestingly, all three of the census tracts identified as "problem tracts" regarding their exposure to Village Creek meet the criteria for an underclass/ghetto neighborhood according to the most recent Census estimates (U.S. Bureau of Census, 2000). In addition to their percentage of Black residents (98 percent) and percentage of households living below the poverty level (33 percent), these three Birmingham neighborhoods meet other underclass criteria: median household income ($15,338), the percentage of vacant housing units (14 percent), percentage of female-headed families with children (53 percent), and median home value ($39,000).

Racial segregation is seen as crucial to both identifying and understanding the urban underclass. The process of segregation helps to explain why the urban underclass consists primarily of Blacks and Latinos—these are the two groups that most often have experienced increases in poverty and residential segregation simultaneously (Fong and Shibuya 2005; Massey and Denton 1993). Evidence seems to point to a recurring theme—in order to address the problem of poverty we must first address the problem of racial segregation.

Context and Health Differences

Based on earlier discussions, we know that racial and ethnic minorities are not randomly distributed in metropolitan areas. Rather, these groups are steered into a small number of neighborhoods characterized as high-risk places with poverty, crime, and illness occurring independently of any individual differences in socioeconomic status (Acevedo-Garcia 2001; Kawachi and Berkman 2003; LeClere et al. 1997). Several studies, while acknowledging that individual differences account for some of the variation in mortality between racial groups, demonstrate that community-level effects are important. Using data on a county in California, Haan and associates (Haan et al. 1987) found that both African Americans and Whites living in a high-poverty area experienced higher mortality rates than those living in non-poor areas. Whites in high-poverty areas experienced almost 50 percent higher mortality than Whites in non-poor areas, and when neighborhood poverty is controlled, the ethnic gap in mortality is reduced by nearly 25 percent. Their argument is that some ethnic groups experience higher mortality because of where they live rather than just because of their ethnicity. Places with low income and high concentrations of African Americans increase the likelihood of death for residents. Just as Jargowsky (1997) argues, these underclass neighborhoods are hazard zones where concentrated "deprivation can do irreparable harm."

Often referred to as "sick" neighborhoods, these places become perfect storm centers where poverty, sickness, lack of access to grocery stores, high density, poor housing, commercial expansion (particularly liquor stores and fast-food restaurants) all converge to have a profound effect on these places and the health of their residents (Morland et al. 2002; Williams and Collins 2001). Recent studies pinpoint these risk environments, specifically examining the relationship between obesity and poverty in specific districts and neighborhoods (Drewnowski et al. 2009; Jeffery et al. 2006; Nelson et al. 2006; Wang et al. 2007). Some studies have established a link between the proximity/density of fast-food restaurants in poor, predominantly minority communities and health problems among residents, particularly but not exclusively among adolescents (Davis and Carpenter 2009; Kwate 2009; Lewis et al. 2005). As expected both racial (African American) and ethnic (Latino) groups are at risk and developmental consequences for youth continue to be well documented in these populations.

When illness and disease are examined the results are similar. The rates of morbidity mirror mortality, and while individual differences (health behavior, beliefs, attitudes, etc.) account for some of the gap existing between Whites and racial and ethnic minorities, community characteristics account for much of this difference. Though we have known for some time now that ecological factors play a significant role in determining physical and mental health, public health policy continues to ignore the power of the community in influencing healthy outcomes.

Health in the 'Hood

In 1900, the life expectancy at birth in the United States was 47.6 years for Whites and 33 years for non-Whites (most of whom were Black). By 2005, life expectancy for Whites increased to 78 years and 73 years for Blacks (Centers for Disease Control and Prevention 2008b). Yet while progress has been made in improving the health status of both races, Blacks continue to bear the burden of premature death, excessive illness, and disability. The differential quality of the residential environments of

Blacks and Whites clearly plays a critical role in shaping health and mortality (e.g. Jackson and Anderson 2000; Schulz et al. 2002).

While these problems are amplified among the Black population, they are not confined to Blacks. Deaths related to heart disease, cancer, and diabetes, as well as infant mortality tend to be higher among Hispanics, Cubans, Native Americans, and even some subgroups of Asian and Pacific Islanders (Acevedo-Garcia 2001; National Association of Community Health Centers 2009; U.S. Department of Health and Human Services 2009a). Additionally, Hispanics and Latinos face unique health challenges, with Latinos' rates for homicide, AIDS infection, and sexually transmitted infections (STIs) increasing, while drug and alcohol use continues to climb, and in some cases, outdistance that among their Black counterparts.

By paying more attention to the local geography and less to individual population differences, traditional explanations give way to more innovative ones. For example, Geronimus (1992) proposed a "weathering hypothesis" as a possible explanation for patterns of high morbidity and infant mortality among Blacks. Focusing on the hostility of the environment within which people live and work, she suggests that as exposure to environmental assaults and deficits increases with age, there is a worsening health status. A similar finding emerges in a recent study on the ethnic and socioeconomic factors that contribute to risk in cardiovascular heart disease (Winkelby et al. 1998). The study finds significant differences in health risks (blood pressure, smoking, etc.) between Whites and racial/ethnic minorities, particularly Mexican Americans and African Americans. The authors argue for exploring alternative causal pathways and suggest that different life experiences as well as economic, time, and most important, residential constraints may be competing with healthy behaviors to further increase the risk of heart disease among minorities.

The Ghetto Resident's Dilemma

Is it possible for an isolated subculture residing in a high-risk environment to establish and maintain healthy beliefs and lifestyles inconsistent with its surroundings? The thrust of our argument up to this point would likely be a resounding no! Chapter 4's discussion of health theories provides a strong theoretical argument for why healthy attitudes and lifestyles are difficult to develop in the face of challenging ecological circumstances. The ghetto suffers from a lethal combination of ecological factors that often promote unhealthy attitudes, lifestyles, and risks, with little protection to circumvent negative health outcomes. Several ecological factors play a significant role in influencing the health and well-being of residents, by constraining residents' choices, limiting their access to health care services, creating unnecessary risks, and nurturing beliefs and attitudes that exacerbate an already desperate situation. The high-poverty ghetto's weakened institutional structures, high degree of segregation, absence of weak ties, limited social support and social capital, and lack of territorial functioning result in concentrated risks and hazards that Andrulis (1997) refers to as the "urban health penalty." The communities suffering most from this penalty are those isolated from the mainstream economy and segregated by race, age, and social class. This penalty only intensifies as urban hospitals continue to close, as urban minority physicians remain in short supply, and as the delivery of medical services remains unresponsive to the needs of people unable to afford health care.

Recognizing the significant interplay of environmental, social, and economic factors is critical to developing strategies that can improve the quality of life and the life chances of those living in disadvantaged neighborhoods. Any serious health reform effort must take into account the multitude of ecological forces and social problems that afflict certain at-risk communities. This "paralysis of place" certainly can be overcome, but not without comprehensive place-based programs that address the multidimensional needs of communities, while at the same time addressing the special needs of the populations that dwell within them.

Needs and Health Risks of the Young and Old

While place matters, its impact on the everyday life of residents depends on a complex interweave of personal and environmental circumstances and events. Place is personal, which is why place-related effects tend to be modest yet persistent. Age is a particularly salient factor in the experience of place. Place of residence has less relevance for some age groups than others, precisely because people of certain ages tend to occupy wider activity spaces (Campbell and Lee 1992) and to participate in a greater variety of what Feld (1981) calls "ecological foci." The two ends of the age structure—youths and elders—share important similarities as ecological actors. The local action space is often more constricted at these two stages of life because of mobility limitations. Due to the limited mobility of the young, the mental maps of children are especially striking in terms of their narrowly constructed bounds (Garbarino et al. 1992; LaGory and Pipkin 1981). The "ignorance surfaces" in the mental maps of elders are also notable, and are the result of reduced mobility, which accompanies old age. The places elders occupy are deeply embedded with memories, and hence, reliving past experiences with a place may intensify environmental experiences. Place experience in the form of reading about other places, or hearing about them through storytelling or conversation may be an especially important mode of environmental experience for both children and elders. Home and neighborhood are critical sources of experience and well-being for everyone, but for those at the beginning and end of the life cycle they retain special significance.

Youth at Risk

In a comprehensive review of research on neighborhood poverty, Brooks-Gunn and associates (1997) note the important role played by neighborhood environments in shaping child and adolescent development. Since that review, a number of studies have further articulated the place–development relationship (Drukker et al. 2003; Evans 2004; Fauth et al. 2007; Leventhal and Brooks-Gunn 2000; Rankin and Quane 2002; Sampson et al. 2008; Shonkoff and Phillips 2000). Despite the mounting evidence that place shapes developmental outcomes, little has been done to modify the harmful environmental circumstances present in America's cities, placing millions of youths at risk. Children living in high-poverty ghettos are confronted with almost impossible odds in successfully maturing into adulthood. All the problems of urban, post-industrial society are localized in these disadvantaged neighbor-hoods, and so its children are exposed to the hazards of the drug epi-demic, rising violent crime, an increase in sexually transmitted diseases, a crumbling infrastructure, schools resembling jails, and vacant lots serv-ing as dumping grounds.

Some two decades ago, in the early 1990s, it was estimated that roughly one in four children in the United States were at risk for some negative outcome (dropping out of high school, drug and alcohol abuse, violent victimization, teenage pregnancy, etc.) (Dryfoos 1990; Millstein et al. 1992). While there have been some dramatic improvements in spe-cific risks over the last two decades, there continues to be overwhelming evidence that the greatest risks faced by youths occur to those living in America's disadvantaged urban neighborhoods (Mather and Adams 2006; U.S. Bureau of the Census 2007; Wolfe et al. 2006). The portrait of at-risk youth that follows describes circumstances heavily concen-trated in the core urban areas of the United States.

(1) Youth at risk are more likely to be living at or below the poverty level

Poverty and community disorganization have grave consequences for the young. In 2006, 17 percent of American youth lived at or below the poverty line (U.S. Bureau of the Census 2007). While a majority of poverty-stricken children are White, minority children are much more likely to live in poverty, with 33 percent of Black children and 27 percent of Hispanic children living in poverty compared to 10 percent of White, non-Hispanic children (Federal Interagency Forum on Child and Family Statistics 2008). These children, living in poor families, often with a single parent, are at significant risk for experiencing difficulty in school, which in turn has implications for their adult futures (Mather and Adams 2006).

Poverty affects children's mental and physical health. Because poor children are likely to live in disadvantaged neighborhoods they are exposed to significant physical hazards as well as multiple stressors. Residence in such places increases their chances of exposure to toxic waste, substandard housing, air and noise pollution, as well as deviant and violent circumstances. These risks and hazards promote illness and disease as well as great psychological uncertainty at a very crucial period in a child's development (Beyers et al. 2001; Evans 2004; O'Campo et al. 2000; Rabito et al. 2003; Wolfe et al. 2006).

(2) Youth at risk are more likely to be without a home

"Placeless" youth face significant challenges. While estimates vary, it is believed that over 1.6 million children and adolescents are homeless (National Center on Family Homelessness 2009; National Coalition for the Homeless 2008). Whether in a shelter or on the street, homeless circumstances are severe and long periods without a home promote a variety of health problems, including increased infections and poor nutrition, distress and anxiety, injuries, and exposure to violence (Health Resources and Services Administration 2001; National Coalition for the Homeless 2008).

(3) Youth at risk are more likely to be abused, neglected, abandoned, or orphaned

In 2006, over 3 million cases of child abuse were reported and, of those, more than 55 percent were substantiated, making for a prevalence rate of 12 per 1,000 children (Federal Interagency Forum on Child and Family Statistics 2008). Forty-nine percent of the maltreatment was the result of neglect, 29 percent physical abuse, 16 percent sexual abuse, and 6 percent emotional abuse. The majority of abused and neglected children live in low-income, principal-city communities where services are overburdened and often inadequate. The impoverishment of these neighborhoods makes effective responses to such abuse unlikely, since poverty burdens families and individuals with significant personal problems, eroding the social capital necessary to promote a blanket of protection (Wolfe et al. 2006).

In addition, empirical evidence suggests that the short- and long-term implications of abuse and neglect are significant. A host of problems including mental health, developmental, sexual, cognitive, and social disorders are associated with child abuse and neglect (e.g. Rankin and

Quane 2002; Repetti et al. 2002; Shinn et al. 2008). A perfect example is the experience of violence. Violent behavior appears to be transmitted from one generation to the next—resulting in a persistent sense of hopelessness and despair that intensifies the problems faced by families and communities struggling to break out of its cycle (Coid et al. 2001; Wolfe et al. 2006).

(4) Youth at risk are more likely to be exposed to drug and alcohol at an early age or, in some cases, in utero

Children are at risk sometimes before being born, and this circumstance is exacerbated in low-income, minority, principal-city communities in the United States. Poverty predicts many negative birth-related outcomes. Whether because of poor nutrition, inadequate prenatal care, smoking, drinking, or drug abuse, poor women are at risk of having more complications during pregnancy and higher rates of infant mortality (Hynes and Lopez 2009; Sims and Rainge 2002).

Smoking and drug and alcohol use among youths remain an important risk factor (Johnston et al. 2003; Federal Interagency Forum on Child and Family Statistics 2008). While long-term trends indicate some decline in drug and alcohol use among teenagers, in 2007, 26 percent of twelfth graders, 22 percent of tenth graders, and 10 percent of eighth graders reported binge drinking (having at least five drinks in a row) in the previous two weeks. Similarly, illicit drug use among teenagers declined in the last decade, but still remained high, with nearly 20 percent reporting having smoked marijuana and 14 percent sniffing glue in the last 30 days prior to the survey (Adlaf et al. 2003; Centers for Disease Control and Prevention 2008c). While estimates of drug use by location among youths are difficult to obtain, the strong relationship between drug use and poverty remains clear, and urban youths are at high risk of exposure to the drug culture (Fauth et al. 2007; Leventhal and Brooks-Gunn 2000). Ecological theories of health (see Chapter 3) further suggest that the risks of exposure to health-compromising circumstances by urban, poor youth will be exacerbated by neighborhood disadvantage, limited collective efficacy, and neighborhood disorder.

(5) Youth at risk are more likely to die while young or give birth while still a teenager

Poverty is often linked to early childbearing. Nearly one-half of children under six living in poverty have mothers who gave birth as a teenager, while only 17 percent of those above the poverty line have mothers who gave birth during their teen years (Centers for Disease Control and Prevention 2002). These children face a double jeopardy—exposure to poverty and a mother lacking the maturity and knowledge to be a good parent. That combination, commonly found among poor, urban Blacks, can have deadly consequences for the child.

While infant mortality in the United States has shown some decline in the last five years, the gap between Whites and Blacks remains significant. Blacks still have an infant mortality rate twice as high as Whites (Sims et al. 2007). The problems of the very young are compounded by health complications related to the circumstances of poverty, the hazards of urban living, and inadequate access to medical care (Centers for Disease Control and Prevention 2005; Fauth et al. 2007; Geronimus 2000). In addition to infant mortality risks, there are significant risks associated with low birth weight or premature delivery (Bauman et al. 2006; Bell et al. 2006; Hoyert et al. 2001; Reichman et al. 2009; Sims et al. 2007). Detrimental health and developmental effects are higher among poor children; low-birth-weight babies are more likely to suffer from disabilities such as asthma, cerebral palsy, mental retardation, blindness, hearing impairment, language dysfunction, and behavioral problems such as attention deficit hyperactivity disorder and oppositional defiance disorder (Almond et al. 2005; Brooks et al. 2001; Case et al. 2005; Costello-Wilson et al. 2005; Hack et al. 2005; Matte et al. 2001; Richards et al. 2001). Research continues to demonstrate how characteristics of inner city neighborhoods, ranging from outdoor air pollution to indoor contaminants, play a role in predicting such detrimental health outcomes for the urban young.

(6) Youth at risk are more likely to be exposed to sexually transmitted infections

While the percentage of 9th–12th graders having intercourse declined in the decade since 2000, still more than a third (34 percent) of young women become pregnant at least once before reaching the age of 20 (Henshaw 2003). Boys report having more sexual contact, and at an earlier age than girls; rates of early entry into sexual intercourse are highest among low-income, minority youths. In addition, more than one-third of teens that are sexually active are having unprotected sex; unprotected sex has significant, sometimes deadly consequences for these youth.

One in four sexually active teenagers contracts an STI each year, with prevalence rates continuing to increase since the end of World War II (Kaiser Family Foundation 2005). Sexual contact and infection is highly correlated with socioeconomic status, race, gender, and age of adolescents, and AIDS has become the fastest-growing cause of death among adolescents and adults. Experts project that in the next 5 to 10 years, AIDS will be the leading cause of death among men of ages 25–44. Those youths at greatest risk of contracting the AIDS virus are runaways, prostitutes, and intravenous drug users. All of these groups tend to be concentrated in low-income, deteriorating neighborhoods of the central city, further promoting the circumstances for a subculture of health risk-taking behaviors in such areas. Once again, there is double jeopardy—those experiencing the most health problems live in the least healthy environments, where there is limited access to medical care (Cockerham 2007; Wolfe et al. 2006). In addition, these environments for socialization and development produce a context of hopelessness and helplessness that results in negative health behaviors.

(7) Youth at risk are more likely to be a witness or a victim of violence

The physical and psychological costs of violence exposure are considerable, particularly for children and adolescents. While violent crime rates among adults show signs of decreasing, juvenile crime and victimization continue to grow, approaching epidemic proportions. In 2005, youth aged 12–19 were twice as likely as adults to be victims of violent crimes (Baum 2005; Beyers et al. 2001). Likewise, the offending rate for youths between the ages of 12 and 17 reached a high of 52 crimes per 1,000 in the early 1990s. Since then the offending rates have declined, yet crime continues to be significant among at-risk adolescents, particularly low-income, minority urban youths.

In addition to more obvious forms of exposure such as victimization, young persons are increasingly exposed to violence as witnesses in their homes, schools, and communities. In a 2008 national survey of exposure to violence, 60 percent of youth reported being exposed to some form of violence in the past year—as either a victim or a witness (Finkelhor et al. 2009; Guterman et al. 2002). In a recent survey of students aged 12–18, nearly 1.7 million reported being a victim of a non-fatal crime in school (Dinkes et al. 2009). Clearly exposure to crime in a variety of social contexts is a significant problem for youth—particularly older adolescents.

In an inner-city Birmingham, Alabama study that included the three high-risk Village Creek communities, 43 percent of youths interviewed said they had seen someone being killed by another person (Fitzpatrick and Boldizar 1993). Children growing up amidst this prolonged daily violence are at risk for serious developmental and psychological harm. A growing body of research shows that chronic exposure to violence increases susceptibility to a wide range of developmental and mental health problems, particularly among adolescents (Buka et al. 2001; Fitzpatrick 1997; Fitzpatrick and Boldizar 1993; Osofsky et al. 1993; Ozer et al. 2004; Richters and Martinez 1993; Salzinger et al. 2006).

(8) Youth at risk are more likely to experience mental health problems

An estimated 15–20 percent of American children suffer from some mental or emotional disorder (Melynk et al. 2003a). In addition, there is a critical need for mental health services to be delivered to young persons, particularly those living in high-poverty ghettos where services are either inadequate or non-existent (Andrulis 1997; Xue et al. 2005). Depression and anxiety disorders are high among young persons; between 15 percent and 20 percent of school-age children and adolescents suffer from one or more mental health problems, with only a small proportion of those receiving treatment for their illness (Garber and McCauley 2002; Kessler and Wallers 1998; Melynk et al. 2003b).

Experts argue that the rising rates of teenage homicide and suicide are a cruel outcome of overwhelming hopelessness, helplessness, and anger (Centers for Disease Control and Prevention 2006). These feelings of despair are amplified in the urban setting where schools are run-down, churches lock their doors at night, stores have moved out of the neighborhood, vacant lots and empty buildings outnumber playgrounds and occupied housing, and fear and distrust permeate everyday life. In the United States, nearly 17 percent of middle/high school students reported thinking about suicide in 2005; and nearly half of those had attempted suicide at least once in the past year (Centers for Disease Control and Prevention 2006). While suicide has declined in the adult population over the last several decades, it remains the third leading cause of death among youth aged 15–24 (Fitzpatrick et al. 2008). These numbers are staggering and deliver a harsh message that the risks associated with adolescence and young adulthood are high, and even higher in certain locations.

(9) Youth at risk are more likely to have difficulty in school and drop out

Poverty severely diminishes a child's ability to learn, his or her overall academic success, and the likelihood of graduation from high school. Family income is one of the strongest predictors of school performance; children from low-income families are five times more likely to drop out of school than children in upper-income families (Mather and Adams 2006).

As expected, this "education effect" is much worse in places where school systems are poor, facilities are run down, deviant subcultures concentrate, and education plays second fiddle to the higher-profile problems of crime, homelessness, and economic decline. While there is some controversy in its calculation and reporting, the national status dropout rate was recently reported to be nearly 10 percent (Laird et al. 2007). This rate measures the percentage of individuals not enrolled in high school and who do not have a high school credential, irrespective of when they dropped out. The measure provides an indicator of the proportion of young people who lack a basic high school education and this average tends to be much higher in urban schools, particularly low-income, predominantly minority schools. Researchers have found that in one-quarter of all poor urban high schools, the dropout rate was 50 percent or higher (Braddock and McPartland 1992). The differences between these poor schools and more affluent ones, however, go well beyond dropout rates. For example, only one-half of graduating seniors in the United States attend college, and fewer than 25 percent receive a four-year degree. The majority of students, particularly low-income minorities, are faced with the challenges of finding work after graduating in a context where local jobs do not often match the skills of those completing school. Thus, high school graduates in disadvantaged neighborhoods are sometimes left to flounder, perpetuating the culture of hopelessness.

(10) Youth at risk are more likely to become an adult who is under- or unemployed

Youths from low-income families, particularly Black and Hispanic youth, are more likely to be neither enrolled in school nor working than White, non-Hispanic youth (Federal Interagency Forum on Child and Family Statistics 2009). Rates of unemployment for high school graduates are high, and in some cases exceed 30 percent (Haggstrom et al. 1991). Rates of inactivity (youths unemployed, not in military service, not attending college) provide further evidence of the growing "placement" problem among at-risk youth. Two years after graduation, the proportion of inactive youth often climbs; youth aged 18–19 (14 percent) are more than three times as likely to be detached from both work and school compared to youth aged 16–17 (4 percent) (Federal Interagency Forum on Child and Family Statistics 2009). What makes the transition from school to work so difficult is the lack of comprehensive job-related programs geared specifically to address the needs of inner-city, low-income minority youths. While unskilled employment is available, it is often part-time, with few or no benefits (Brewer 2004).

The word "epidemic" is often used to describe many of the contemporary problems facing young persons in high-poverty neighborhoods. The large number of single-parent families concentrated in disadvantaged

neighborhoods, along with the social disorder and limited collective efficacy found in some of these places, provide the necessary circumstances
for the "contagion" to spread. Clearly, the number of risks and hazards
confronting urban youth in such neighborhoods is considerable, particularly given their developmental capacity to cope with stressful circumstances. As a result of their limited mobility, immaturity, and
dependency on others, these youthful ecological actors are often at the
mercy of their surroundings and circumstances.

Elders at Risk: Physical and Mental Health Aspects of Aging

Just as youths are particularly sensitive to environmental factors, so
are the elderly. While the majority of persons over 65 are healthy, significant physiological changes accompany the aging process, and in some
cases affect everyday activity and transform place experiences. Such
changes place elders at greater risk for certain environmentally related
health challenges. For example, people at age 75 typically have 92 percent
of the brain weight they had in their 30s, 84 percent of former
basal metabolism, 70 percent of kidney filtration rate, and 43 percent of
maximum breathing capacity (Kart 1990). Gerontologists suggest that
changes in the skin, skeletomuscular, neurosensory, and cardiopul-
monary systems associated with aging have the possibility of directly
affecting elders as ecological actors (Satariano 2006). Mobility is
sometimes reduced by neurosensory changes, loss of muscle power,
osteoporosis, arthritis and rheumatism, and chronic muscular and joint
pain (Roubenoff and Hughes 2000; Sharma et al. 2003; Sternfeld et al.
2002).

While many of these physiological changes are observable, others
associated with aging are less so. Most notable in this less visible category
of health declines are those related to the individual's ability to achieve
physical equilibrium (homeostasis). As people age, their ability to "get
back to normal" after stressful events is reduced (Brunner 2000). Various
systems and organs operate at reduced capacity. Blood pressure and heart
rates take longer to return to pre-stress levels. The immune system is less
able to protect persons from contagious diseases.

Old age, then, is not for the faint of heart. It can take a toll on mental as well as physical health. A range of stressful, age-related experiences are presumed to interfere with some people's ability to age successfully (Aldwin and Gilmer 2004; Aldwin et al. 2006; Chen and Wilmoth 2004; LaGory and Fitzpatrick 1992; Moos et al. 2005). These can include increases in age-connected stressful events or life circumstances such as the loss of friends or spouse, hospitalization, relocation, retirement, reduced income, chronic pain, or declining health. But they may also be due to changing physical and social environments such as a declining neighborhood, an aging house, poor access to transportation, or reductions in social support because of overtaxed social support systems or the loss of sources of support through death or illness.

Those caring for elders carry a heavy burden, too. This burden increases the likelihood of depression among caregivers, which in turn produces a "depressing" environment within the household (Ferrell and Mazanec 2009; Kurtz et al. 2005; Matthews et al. 2003; Whitbourne 2008). Events and circumstances associated with aging produce higher rates of depression in persons beyond retirement age (Aldwin et al. 2006; Karp and Reynolds 2009; Zarit et al. 2004). Indeed, of the non-organic mental disorders such as anxiety, paranoia, schizophrenia, and depression, depression is the most likely to have its onset in later life.

Besides depression, various forms of dementia are associated with aging. While a relatively small number of elderly exhibit any symptoms of dementia, currently over 5 million persons have Alzheimer's disease (Alzheimer's Association 2009; Esch et al. 2002), the most common cause of dementia among older persons. The disease develops gradually over an extended period of time with the duration of noticeable symptoms usually occurring within four to eight years (Administration on Aging 1998). Early symptoms include forgetfulness and some difficulty negotiating unfamiliar spaces, but as the disease progresses the individual becomes increasingly dependent on others for even the most basic needs.

While the majority of elders are independent and competent, some gerontologists have argued that they have a higher probability of becoming environmentally sensitive or docile (Balfour and Kaplan 2002;

Kawachi and Berkman 2003; Lawton and Simon 1968; Satariano 2006). They suggest that the reduced physical and cognitive competence associated with aging causes some elders to become more vulnerable to environmental factors. Coinciding with this increased sensitivity is a reduced ability and interest in manipulating and changing their environments. With age, the threshold of place awareness shrinks, and the potential for being more vulnerable to negative aspects of place grows. Spatial imprisonment puts the elderly at a disadvantage relative to other residents in communities where the range of personal support networks and social capital often extends beyond localized neighborhoods (Berkman and Glass 2000; Satariano 2006; Wellman 1979). The reduced mobility of some older people, perhaps because of losing the ability to drive, means that the aged are more likely to rely on neighborhood services and neighbors to support their needs, while the majority of metropolitan residents reach far from home to meet the needs of everyday life.

Lawton and Nahemow's (1973) theory of "environmental press" suggests the effect that environmental forces may have on the aged. In their thesis, person–environment relations are a function of the environment's capacity to challenge the individual (its "press" level), as well as the individual's ability to deal with these challenges ("competence"). Physical and mental health, sensorimotor functioning, cognitive skills, and personality factors such as mastery and hardiness can affect individual competence. Competence in dealing with the environment is often discussed in terms of the activities of daily living and the instrumental activities of daily living, which are all affected by the aforementioned factors. Can the person get by on his or her own, and what will the cost of limits to this independent living be to the person's general well-being? Is mobility impaired, and by how much? Can the person be independent physically? Can he or she take care of personal finances and access needed services? Approximately 20 percent of persons 65 and over have some limitation in their daily activities. By age 85, nearly half of all elderly have some impairment (Soldo and Longino 1988). Levels of impairment vary by income. Among men over 70 years of age, poor men are 1.8 times more likely to have some impairment, and poor women are more than 1.5 times more likely to be impaired (National Center for Health Statistics 1998).

Of course the individual's ability to live out a life in a given place also depends on the qualities of the local environment itself. The so-called environmental press level is gauged by how behaviorally demanding the environment is to residents. Are there significant hazards present that challenge the physical and mental health of the person? Is the environment dangerous in the sense that it has high levels of noise or chemical pollutants? What are the levels of local crime? How far away are the resources and services that the person needs in order to get by on a daily basis? Is the home and neighborhood physically deteriorating so that mobility may be constrained? Is transportation readily available? Are sidewalks and streets congested? All these questions concerning the state of the person and the environment relate to factors that determine the individual's ability to adapt to their environmental circumstances.

Space constricts with age as role loss, reduced income, decreased physical and mental competence, and increased fear take place. As people age, the distance traveled to get needed services and resources shrinks (Carp 1976; Ward 1984). Hence, for many elderly people, home and neighborhood become even more meaningful and consequential with time. Such places are often imbued with rich memories, since many people age in place. Indeed, the likelihood of a person moving within a five-year period declines significantly after the age of 30, and those least likely to move are over 55 years of age, a trend particularly accentuated for African Americans (Atchley 1991). Both of these consequences of aging, increased environmental sensitivity and constricted action space, suggest that elders are more likely to be at risk from the hazards present in their residential environments. Place means more for them, and as such, an ecological view of aging is most appropriate (Kawachi and Berkman 2003; Satariano 2006; Smedley and Syme 2000).

Neighborhood as a Healthy Place for Aging—Hazards and Risks

As their action space constricts with age, inertia takes on greater significance. Home and neighborhood matter more, particularly for those with limited spatial options. People age in place, and these places also age and sometimes deteriorate. What are the hazards and risks affecting homes and neighborhoods as contexts for healthy aging?

Places like Village Creek contain physical, psychological, and social hazards for the elderly. Housing in such areas tends to suffer from age and deterioration, and these factors may be exaggerated for older, frail elderly (Iwarsson 2005; Oswald et al. 2007). Reschovsky and Newman (1991) have demonstrated a strong correlation between age, home maintenance, and housing quality. These hazards extend into the larger residential space of the neighborhood. High-poverty areas have a significant concentration of aging, dilapidated structures—poorly maintained residences, crumbling sidewalks, vacant buildings, etc. They also have higher densities of older persons than is typical for the metropolitan area (Fitzpatrick and Logan 1985; LaGory et al. 1980, 1985). Village Creek's high-poverty tracts are home to nearly 34 percent more elderly than the average tract in the Birmingham Metropolitan Area. Additionally, these high-poverty tracts have nearly 14 percent of their housing units vacant compared with only 9 percent in the Birmingham Metropolitan Area. When focusing specifically on households with persons aged over 65, 43 percent of these households in the Village Creek area have no car available to them, a figure nearly twice as high as that for the average elderly household in the metropolitan area (U.S. Bureau of Census 2000).

Age density also affects the character of a neighborhood. In such places, people deal with the consequences not only of their own aging, but also that of the neighbors who surround them. High age densities may create a local culture of vulnerability and an inability to respond to the changing circumstances in the neighborhood. The effects of age segregation can be further exacerbated by the fact that neighborhoods with a high concentration of older persons (both in central cities and in older, inner-ring suburbs) are also typically in places with higher levels of poverty, aging buildings, and larger numbers of unattached persons (Fitzpatrick and Logan 1985; LaGory et al. 1980). In central cities, these areas of concentrated aging also contain high concentrations of minorities, generally fitting the characterization of a ghetto (Jargowsky 1997). Thus, people find themselves addressing their own potentially stressful personal issues as well as the larger stressful context.

The concentration of hazard present in high-minority, high-poverty ghetto areas has already been explored in Chapters 3 and 5. Such areas tend to have high levels of violence, weak political ties, low territorial functioning, high degrees of transience, high vacancy rates, and extremely weak economies. Services are uniformly inferior to those available in other parts of the metropolis. Levels of fear are predictably higher, as are the stressors associated with daily living in such areas (Ward et al. 1986). These areas are "risk spaces." Environmental forces in these risk spaces are stressful for all, but even more so for the elderly. As the docility hypothesis suggests, the elderly have a significantly higher risk of chronic degenerative diseases and cognitive impairments, making them more vulnerable to factors in the local environment (Lang et al. 2009). That vulnerability to environmental hazards connected with residence in disadvantaged neighborhoods is further intensified by elders' tendency to age in place.

It is no surprise, then, that research finds great differences in the environment for aging in central cities versus that of suburban and rural communities (LaGory and Fitzpatrick 1992; Reitzes et al. 1991; Ward et al. 1988). Reitzes et al. (1991) showed that while personal factors such as physical health and personal assets were important for overall well-being, place of residence was even more important. Most notably, the well-being experienced by elderly people living in cities was significantly lower than for those residing in suburban or rural areas. As noted in Chapter 3, cities concentrate diversity, strangers, and highly complex environmental stimuli. Older persons may perceive principal-city spaces and organizations as large, impersonal, and threatening, and thus participate less actively with their surrounding environment (Reitzes et al. 1991). The negative aspects of urban location, however, may not always outweigh the benefits accruing to residents in certain parts of the central city.

The accessibility of an area to other places (good, reliable, and available transportation) is also a critical factor in both general well-being and levels of depression, particularly for the less healthy elderly (Aneshensel et al. 2007; LaGory and Fitzpatrick 1992; Lang et al. 2009). The central city may be convenient for some residents, even more convenient than suburban and rural communities. In the case of disadvantaged neighbor-hoods, however, accessibility may be extremely problematic. These areas can promote higher levels of depression and lower levels of well-being for vulnerable elderly because they are essentially cut off from access to other parts of the metropolis due to high crime, fewer personal forms of trans-portation, and high levels of mistrust. Lack of access may also exacerbate the physical health risks associated with the frail, less competent elderly. This group of individuals is usually not just physically disabled but also socially, economically, or environmentally impoverished as well. These deficiencies may be extremely low income, incomplete care-giving arrangements, limited social contacts with friends or family, inaccessible homes for persons with disabilities, or inconvenient, high-crime neighborhoods that limit people's ability to effectively use their sur-roundings.

Conclusion

These four groups: the homeless, the poor, youth, and elders, experience similar spatial constraints. They are more dependent on others to gain access to opportunities afforded in other parts of the metropolitan area. Their constrained action spaces limit their options and experiences, and reduce the ability of the city to work effectively for them as a "machine for living." At the same time, because of limited action spaces, their health is more likely to be threatened by the hazards and risks present in the local residential area. Clearly, place matters more for them than for others, and their place in the world is governed by both geography and their unique physical, psychological, and social circumstances.

7

PROMOTING HEALTH

PLACE-BASED SOLUTIONS TO PLACE-BASED PROBLEMS

One number may determine how long you live and how good you feel. It's not your weight or your cholesterol count. In fact, it may help determine those too. It's your address.

Bell and Rubin

The warehouse fire that released nearly 5,000 gallons of highly concentrated toxins into Village Creek more than ten years ago is long-forgotten news, but the story is far from over. There is some good news in this story. The Village Creek Acquisitions Project removed over 700 structures from the creek's floodplain, preventing the displacement of residents during frequent flash-flooding. Volunteers working with the Village Creek Society and Alabama Power's Renew Our Rivers Project removed over 30 tons of debris from the creek. At the same time, however, too much of the story remains the same. Several studies in the decade after the fire reported significantly degraded water quality with elevated concentrations of heavy metals, organic contaminants, and a deteriorated aquatic community (Spencer 2008).

The daily challenges confronted by several thousand residents continue. Poverty-stricken, minority-concentrated neighborhoods like Village Creek face unhealthy futures unless comprehensive, place-sensitive programs are designed and implemented to assist residents. Around the United States universities, schools, churches, and neighborhoods have begun to form successful partnerships aimed at addressing place-specific health risks and hazards (National Association of County and City Health Officials 2009; Bell and Rubin 2007; Robert Wood Johnson Foundation 2009).

Youth crime, teenage drug and alcohol abuse, high school dropouts, teenage pregnancy, unemployment, environmental pollution, and homelessness are just a few examples of the problems that have benefited from intensive, place-based approaches to problem solving. Where large-scale federal and regional programs sometimes stumble, local community action continues to record successes. A recent story about a community in California underscores how home grown solutions can have a significant impact on the health and well-being of a community.

Nearly two decades ago, a public health worker, America Bracho, a Venezuelan physician, showed up in the border town of Santa Ana, California with a mission. In the same county as Disneyland, Knott's Berry Farm, and Saddleback Church, Santa Ana just a few years ago was ranked the toughest city in the United States (based on weighted levels of crime, poverty, disease, etc.). Santa Ana wasn't just any little border town; it had over 350,000 residents, 70 percent of which were Latinos, with an average family of four barely making enough wages to keep them above the federal poverty level. Like many places around the country, Santa Ana was fraught with health risks that were creating a major problem for the community and its residents—particularly its youth. America Bracho's mission was about turning this community's health trajectory around and in 1993, she helped found a non-profit organization called Latino Access (Latino Health Access 2009; Moyers 2009). Facing so many health crises, Latino Access began by first addressing adult diabetes and then watched over the next decade as that one outreach program grew into another and an innovative community outreach system was born. Training residents to be part of an outreach team became a very successful strategy and Latino Access started tackling even bigger, tougher community health issues.

After developing a number of successful outreach programs, Latino Access began to notice how hard it was for residents to maintain healthy lifestyles in an unhealthy environment. Apartment complexes had no free play zones set aside for children, no parks for families to exercise or children to play; vacant lot after vacant lot, bordered by fast-food restaurants and liquor stores, Santa Ana was a community "designed to be sick." But with a community-wide outreach organization in place, and a core of mothers committed to finding healthy outdoor play alternatives for their children, city hall would end up being an unworthy opponent. Just recently, a park began to take shape and land was cleared in an area once made up of abandoned buildings and vacant lots. With private funds, along with city and county support, a play zone and community center are being planned. The story of Latino Access's struggles and successes in promoting a healthy community highlights a critical fact about health in America—there are dramatic health disparities in the United States that can only be overcome by developing strategies that attack the underlying social conditions causing them. As Bruce Link (2008) argues forcefully: "The health of the U.S. population and the health of other countries around the world is substantially worse than it might have been had the influence of social factors been recognized and harnessed to achieve optimal health for the citizens of the world" (p. 368).

The growing recognition that Americans' health status is associated with complex social phenomena such as poverty, inadequate housing, racism, and segregation has led health scientists to call for a renewed focus on an ecological approach to addressing health inequalities (Fitzpatrick and LaGory 2000; Hynes and Lopez 2009; Kawachi and Berkman 2003; Robert Wood Johnson Foundation 2009). By recognizing that individuals are embedded in a nexus of social, political, economic, and cultural systems that shape their behavior and often obscure healthy choices, public health faces new challenges. In part because public health has been burdened with a tradition that overemphasizes individual-level risk factors, the consequences of social and environmental conditions for health promotion and illness have been overlooked. Earlier works by Wilkinson (1996) and Beck (1995), however, clearly articulate the significance of context in promoting a society's overall health. The perspective presented in this book identifies a critical aspect of context that impacts not only the health of individuals, but the health of society as well.

At the risk of sounding like a broken record, we'll say it again: *place matters*. The central theme, laid out in earlier chapters, focuses on bringing place back into discussions that traditionally have been dominated by an individualistic, behavioral interpretation of health. More than just emphasizing the importance of place, we've attempted to integrate several bodies of literature and synthesize these various traditions into a common approach with a common language. Thus, health becomes more than an individual characteristic. The health of places and their capacity to impact on risk and promote protection represent a renewed focus on an old problem—how to improve the health of a nation. The literatures of medical sociology, urban sociology, community psychology, medical geography, and public health all provide important perspectives on this problem, all of which can be integrated into a place-based approach to understanding and addressing critical national and international health issues.

In earlier chapters we reviewed research from these various perspectives pointing to the significant role context plays in a population's health. This work often finds, however, that while a contextual effect on health is present, individual-level variables' contributions to health behaviors and risks are much stronger. Although this conclusion is statistically accurate, it has the potential of misleading readers and misdirecting health policy. In many cases, the analyses are predisposed to these results. Generally, individual variables are entered first, in order to "control" for their impact and to detect "real" contextual effects. The contextual effect is the impact of individuals' presence in the group, over and above the aggregate of the individual-level variables' effects. Intuitively, it could be expected that this aggregate of individual effects would be rather large while the remainder of the "group" effect (the contextual effect) would be smaller. The small contextual effect is, to a degree, predetermined by analytical assumptions about the "real" group effect. While analytically correct, the research outcome has the possibility of being mistranslated when policy strategies are proposed.

Traditional regression approaches typically have been used to examine the "context" effects and this approach operates on the assumption that observations used in regression analyses are *independent*. Thus, observations of any one individual are not systematically related to observations of any other individual. Yet practically speaking, that assumption is often violated when adults are sampled from the same neighborhood, or children from the same school, etc. When this assumption of independence is violated, regression coefficients can be biased, standard error estimates artificially are smaller, and consequently there is a risk of inferring that a relationship is statistically significant when it is not.

One recent methodological advancement that has helped to correct this flaw in "contextual" analysis has been hierarchical linear modeling (HLM) (Raudenbush and Bryk 2002). HLM is a technique developed to address the larger question of context's importance, above and beyond the individuals in that context, for predicting some outcome. Not only in social research but in other fields, data often have a hierarchical or nested structure. Individual subjects are classified or arranged in groups with qualities that influence an outcome. In HLM individuals are seen as level-1 units of study. The groups in which they are members (e.g. organizations, schools, neighborhoods) are level-2 units. The analysis enables the researcher to simultaneously assess relationships within a certain level as well as between or across hierarchical levels (Raudenbush and Bryk 2002; Subramanian et al. 2003). Throughout this book we reference research that has examined these types of nested relationships/multilevel models where individuals are at level 1 and neighborhoods are at level 2. While this modeling strategy has provided key insights into the relationship between neighborhood and health in recent studies, its use is still not standard practice among community and health researchers (Subramanian et al. 2003).

Methodological issues aside, the fact that individual-level effects are often noted as being stronger by no means implies that individual-level strategies are the most appropriate for risk reduction, health promotion, or service delivery in the high-poverty ghetto. Indeed, well-designed, place-based approaches to health can serve two functions—promoting healthy places while at the same time serving as sites for delivering information and services to high-risk individuals. When certain places are used as dissemination points for services and information, for example schools or churches, they provide services to the community while strengthening central institutions. In this process of institutional support, local communities are empowered, promoting an atmosphere of deeper attachment and healthier social ties.

The goal of this final chapter is to demonstrate the crucial role of place for health by concentrating on specific place-based health strategies. While our focus is on high-poverty ghettos, the framework developed in this book has relevance for the health and well-being of residents in other places as well. Not only is such an approach vital to understanding the health of specific at-risk groups, but place-based policies are critical to promoting the health of these groups in the whole society. Indeed, in the divided health worlds of contemporary urban America, without such a strategy our society's health is at risk.

There is reason to be both optimistic and pessimistic about the political commitment to place-based approaches. At the federal level, there is growing recognition of the importance of ecologically targeted strategies to address urban poverty and health problems. Over the last several decades, the philosophy at Housing and Urban Development (HUD), Departments of Justice and Education, and the Centers for Disease Control and Prevention all have shifted toward the development and support of comprehensive, community-based strategies to solve complex social problems. At HUD, for example, local communities have been asked to develop comprehensive programs to work on local housing problems. In the area of homeless service provision, the community's agencies, as a group, are required to develop a single funding proposal annually to address homelessness. In these funding proposals, agencies must work together to identify local needs and agree on a comprehensive strategy (a "Continuum of Care") to address these needs. These programs continue to be effective at addressing local housing needs because they are locally designed. A new federal stimulus package ($1.5 billion) being administered by HUD has an even greater potential to impact on communities and their affordable housing and homeless problems. This program, the Homelessness Prevention and Rapid Re-Housing

Program, is designed to provide homelessness prevention assistance for the precariously housed, and rapid re-housing assistance for persons who are already homeless.

Not only are such place-based approaches becoming more common, but urban scholars continue to gain an important voice in the policy arena. At the heart of this shift in favor of ecologically based social policy was William Julius Wilson's (1987) *The Truly Disadvantaged.* Its publication, Lehman and Smeeding write,

> was a significant event on many levels. It had a substantial impact on public debate about race and urban poverty; it had a clear impact on the thinking of then Arkansas governor Bill Clinton; and it triggered a resurgence of foundation support for social science research in those domains. Not the least significant of the book's effects was to stimulate renewed and heightened interest in the sociological and ethnographic investigation of neighborhoods.
>
> (1997:256)

The research stimulated by Wilson's work provides growing evidence that the metropolis is being dramatically restructured (Brooks-Gunn et al. 1997; Jargowsky 1997). While segregation is actually declining in many MSAs, economic segregation by race is increasing significantly, poverty is concentrating in inner cities, and the number of high-poverty minority neighborhoods is growing. In addition, as the metropolis continues to decentralize, this highly concentrated minority poverty has increasingly deleterious effects on the physical and mental well-being of its residents (Browning and Cagney 2003; Jackson and Anderson 2000; Massey 2001; Sampson et al. 2002; Smedley et al. 2003). How can these restructuring trends and their health consequences be addressed effectively?

Removal Strategies

While most agree that place matters for some in the metropolis, there continues to be some debate over the specific programs that should be developed. Two broad options have typically been discussed as popular strategies in the place-oriented policy repertoire: (1) removal strategies that either disperse concentrated at-risk populations or remove the existing concentration of a particular hazard, or (2) local community development strategies that attempt to reduce various risks or provide additional sources of protection through promotion of human, physical, or social capital in local areas.

We have noted in earlier chapters the significant health-related problems associated with the concentration of minority poverty in cities. This association has led some federal and local policy makers to focus on the dispersal of the poor through housing voucher programs or scatter-site public housing (Brown and Richman 1997). The Gautreaux Assisted Housing Program in Chicago provided some encouraging evidence for the benefits of housing dispersal programs for the well-being of the poor. Gautreaux participants were placed on a waiting list and offered housing as it became available rather than allowing them to exercise site preferences. This effectively randomized the location process, some being placed in suburban and others in urban settings. While all were placed in private-sector apartments in various sections of the metropolitan area, more than half of the participants were relocated to middle-class suburban neighborhoods (Brooks-Gunn et al. 1997). Follow-up research on residents in the program over the last several decades showed positive effects of suburban residential shifts, particularly for development and educational outcomes (DeLuca and Rosenbaum 2003; Gephart 1997; Rubinowitz and Rosenbaum 2000). Children from the ghetto who moved to the suburbs often benefited in dramatic ways from these moves—with considerably lower dropout rates (5 percent for suburban Gautreaux youths versus 20 percent for urban youth), higher rates of college completion (40 percent versus 20 percent), and a much greater likelihood of employment (75 percent versus 41 percent). These factors are associated with improvements not only in general well-being, but also in physical and mental health.

Although the Gautreaux program seems to have worked, there are a number of reasons to believe that, at least for now, dispersal programs are not the most desirable option. While high-poverty ghetto residents' well-being has clearly been compromised by the accident of place, there are still individual-level correlates of well-being (demographic factors such as age, race, gender, and so on) that cannot be altered by a change of scenery. Even the Gautreaux program had challenges (Keels et al. 2005).

In an effort to better understand whether assisted housing mobility programs can succeed on a large scale, HUD piloted the Moving to Opportunity (MTO) program in five metropolitan areas in 1994 (Comey et al. 2008). Similar to the Gautreaux project, the MTO program was intended to give those persons living in high-poverty, high-crime neighborhoods an opportunity to move to safer, more economically stable communities. The targeted neighborhoods were in some of the worst inner cities in America—Baltimore, Chicago, New York, Los Angeles, and Boston. Over 5,300 low-income families volunteered for the program in these five cities. More than 4,000 families were screened and randomly assigned to a control group, a Section 8 housing group, and the experimental MTO group (Comey et al. 2008). While the results of this relocation experiment were mixed, evaluators concluded that in tight housing markets or uncertain fiscal times, a relocation-only program was likely not enough to help residents develop stable housing out of their original low-income, high-risk neighborhood (Comey et al. 2008). Evaluators further noted that transportation assistance, greater landlord participation, and relocation/housing counseling were all important components to improving relocation successes.

In addition to these problems, large-scale dispersal efforts are not generally feasible, and they often can do serious harm to the neighborhoods of origin. Brown and Richman (1997) point out that even if all public housing residents were given housing vouchers and could be moved to suburban housing, only a fraction of the urban poor would be affected. Dispersal efforts can also lead to further weakening of neighborhood community structure, with those left behind having to confront higher vacancies and more deteriorating structures. Such has been the case with Village Creek. Since hazard removal was not feasible, the Army Corps of Engineers and the city of Birmingham concentrated their efforts on a residential dispersal strategy. In order to reduce residential health risks, less than 15 percent of the 5,000 local households in the Village Creek high-poverty communities were relocated to other areas over the decade following the incident. Removal efforts, however, have been at best haphazard and modest, with little thought given to the consequences of removal on the 85 percent of Village Creek residents left behind. Indeed, instead of strengthening these neighborhoods, evidence suggests this effort to redress the problems of Village Creek residents may actually have intensified the risks and hazards inherent in the area. Increased vacancies, decreasing population, and a growing sense of a community without a future generate an environment that discourages territorial functioning and increases opportunities for victimization. In addition, self-selection biases may have resulted in the loss of important local actors, including cross-generational role models as well as residents aware of environmental risks and hazards and committed to change.

The attempts to deal directly with the environmental hazards of Village Creek include: a monitoring program designed to detect pollution levels in the water, a weekend volunteer-based effort by the Save Our Rivers program to clean up sections of the stream, and a program to prevent flooding. Scientific studies mentioned earlier in this chapter, however, indicate that pollution problems persist, and anecdotal evidence from those who make the mistake of swimming or wading in Village Creek suggest that it is still a major hazard to residents—producing acid burns for some and crippling nervous-system damage for others. The Village Creek experience seems to be indicative of deeper problems entrenched in our current "risk society." While the Environmental Protection Agency has responsibility for oversight of hazardous waste areas through Superfund legislation, complete cleanup of such sites would likely address only a small fraction of the environmental hazards and risks confronting high-poverty ghetto residents (Greenberg and Schneider 1996).

In addition to physical hazards, residents face a myriad of social, psychological, and economic challenges to their health and well-being. In such cases, hazard removal is not the appropriate strategy. Researchers and program developers around the country argue instead for programs that promote neighborhood development by rebuilding institutions, strengthening social support systems, and designing local initiatives in poor minority neighborhoods, rather than dispersing residents or removing specific hazards (e.g. Bell and Rubin 2007; Berlin et al. 2001; Hood 2005). Hazard removal does not create healthy places. Residents of high-hazard, high-risk communities face complex health challenges (Cagney and Browning 2004; Downey and Willigen 2005; Jacobs et al. 2002; Palmer et al. 2009; Shaw 2004). These areas usually combine technological hazards (toxic waste sites, incinerators, polluted water or air, heavy traffic, etc.) with blight (vacant structures, dilapidated or poorly maintained buildings, littered streets, sidewalks, and alleys, poorly maintained infrastructure), and behavioral problems (crime, unfriendly neighbors, and strangers). High-poverty hazard zones cannot suddenly become healthy with narrowly focused programs that address only a single health-compromising issue.

> Is it prudent to spend millions of dollars building noise barriers along roads, remediating waste sites to minimize risk, or reducing odors from sewage treatment plants while doing nothing about blight and crime in the neighborhoods? Likewise is it logical to increase police surveillance, fix streets and street lights, and rehabilitate housing while continuing to allow odors from sewage treatment plants or petrochemical complexes to make the neighborhood unpleasant . . .?
> (Greenberg and Schneider 1996:206)

A comprehensive approach is clearly called for, one that addresses developing both social and physical capital investments in local areas.

Even the best family-oriented or individually targeted programs cannot succeed in neighborhoods where social support systems and local institutions are weakened or where the neighborhood is incapable of promoting territorial functioning (Brown and Richman 1997). Putnam (1993:41) argues forcefully that "in any comprehensive strategy for improving the plight of America's communities, rebuilding social capital is as important as investing in human and physical capital. Investments in jobs and education, for example, will be more effective if they are coupled with reinvigoration of community associations." Integrated strategies are becoming more commonplace and are founded on the

principle that health programs of all types will have the greatest likelihood of success in neighborhoods that function territorially, are well
organized, maintain strong social support systems, and have a strong
voice (Bell and Rubin 2007; National Association of County and City
Health Officials 2009; Robert Wood Johnson Foundation 2009).

Clearly, the most important target areas for a comprehensive strategy
are those areas containing concentrated minority poverty, with limited
collective efficacy and poor resources. In these neighborhoods, a categor-
ical, piecemeal approach is unlikely to be successful because it addresses
only one of a complex set of needs. Comprehensive programs should
attend to the interrelated assets necessary for a healthy community: (1)
Human and physical capital factors such as economic opportunity and
security, affordable housing, physical security, safety, lower dropout rates
and (2) *Social capital* in the form of opportunities for social interaction
and support, opportunities for a sense of territorial identity and local
participation, and access to beneficial role models (Bell and Rubin 2007;
Brown and Richman 1997).

In the next section, we examine some targeted health programs that
contain clear community-building components, which when introduced
into the fabric of local life promote social interaction and support, local
participation, and help develop a sense of local identity. Placing programs like these into a general framework such as *Building Healthy
Communities* could be the basis for a successful place-based approach to
promoting a "healthy society" (Bell and Rubin 2007; National
Association of County and City Health Officials 2009; Robert Wood
Johnson Foundation 2009).

Community Development Strategies

Promoting Health in Schools

Schools have played a critical role in health promotion in the United
States since the late eighteenth century (Allensworth et al. 1995) and in
this century they have been an integral part of strategies for promoting
and protecting the health of young persons. With nearly 50 million

young people attending more than 98,916 schools around the country, schools represent an ideal opportunity to influence the health trajectory of our nation's youth (U.S. Department of Education 2009). Indeed, when school immunization programs were introduced to fight polio in the 1950s, schools were seen as a front line in the fight against deadly diseases. Today, with the present H1N1 influenza pandemic, schools are again seen as a critical entry point for prevention and are viewed as hubs in a delivery network of comprehensive services aimed at improving the health and well-being of students, families, and communities. Whichever perspective one adopts (focused vs. comprehensive), schools, sometimes along with churches, are a focal point for the implementation of place-based strategies for health promotion.

Using schools as central points for service delivery is important not only because of public accessibility, but also because so many of youths' risk-taking behaviors are addressable through prevention programming in schools. The challenge, however, is daunting. What makes it difficult is that it requires schools to juggle several curricula at once. While the academic development of students is critical to the school's mission, broader social development is central to the students' overall integration into society. The statistical portrait of youth health behaviors is alarming, and it is essential that schools recognize the vital role they can play in health promotion and disease prevention. The following few statistical examples help underscore the importance of addressing health concerns in the school setting:

- Every day, nearly 4,000 adolescents smoke their first cigarette.
- Nearly two-thirds of high school seniors do not meet the currently recommended levels of physical activity.
- Nearly 80 percent of school-age youth do not eat the recommended daily amounts of fruits and vegetables.
- Over one-third of high school students reported being in a physical fight one or more times over the last year.
- Every year, more than 3 million teenagers become infected with a sexually transmitted disease (Centers for Disease Control and Prevention 2006).

Many of these health-compromising behaviors can be addressed either in standard curricula or in prevention-based programs for at-risk populations. Regardless of the strategy adopted, schools continue to demonstrate the crucial role they can play in place-based health delivery systems. What follows are just a few examples of school-based programs that have been successful in reaching young populations at risk.

Safe and Drug-Free Schools The safe and drug-free school program was initiated in 1994 following enactment of the Safe and Drug Free Schools and Communities Act. The purpose of this federal mandate was to provide support to programs designed to meet the National Education goal aimed at violence prevention in and around schools, and reduction in the illegal use of alcohol, tobacco, and drugs. State-based safe and drug-free school programs rely on existing resources and supplemental funds from the United States Department of Education. Funds must be used to develop age-appropriate, comprehensive education/prevention curricula to combat violence, the use of drugs and alcohol, improve health and well-being, and develop character and civic participation among school-age youth. While these programs are primarily school-based, they are designed to involve parents, businesses, and communities in a coordinated prevention effort, using the school as the center in the service delivery hub. Specific programs use parents as mentors and tutors, while businesses are asked to provide financial assistance as well as job training and employment opportunities. Police, fire, and other city personnel are invited to participate in programs aimed at involving youth in their community through a variety of hands-on programs.

Evaluation research shows that ineffective school-based prevention programs tend to either neglect or have difficulty enlisting the help of parents and the larger community. Researchers have proposed an environmental approach to prevention planning that encourages a community-wide effort to combat adolescent problems such as violence, teen pregnancy, and drug or alcohol abuse (Hawkins and Catalano 1992; McKnight and Kretzmann 1990; Wittman 1990). In some instances, these prevention plans have included the development of neighborhood needs-and-assets maps to help communities visualize their strengths and weaknesses within geographic boundaries. By mapping problems, the community is able to identify critical issues, and begin addressing them with local resources. Whether the school is physically located in the center of a neighborhood or community is not nearly as important as its location in the center of the service delivery system.

The guidelines for building safe and drug-free schools are straightforward and rely heavily on schools, parents, businesses, and students all working together to create the desired environment. It requires an articulation of community needs and responsibilities. The United States Department of Education in conjunction with the Office of Juvenile Justice and Delinquency Prevention created an action guide for schools in developing safe and drug-free schools (U.S. Department of Justice 1996). In a list of "essential ingredients" the guide underscores the importance of a combined effort on the part of multiple actors in making place-specific prevention programs work.

These programs are examples of place-based approaches that can play a critical role in administering and coordinating community-wide prevention efforts. However, these efforts are sometimes ineffective. A comprehensive evaluation of the safe and drug-free programs concluded that while schools nationally were implementing a large number of prevention efforts, the quality of those efforts was low overall (Crosse et al. 2001). Evaluators further urged schools to improve programming by using an evidence-based approach, in which prevention efforts are adopted, retained, or discarded on the basis of research evidence of program effectiveness. This type of "self-correcting" effort remains a critical component for successful programming, not only in schools, but in community-wide efforts as well.

School-Based Health Clinics In 1840, Rhode Island passed the first legislation making health education mandatory in public schools. Many states followed, and by the turn of the century most states had adopted the idea that schools were important centers for the delivery of health information and care. Since then, school health education and service delivery have gone through considerable transformation (Means 1975). Beyond basic health education, schools were always viewed as important venues for introducing programs designed to prevent malnutrition, screen for visual and hearing defects, and serve as a first defense against a variety of illnesses and infections. By the early 1900s, school nurses, acting as both education coordinators and practitioners, became the key health care personnel for the school. Not until the early 1970s did the school nurse's role begin to change.

In 1972, the Robert Wood Johnson Foundation reviewed state legislation, searching for laws prohibiting the delivery of comprehensive health care services in the school. Unable to find any such legislation, they argued that schools were the ideal place to introduce primary health care activities (Allensworth et al. 1995). The Robert Wood Johnson Foundation stepped up their involvement and funded several school health programs setting up a health center for children from impoverished families in two small towns near Chicago (Brodeur 2000). By the late 1970s and early 1980s, the school clinic was well rooted in the secondary education system. With a growing awareness of and concentration on the multiple physical health, mental health, and social needs of adolescents, the school-based clinic began to represent an excellent alternative to a fragmented health care system that often failed to deliver comprehensive health care services to adolescents. No longer would transportation, school time, or parents' lost work time be a problem for adolescents seeking health care services. These services would now be made available on a routine basis in the schools.

Growing from 20 clinics in 1980 to nearly 2,000 clinics serving more than 2 million children in 44 states (National Assembly on School-Based Health Care 2008; Schlitt 1994), the school-based clinic occupies an important niche in the health care delivery system. By relying on a place-based approach to health care delivery, these clinics have been able to reach thousands of students who otherwise would not have had access to health care because of where they lived. Adolescents often are reluctant to seek health care, and subsequently their health status is jeopardized, particularly as a result of risk-taking behaviors such as drug and alcohol use, sexual behavior, cigarette smoking, insufficient exercise, and poor diet. However, with convenience, confidentiality, and a non-judgmental staff available in clinics at school, adolescents can benefit from comprehensive services that directly and indirectly address many of their risk-taking behaviors (Brindis and Sanghvi 1997). While a majority use the clinics for acute care, a large percentage receive preventive care, counseling, reproductive and sexual health care, and treatment for chronic illnesses. Clearly, this approach to reaching a population in need has great potential, particularly in high-risk high-poverty ghetto schools and neighborhoods.

While the long-term effectiveness and viability of school-based clinics is uncertain, school clinics have become a critical place-specific service reaching thousands of students every year. As a central community institution they provide access, as well as information and role models for disease prevention and health promotion.

School Spotlight: Making a Difference in One Community

Poor nutrition can lead to a number of health problems during adolescence and, if left unattended, can create major health problems into adulthood. For decades, schools have continued to play an important role in developing a health conscience for the communities they serve. Changing food policies, while controversial, have clearly had an impact beyond the walls of the school. Those changes have improved the way parents generally perceive the school, improved the health lifestyles of students, and in some communities, helped set new standards for other community food vendors (restaurants, grocery stores, etc.) in promoting healthy lifestyles among the residents of the local community they serve (Bell and Rubin 2007).

One "school" working to make a difference in the health and well-being of their students, families, and community is the Los Angeles County School District, the second largest school district in the United States. Serving more than 735,000 students, with more than two-thirds eligible for free or reduced lunch, schools throughout the district argued that the eating and exercise patterns of students and the sale of junk foods in the school were contributing to unhealthy "places." Through collaboration between administrators, teachers, health professionals, parents, and students, food policies across the district were changed. All soda sales were banned in Los Angeles County schools. In addition, all à la carte foods were required to have certain nutrient standards and portion sizes, with at least one vegetarian option offered through the school meal program. While these changes may seem small, they had significant ripple effects into the community (Samuels et al. 2007). Parents reported healthier outcomes at home, schools reported increased participation in the school lunch program, and communities developed healthier food alternatives with additional neighborhood farmers' markets being funded. Targeting a wide range of health problems/risks including obesity, sedentary lifestyle, and poor nutrition, schools continue to play an important role in the health of their students, families, and communities.

Promoting Health in Neighborhoods

Neighborhoods have always played a vital role in the delivery of services to local residents. Specifically, in an effort to promote health, neighborhoods have been an important location for development of place-based health care programs, violence prevention, health education, and a cadre of other services. While there is considerable variation from one neighborhood to the next, many neighborhood residents are place bound, depending heavily on localized service delivery because of accessibility limitations ranging from transportation to information, income, and physical impairments.

Since the passage of the Better Communities Act of 1974, cities have received billions of dollars to develop neighborhood programs aimed at resolving urban social problems. Thus the neighborhood became the primary point of attack against problems of crime, poverty, racism, housing, and health care (Schoenberg and Rosenbaum 1980). Neighborhoods, seen as cohesive and independent units within the metropolitan area, faced difficult decisions and choices as the problems of the urban area began to multiply. Not all problems received the same attention, and unfortunately many remained unresolved.

Neighborhoods vary in their ability to solve problems (see Chapter 3). Research suggests that the most viable neighborhoods are those where residents control the social order, set goals for the collective neighborhood life, and implement programs that help to achieve those goals

(Schoenberg and Rosenbaum 1980). In addition, neighborhood areas with extensive bonding social capital also tend to be better able to elicit necessary resources (Putnam 2000). As a result, viable neighborhoods have become models of collective problem solving, introducing health clinics, job corps, education programs, and a variety of prevention strategies tailored specifically to address social problems at a local level. This specific place-based approach has been embraced by many policy makers, planners, and service delivery agencies, who are starting to realize that providing tailored services at a local level is perhaps the most efficient way of reaching segregated, impoverished, predominantly minority communities.

The most viable neighborhoods typically are the ones where formal organizations have been permanently established within the neighborhood. We discussed earlier in this book the importance of an institutional presence for the success of certain places and their delivery of services to residents. For example, without a hospital or primary care facility in or near an inner-city neighborhood, residents are forced to look outside their residential area for health care services. Identifying the needs of a localized population and then working to develop comprehensive programs of service delivery that are "place-sensitive" may be the most successful strategy for addressing problems related to health promotion, disease prevention, and risk-taking behaviors. Such needs identification, however, must evolve at the grassroots level, rather than percolate down from above. Outlined below are a few examples of neighborhood-based programs aimed at addressing local health needs.

Community Housing Programs Good housing is essential to the promotion of health in high-poverty urban areas. But as we have already seen, housing in these areas is often inadequate and dangerous, and public housing has often actually contributed to the problems of ghettoization rather than improved the situation. Because of that fact, in 1989 the U.S. Congress established the National Commission on Severely Distressed Public Housing to assess the quality of public housing and to develop strategies to improve conditions in public housing communities. The Commission concluded that roughly 7 percent of existing units in the 1.3 million unit public housing stock were severely distressed, and that serious efforts were needed to address problems in existing developments (Popkin et al. 2004).

The HOPE VI program is a response to these problems. Its stated goals are to: build sustainable communities, provide housing that reduces the concentration of very low income families in the community, revitalize declining public housing communities and in the process improve the surrounding neighborhood. To date roughly 450 projects have been funded in 166 cities. The program is based on the "new urbanism" philosophy that strives to encourage an urban village-like feel to a community by promoting high-density, low-rise, pedestrian-friendly, public transportation-accessible developments. Housing developments in the new urbanism style typically are close to the street, and have porches and small yards. HOPE VI generally mixes low-rise row houses with some apartments built over garages. The emphasis in HOPE VI is on building safe, defensible neighborhoods and promoting community efficacy. It does this by requiring a diverse mix of household incomes and encouraging a sense of private custodianship through resident assistantship programs that teach people to take care of their homes.

While these projects are based on sound principles, their implementation has not been without significant controversy. The Urban Institute (Popkin et al. 2004) attempted a systematic review of the program. They concluded that HOPE VI has made a positive difference in many communities, reducing concentrated poverty in urban areas and replacing some severely distressed residential areas with more viable mixed-income neighborhoods and higher quality housing. The downside, however, has been obvious and distressing; while HOPE VI focuses on building neighborhoods that promote collective efficacy and safety, these projects often serve as mere removal strategies for low-income minority households. As a consequence, many of the original residents wind up living in equally or even more deplorable conditions than before. Because of this the Urban Institute urges that while the program should continue, significant reforms must be implemented that improve relocation strategies and services and better integrate residents in the planning process (Popkin et al. 2004).

Community Health Clinics A more focused effort to promote healthy neighborhoods is the community clinic program. Community health clinics have traditionally played important roles in neighborhoods around the country. By replacing family physician home visits, these clinics provided a sense of ownership to community residents while at the same time allowing them access to a staff of health care professionals. Considered a success in many urban areas, the viability of community health clinics recently has been threatened. As a result of major shifts in the economy and managed health care, problems with health service access and use are plaguing the high-poverty ghetto. A 1993 report, *Lives in the Balance*, documented the extent of this problem for the under-served in urban areas by suggesting that more than 500 metropolitan locations were classified as "medically underserved areas" (Hawkins and Rosenbaum 1992). Thus, whether a function of physician shortage, lack of medical technology, or limited medical facilities, it appears that those neighborhoods and residents in greatest need suffer the most from current managed health care policies.

Although it is extremely inefficient, primary health care for many low-income and minority residents of the inner city is provided by emergency departments of local hospitals. Hospitals serve as screening centers and primary care facilities for many residents because there is no other place nearby to provide for their health care needs. The National Center for Health Statistics (Nawar et al. 2007) reports that emergency room visits continued to increase over the last decade, and millions of emergency visits made were non-urgent and should have been treated in less expensive, more localized facilities. Indeed, in many communities, hospitals remain the major provider of health care, and in the case of communities of mostly low-income, minority, uninsured residents, they are often the only source of care (Nawar et al. 2007). The economic inefficiency of this arrangement has continually been demonstrated, yet little can be done without major health care reform.

In an attempt to address some of these service delivery problems, community health clinics have grown to number more than 1,200, caring for more than 20 million people. Nearly half of these centers are located in impoverished inner cities (National Association of Community Health

Centers 2009). Typically, the patients are young, poor, unmarried, and often uninsured, creating fiscal instability—an even greater challenge for these localized points of health care delivery. In addition to community clinics, local health departments also deliver primary and preventive health care to those with limited means to pay for such services. In a survey of 176 health departments in metropolitan areas with more than 100,000 persons, 56 percent reported providing primary and preventive care services, including immunizations, family planning, and STI screening (Peck and Hubbert 1994). While such programs offer a safety net, the current structural arrangements do not adequately address the comprehensive health care needs of high-poverty ghettos.

The American Hospital Association (1992), after an extensive review and assessment of urban hospitals, concluded that although inner-city institutions face major problems, they remain the best-equipped places to serve the underserved community (American Hospital Association 1992). While health care solutions for the urban poor require a comprehensive, collaborative strategy involving communities, health care providers, businesses, and residents, something can and must be done to avert further disaster in an already "fragile" system of care. The study mentions several model programs that can be applied in communities. The first one, in Dallas, Texas, is the Parkland Health and Hospital System, which blends primary care with public health services while capitalizing on community involvement (Anderson and Anderson 1990). Health clinics are located in strategic places in neighborhoods and become the primary point of contact between the central hospital and patient. As an extension of the larger hospital system, this local neighborhood site must be able to accommodate a wide range of patient needs, be open on weekends and evenings, and provide preventive as well as acute and chronic health care. This type of arrangement takes the pressure off the hospital system to serve as the catchall health care provider for everyone in the neighborhood. It has been shown to be more cost-efficient while at the same time promoting better interaction between the community and medical personnel, and providing an excellent training ground for medical students interested in family and community medicine.

Similar to the Dallas model is one initiated by the Denver Health Medical Center (Andrulis 1997). This program developed a network of neighborhood clinics and a community health network emphasizing local over regional health care. The mission is community oriented, recognizing that not every neighborhood experiences the same set of health care problems. Thus, clinics have a responsibility to know their patients, the population they serve, and the peculiar characteristics of the residential environment. This type of approach underscores the importance of physician recruitment and retention programs that make a concerted effort at matching physicians to populations. This becomes particularly important in predominantly low-income, inner-city, minority neighborhoods where there is a current shortage of physicians, especially African Americans (Andrulis 1997). In addition, training programs that improve physicians' ability to communicate and interact with their patients must also be incorporated into the mainstream educational programs that are training physicians to serve in predominantly low-income, urban, ethnic neighborhoods.

Neighborhood Crime Prevention Over the last few decades, neighborhood-based crime prevention programs have developed in an effort to localize prevention, giving residents a role to play in maintaining the safety and well-being of their neighborhoods. An excellent example of this localized approach to crime prevention is Neighborhood Watch, a program in which neighbors and the local law enforcement agency work together in detecting and preventing crime. While there have been a variety of spin-off programs from the traditional Neighborhood Watch (Fathers and Mothers Against Violence, Guardian Angels, Dads on the Street, etc.), no other local effort has been as successful.

With the ratio of police officers to citizens approximately one per 2,000 people in the United States, local involvement in crime prevention efforts has become critical to the health of communities. They are a particularly effective deterrent against property crimes. Neighborhood Watch participants post signs in their windows, and are instructed to immediately report any suspicious or criminal activity to their local law enforcement agency. In addition, local citizens work collectively to maintain safety on their streets and security in their homes by conducting home security checks, neighborhood cleanups (alleyways, abandoned buildings, parks, empty lots), and by participating in a program known as Operation Identification (marking personal valuables with ID numbers so they can be tracked if stolen). These activities, along with the signs posted in the neighborhood, actually give the neighborhood a distinctive identity that helps promote territorial functioning.

A similar effort to Neighborhood Watch is the Block Home program. Started by local police departments around the country in the early 1980s, the purpose of the program is to provide children a safe place to go when lost, scared, hurt, threatened, or involved in some emergency situation. It was originally designed to make children and adolescents aware that members of their community were watching out for their safety and health. As an extension of Neighborhood Watch, the Block Home project has also relied heavily on community participation and encouraged territorial functioning. The program reinforces social support systems and builds trust among neighbors.

Perhaps the most significant prevention program in the local community has been the nationwide effort to introduce community policing. Community policing is a place-based strategy of crime and violence prevention. It can be characterized as a personalized, full-service policing effort, where the same officers patrol the same areas on a relatively permanent basis (Trojanowicz and Bucqueroux 1994). That strategy encourages a problem-solving relationship between citizens in a location and their law enforcement partners. By making officers responsible for relatively small territories, the community policing approach promotes officers' knowledge of the local area, and builds direct social ties between officers and residents. This creates an environment that supports crime prevention and control strategies. As officers' relationship with the public grows, they become an integral element in service delivery for the neighborhood. Thus, not only do they serve as a deterrent, but they also play an important role in minimizing risk-taking behavior and improving the overall quality of life and well-being of the community. These programs can be targeted for specific high-risk groups within a larger area such as youth, elders, or homeless.

While "crime fighting" is not usually equated with the overall health of a particular place, community policing has generated a renewed interest in the potential role that law enforcement can play in improving community health. When community policing is used in high-poverty, high-risk neighborhoods, its direct and immediate impact can be seen in obvious ways (reduction in crime rates, lowered risk-taking behaviors, etc.). Quite apart from these effects, the presence of local patrols has a larger impact on well-being, reinvigorating neighborhood identity and promoting a sense of being linked to the larger urban community. Many neighborhoods have lost the collective will to fight the difficult battle against drugs, decay, disorder, and health-compromising behavior. By helping local communities examine their problems from within, programs like these become important to the revitalization and rebuilding of local infrastructures responsive to residents' social, psychological, physical, and economic needs. They promote community efficacy and build the community's social capital.

As suggested throughout this and earlier chapters, the most effective prevention and intervention programs are those that engage multiple actors in addressing a wide range of problems (Bell and Rubin 2007; Greenberg and Schneider 1996). While there are numerous programs around the country designed to address a variety of crime-related issues, the successful ones tend to be localized efforts that seek to enable and empower local residents. They engage local residents directly in the solution of their own problems. In so doing, they build healthy communities, capable of responding to future hazards and risks. In addition, they tend to be comprehensive, requiring multiagency collaboration to attend to complex health-related problems. As Hawkins and Catalano (1992) propose in their monograph *Communities That Care*, communities can become healthier, more productive places for youths and adults if the community as a whole is involved in prevention efforts and stays involved long enough to make a difference. Thus with a comprehensive, consistent strategy in place, local stakeholders emerge at all levels in the prevention process. Families, schools, teachers, counselors, administrators, students, health care workers, law enforcement, businesses, and clergy all have a stake in maintaining the overall health and well-being of the community.

Building this type of community-wide initiative is crucial to developing a place-based approach to health. Promoting neighborhood participation is essential to establishing locally successful programs that address the physical and mental health needs of a neighborhood. Successful neighborhood mobilization uses at least four mechanisms: (1) community organization and development; (2) service delivery collaboration; (3) implementation of community-based programs; and (4) involvement of families, schools, clergy, and other institutions in the broad-based initiative (National Research Council 1993).

As we have suggested before, traditional approaches to place-based urban problems need to be revisited. For example, while the health care system relies heavily on treatment in traditional settings, such as hospitals and physician's offices, many residents' access to these services is limited. In addition, these settings are inappropriate for numerous necessary comprehensive services. Thus, communities need to develop alternatives that address the specific needs of the local community, while at the same time working with other institutions in the provision of care. School-based or school-linked clinics are an example of some communities' effort to develop comprehensive health services for the difficult-to-reach populations. Other communities have relied on building community-based multiservice centers that provide access for the general population as well as special-need populations such as the uninsured, homeless, elderly, and youth. These multiservice centers act as "cafeterias of care" where local residents receive a wide range of services under a single roof without having to deal with more than one organization. Thus, access is improved, and transportation problems minimized. Unfortunately, these centers are expensive and require a great many resources that local communities often do not have. Nevertheless, they are one strategy to consider when asking the question: How best can we address the complicated health needs of our diverse community population?

Neighborhood Spotlight: Making a Difference in One Community

In the Sandy Bottom neighborhood of Birmingham, an area within Village Creek, a local minister, the Reverend Ron Nored, formed

B.E.A.T. (Bethel Ensley Task Force). The neighborhood around his church, Bethel AME, was like many aging high-poverty areas throughout the United States—a crime-ridden, drug-infested, high-minority, high-poverty, blighted area, with no promise of economic opportunity and no sense of shared trust or obligation. It seemed helpless and hopeless. For many years, the church had been the only viable institution in the area, but as members' economic status improved, they moved away to better neighborhoods. As Nored notes:

> When I came to Birmingham to pastor Bethel AME Church in 1987, Sandy Bottom was indeed a tough neighborhood. Many very low-income senior citizens lived in the neighborhood, and they had to contend with transients, drug dealers and bootleggers. Few residents had any relationship to the church. For most in Sandy Bottom, neighborhood pride and hope had become foreign concepts. Dilapidated shotgun houses . . . made up Sandy Bottom's substandard housing stock. Lots were overgrown and filled with trash. The infrastructure was sorely inadequate. On rainy days water covered the front yards due to poor sewer and drainage systems. There were no sidewalks, curbs or gutters. Utility lines hung literally at eye level, so you had to duck your head to walk from yard to yard. . . . The Ensley Works, a huge steel plant that once employed 15,000, shut down in the early 1970s. That shutdown signaled a slow death for [the area]. Once-thriving businesses in the community closed. Whole sections of the nearby retail area became vacant.
>
> (1999:1c)

Nored had a big dream. Using the model of Habitat for Humanity, he received a HUD grant to purchase six city blocks of land in Sandy Bottom. He then went to local churches, non-profits, architects, and housing experts in Birmingham to seek assistance in building a revitalized community in the six-block area around the church. A significant number of new homes were built using volunteers and homeowner sweat equity. Prospective homeowners worked together on each other's homes, and in the process trust was built between neighbors. They worked with sponsoring agencies selecting design features, worked side by side with volunteers to build their houses, and committed to paying low-interest home mortgages. Clearly, this is a strategy that worked not only because of understanding the limitations and resources in the environment but also by recognizing the importance of teaming together with other local actors to make a difference; it was an example of how a local community can build its own assets up by relying on the resources contained in their bridging social capital.

Promoting Health through the Church

America is a religious country, and churches may be "the single most important repository of social capital in America" (Putnam 2000). A church is not a building, but a congregation—a group of people. The value of the churches' role in building healthy communities is obvious. Like schools, they represent a central institution in the local community. Congregations with denominational affiliations possess ties to the outside community necessary for local problem solving and initiating the involvement of outside agencies. They are a critical source of bridging social capital. In addition, unlike schools, churches are not limited by a public charter, so they can provide a great variety of services and programs that go beyond health service provision and health promotion. The ideology underpinning the church also encourages it to, in the words of Habitat founder Millard Fuller, "make no small plans."

Historically, the church has been concerned with the public good. Since the days when Quakers called for the abolition of slavery in the colonies, clergy and their supporting institutions have often been at the forefront of social discourse (Bellah et al. 1991). In some communities, particularly low-income, minority ones, the church has played a vital role in sustaining the life of the larger community. Churches have helped to fight the battle against poverty and the debilitating conditions that accompany it (Andrulis 1997). As noted in Chapter 5, the Cooperative Downtown Ministries, a collection of churches in Birmingham, Alabama, formed an alliance in the middle 1980s to fight the problem of homelessness and since then has developed a successful multiagency service program attending to the needs of thousands of homeless every year. Church-initiated coalitions like Cooperative Downtown Ministries have been formed in cities across the country. They have done an outstanding job in not just addressing homelessness, but also AIDS, violence, and a variety of other social problems.

In rebuilt neighborhoods, churches often serve as a visual and symbolic focal point, as well as a center for social action and advocacy. They coordinate the provision of local services already present in the community, and make them more user-friendly and accessible. Churches are good at coalition building. One example of this is the Communities of Shalom initiative started in 1992 by the United Methodist Church in response to the devastation experienced after the Los Angeles riots. Particular areas known as "shalom zones" were identified and targeted for assistance. The shalom zone is a geographic area within a community where churches work toward systemic change through collaboration with residents, service agencies, government, and local businesses to develop economic prosperity, resource coordination, and creation of a systematic plan for the community's future. The United Methodist Church organized over 300 Communities of Shalom throughout the world by the beginning of the twenty-first century. With the local church serving as the catalyst for development, collaboration becomes the path to revitalization in struggling neighborhoods. More than 265 shalom zones have been developed in the United States and South Africa; new sites continue to start up at the rate of 15 per quarter (Communities of Shalom 1998). The targeted high-risk poverty areas have benefited greatly from this intensive service effort. For example, in Houston, Texas, a group of neighborhoods have formed a "shalom health zone" where a mobile medical unit is providing state-of-the-art medical services to residents who do not have either health insurance or ready access to traditional health care facilities.

Though using the church as the central delivery point for health promotion and disease prevention is an unusual approach, for many minority communities the church remains one of the most trusted and respected local institutions. In churches, residents feel that they can receive assistance without barriers. Centrally located within the neighborhood, churches represent an excellent opportunity for developing a place-based strategy of health promotion, much like the school or the neighborhood health clinic.

Whether the local unit is the school, church, or neighborhood, carefully designed place-specific strategies for health promotion not only make sense but have been demonstrated to be highly effective. Thinking at the broader municipal level, during the last 30 years, a number of cities have developed successful strategies to solve area problems (Goldsmith and Blakely 1992). As the federal government became a less active partner in social reform, cities had more discretion in designing solutions to local problems. The severe global recession, however, reversed this trend. At least in the near future, local government is unlikely to have the resources necessary to orchestrate a health promotion strategy for its disadvantaged neighborhoods. New local partnerships must develop. Among the most likely institutions to accomplish this are America's urban universities, where significant human capital is heavily concentrated near neighborhoods with the greatest needs. The following example involves a unique partnership between a set of inner-city neighborhood churches and an urban university.

Church Spotlight: Making a Difference in One Community

In 2004 the University of Alabama at Birmingham's School of Public Health established Congregations for Public Health (CPH) as a tax-exempt non-profit organization to address the health concerns and needs of residents in Birmingham's eight poorest minority neighborhoods. CPH is a consortium of eight African American churches who partner with the School to identify health needs and develop programs and services for residents living within a one-mile radius of the church. These eight neighborhoods have poverty rates ranging from 44 percent to 85 percent, with a modal rate above 66 percent. The areas surrounding these eight churches include over 115,000 low-income African Americans, 60 percent of Birmingham's African American population, and 80 percent of its school-age children. Only 25 percent of adults age 25 and older in these areas have a high school degree. These communities contain all the health challenges of high-poverty neighborhoods. Crime rates are high. Residents have considerably higher rates of morbidity and mortality associated with chronic diseases such as cancer, heart disease, and diabetes as well as risky lifestyle behaviors linked with addiction, lack of exercise, and lack of good nutrition. Their access to health care, and to health information related to prevention and disease control, was limited until the formation of CPH.

CPH uses community residents who are hired to manage program activities and outreach in the neighborhood. These Neighborhood Outreach Specialists complete 60 hours of training in health outreach and learn the basic skills necessary to gather data and implement best practice programs in the neighborhood. Six programs are currently in place to address the communities' complex health problems:

1. Search Your Heart is a heart-health stroke-prevention community education program aimed specifically at African Americans.
2. Your Community, Your Health is a radio talk show featuring a locally written and acted soap opera that draws attention to various public health problems such as diabetes, addiction, unprotected sex, etc. In addition to promoting awareness of these problems, it offers examples of the everyday battles of people struggling to adopt positive health behaviors.
3. Community Public Health Certificate Program is in partnership with a church-based Bible College. It teaches congregation members and ministers about the health issues and prevention programs directly related to the health of their neighborhood, and raises health awareness in the community.
4. CARES (Congregational Advocates Reaching and Empowering Survivors) is funded by the Lance Armstrong Foundation and other groups to provide information to cancer survivors and their families. It trains Neighborhood Outreach Specialists to give patients, caregivers, and families the information access to services, and program referrals needed, to cope with the circumstances of their illness.
5. Health InfoNet is a Robert Wood Johnson-sponsored program that teaches congregations and neighborhoods how to access

health-related information via the web. Partner churches have computers in their resource centers and provide trained volunteers to help individuals get the health information that they need.

6. CPH CARES about Breast Cancer trains Neighborhood Outreach Specialists to conduct breast cancer awareness programs, one-on-one interventions, and service referrals. Free or low-cost breast cancer screening programs are also offered.

7. Sing for the Cure raises awareness about the importance of early breast cancer detection by performing in local venues and churches. The choir is made up of breast cancer survivors who sing and give their personal testimonies.

Healthy Places: Building a Healthier America Programs

Up to now, we have explored several successful place-based, but highly focused strategies for health promotion. Many of these programs are geographically constrained and problem focused; thus their ability to reach large populations and address a wide range of health-related problems is limited. How can we serve the health needs of a large, diverse population and at the same time avoid sacrificing the quality and extent of service delivery? This question continues to challenge health planners as they strive to develop service delivery plans that are both functional and efficient. Designing such programs, particularly for use in America's inner cities, has not been easy. Clearly, the more comprehensive and holistic the plan, the greater its potential to impact a large number of high-need areas and subpopulations. Its drawback, on the other hand, is that measures and goals are often so vague that all they do is give mere lip service to the difficult problems facing society. Such "bold initiatives" often become dust catchers on the shelves of libraries.

A number of these comprehensive, place-sensitive health programs have developed over the last several decades. One such program was the Healthy Cities Project (HCP). Initiated by the World Health Organization in the 1980s, HCP was a long-term developmental project that attempted to put health at the front of the policy maker's agenda. The project has since grown exponentially, with networks in nearly 1,000 cities worldwide. A place-based approach to health like that of HCP is the type of program that the residents of Village Creek and the larger Birmingham community might benefit from. HCP reminds local constituencies that *place matters*, and notes the importance of being sensitive to the settings in which people live, work, and play. By modifying the physical environment and the social and economic conditions of places, the health status of local residents can be improved. Without some planned sensitivity to the social topography of the local landscape, health strategies are doomed to fail. Many will miss the opportunity to fill a gap in our system of health care, particularly for those whose needs are the greatest (homeless, youth, elderly, disabled, racial and ethnic minorities, etc.).

Another program that has been expanding since its development nearly a decade ago has been the Center for Disease Control and Prevention's (CDC) Healthy Communities project (Center for Disease Control and Prevention 2009a; Giles et al. 2009). In an effort to combat chronic disease at the local level, through this plan, the CDC has partnered with hundreds of local communities in an effort to develop place-based strategies for improving health. Investing in the local community has had a profound impact on chronic disease prevention. In addition, mobilizing local officials, health care providers, practitioners, parents, elected leaders, etc. becomes an important part of the change process. Local actors need to understand both the environment for policy change as well as health improvement. Finally, mobilizing networks, pouring resources into the local health effort, and providing communities with the tools to assist them in achieving health equity and preventing chronic disease, have all been critical elements to these successful place-based programs for healthy living (Giles et al. 2009).

Just recently, the Robert Wood Johnson Foundation Commission for a Healthier America released a series of recommendations for creating a healthier nation (Robert Wood Johnson Foundation 2009). Of the ten major recommendations that the commission makes, the majority are place relevant. In addition, they are very much focused on the types of program intervention that promote childhood development and support children and families. This reflects a long tradition of investing in the health and well-being of local communities; the Robert Wood Johnson Foundation remains a leader both in funding innovative strategies as well as in mobilizing resources and local actors in impacting on the local environment. The commission's ten recommendations are worth noting:

1. Ensure that all children have high quality early developmental support
2. Fund and design WIC and Food Stamp (SNAP) programs to meet nutritional needs of hungry families
3. Create public–private partnerships to open and sustain full-service grocery stores in communities without access to healthy foods
4. Feed children only healthy foods and snacks in school
5. Require all K-12 schools to include daily physical activity time for youth
6. Become a smoke-free, clean-air nation
7. Create healthy communities that demonstrate a full complement of health-promoting programs
8. Develop a housing and infrastructure program that reflects the effects of the built environment on health
9. Integrate safety and wellness into community life
10. Ensure decision-makers have the evidence they need to build health into public and private practice and policy (Robert Wood Johnson Foundation 2009).

The commission recognizes that the existing urban ecology impacts on health and promotes health disparities. The report notes:

> Poorer neighborhoods have weaker tax bases, which can mean limited support for public schools and community programs; crime and social disorder; and limited access to fresh groceries. Low-income neighborhoods have often served as locations for toxic waste dumps or have bordered freeways, refineries, and other sources of pollution. Neighborhood conditions contribute to disease, such as asthma, as well as limit ability to make healthy choices in daily life.
>
> (Robert Wood Johnson Foundation 2009:22)

Highlighting the risks related to where we live, endorsing place-based initiatives to help those who often cannot help themselves, and helping communities garner the resources and social capital necessary to change their health trajectory, is at the core of these Robert Wood Johnson Foundation programs.

Planning for the Future: Minimizing the Urban Health Penalty

Numerous scholars have noted that over the last 50 years our nation's inner cities have become increasingly unhealthy places. The dimensions of this seeming crisis have broader implications for the health of the nation. As noted previously, for example, the rise of drug-resistant strains of tuberculosis has its origin in the growing prevalence of inner-city homelessness. That is, there are public health consequences to these concentrations of high hazard and risk that go beyond the boundaries of any one place in the city. These "hazard zones," where social, psychological, economic, and political factors intersect with physical and mental health deficits, create challenging circumstances for the health of the larger society. As Wilkinson (1996) noted, highly developed societies with wide gaps between socioeconomic groups tend to demonstrate poorer overall health. The stress of living in cities where such gaps exist produces mental and physical health challenges that belie the overall circumstances of wealth in the nation. In short, the existence of these unhealthy places is a national health issue that demands a comprehensive approach that accounts for the interplay between place and health. As argued throughout this book, a place-based approach to health is critical to the development of a national health policy in the twenty-first century.

Given the current political climate, place-based strategies for addressing health needs have generated mixed responses. On the one hand, federal programs have become more sensitive to the need for local strategies to address local expressions of societal problems. On the other hand, however, the place-based problems identified in this book are concentrated in populations with limited political influence and resources—the minority poor, youth, and homeless. Political issues with smaller constituencies and a minority voice may not be acceptable to the majority.

William Julius Wilson (1996) noted that racial attitudes continue to be a substantial factor in the degree to which Caucasian Americans support race-targeted and class-targeted social policies. In order to counteract this bias, Wilson suggests that a "broader vision" is most appropriate for addressing the problems of the new urban poor. This vision would include broad-based national programs that enhance opportunity among all groups. Opportunity-enhancing programs fit well with the current climate in that they do not challenge the principles of equity, they continue to reward people on the basis of individual effort, and unlike targeted programs, they appear to be unrelated to anti-African American attitudes (Bobo and Kluegel 1993; Wilson 1996). These policies include a national jobs program (Works Progress Administration-style work projects), national performance standards for the classroom, support for development and expansion of public transportation, and school-to-work transition programs.

While these national programs are critical to alleviating the health burden of the high-poverty neighborhood, it becomes very clear that they cannot succeed without simultaneously implementing comprehensive, place-sensitive strategies for healthy communities. Such an approach must include programs to promote both social capital as well as the human and physical capital contained in the community. The local place is a multidimensional space that orients individuals to the resources present. It consists of defensible home bases, social networks and supports, a cultural milieu, and a political base that either impedes or promotes access to opportunities. This complex "opportunity space" cannot be transformed through national policy without local strategies and significant local community participation. If, as we contend, place matters, then a place-based policy becomes essential to promoting national health and well-being. Without that strategy the potential for growing opportunity spaces will not be realized, and only hazard spaces will flourish, and a never-ending ecology of fear and hopelessness will be their progeny.

REFERENCES

Aalbers, Manuel B. 2006. "'When the Banks Withdraw, Slum Landlords Take Over':
  The Structuration of Neighbourhood Decline through Redlining, Drug Dealing,
  Speculation and Immigrant Exploitation." *Urban Studies* 43:1061–86.
Abel, Thomas and William Cockerham. 1993. "Lifestyle or Lebensfuhrung? Critical
  Remarks on the Mistranslation of Weber's Class, Status, Party." *Sociological Quarterly*
  34:551–56.
Acevedo-Garcia D. 2001. "Zip Code-Level Risk Factors for Tuberculosis: Neighborhood
  Environment and Residential Segregation in New Jersey, 1985–1992." *American
  Journal of Public Health* 91:734–41.
Adlaf, E. M., A. Paglia., and F. Ivis. 2003. "Drug Use Among Ontario Students,
  1977–1999: Findings from the Ontario Drug Use Survey." In Research Document
  Series. Toronto: Center for Addiction and Mental Health.
Administration on Aging. 1998. "Alzheimer's Disease." *Fact Sheets* Washington, DC:
  Administration on Aging. Retrieved on November 22, 1998. (www.aoa.dhhs.gov/fact-
  sheets/alz.html).
Aitken, Campbell, David Moore, Peter Higgs, Jenny Kelsalla, and Michael Kergera. 2002.
  "The Impact of a Police Crackdown on a Street Drug Scene: Evidence from the Street."
  International Journal of Drug Policy 13:189–98.
Aldgate, John L., Timothy R. Church, Andrew D. Ryan, Gurumurthy Ramachandran, Ann
  Frederickson, Thomas H. Stock, Maria T. Morandi, and Ken Sexton. 2004. "Outdoor,
  Indoor, and Personal Exposure to VOCs in Children." *Environmental Health
  Perspectives* 112:1386–92.
Aldwin, Carolyn M. and Diane F. Gilmer. 2004. *Health, Illness, and Optimal Aging*.
  Thousand Oaks, CA: Sage.
Aldwin, Carolyn M., Avron Spiro, and Crystal L. Park. 2006. "Health, Behavior, and

Optimal Aging: A Life Span Developmental Perspective." Pp. 85–104 in *The Handbook of The Psychology of Aging*, edited by J. E. Birren and K. W. Schaie. 6th ed. Burlington, MA: Elsevier Academic Press.

Allensworth, Diane, Elaine Lawson, Lois Nicholson, and James Wyche, eds. 1995. *Schools and Health: Our Nation's Investment*. Washington, DC: National Academy Press.

Almond, Douglas, Kenneth Y. Chay, David S. Lee. 2005. "The Cost of Low Birth Weight." *The Quarterly Journal of Economics* 120:1031–83.

Alzheimer's Association. 2009. "Alzheimer's Disease." Chicago, IL: Alzheimer's Association.

American Heart Association. 2009. *Heart Disease and Stroke Statistics: 2009 Update*. Dallas, TX: American Heart Association.

American Hospital Association. 1992. *Environmental Assessment for Urban Hospitals*. Washington, DC: American Hospital Association.

American Jewish Committee. 2003. *American Jewish Year Book 2002: The Annual Record of Jewish Civilization*. American Jewish Committee: American Jewish Year Book.

American Lung Association. 2009. *Children and Ozone Air Pollution Fact Sheet*. New York: American Lung Association.

Anderson, D. R. and R. J. Anderson. 1990. "Community Responsive Medicine: A Call for a New Academic Discipline." *Journal of Health Care for the Poor and Underserved* 1:2.

Andrulis, Dennis P. 1997. "The Urban Health Penalty: New Dimensions and Directions in Inner-City Health Care." American College of Physicians Position Paper, No. 1. Washington, DC: National Public Health and Hospital Institute.

Aneshensel, Carol S. 1992. "Social Stress: Theory and Research." *Annual Review of Sociology* 18:15–38.

Aneshensel, Carol S. and Clea A. Sucoff. 1996. "The Neighborhood Context of Adolescent Mental Health." *Journal of Health and Social Behavior* 37:293–310.

Aneshensel, Carol S., Richard G. Wight, Dana Miller-Martinez, Amanda L. Botticello, Arun S. Karlamangla, and Teresa E. Seeman. 2007. "Urban Neighborhoods and Depressive Symptoms among Adults." *Journal of Gerontology Series B: Psychological Sciences* 62:S52–59.

Ardrey, Robert. 1966. *The Territorial Imperative*. New York: Atheneum.

Atchley, Robert. 1991. *Social Forces and Aging*. 6th ed. Belmont, CA: Wadsworth.

Athanasiou, Robert and G. Yoshioka. 1973. "The Spatial Character of Friendship Formation." *Environment and Behavior* 5:43–65.

Avison, William R. and R. Jay Turner. 1988. "Stressful Life Events and Depressive Symptoms: Disaggregating the Effects of Acute Stressors and Chronic Strains." *Journal of Health and Social Behavior* 29:253–64.

Baldassare, Mark. 1977. "Residential Density, Household Crowding, and Social Networks." Pp. 101–16 in *Networks and Places*, edited by Claude Fischer. New York: Free Press.

———. 1981. "The Effects of Household Density on Subgroups." *American Sociological Review* 46:110–18.

Balfour, J. and G. Kaplan. 2002. "Neighborhood Environment and Loss of Physical

Function in Older Adults: Evidence from the Alameda County Study." *American Journal of Epidemiology* 155:507–15.

Balshem, Martha. 1991. "Cancer, Control, and Causality: Talking About Cancer in a Working-Class Community." *American Ethnologist* 18:152–71.

Bandura, Albert. 1986. *Social Foundations of Thought and Action: A Social Cognitive Theory.* Englewood Cliffs, NJ: Prentice Hall.

Barker, Roger. 1967. *Ecological Psychology.* Stanford, CA: Stanford University Press.

Barrow, Georgia. 1992. *Aging, the Individual and Society.* St. Paul, MN: West.

Baum, K. 2005. *Juvenile Victimization and Offending, 1993–2003.* Washington, DC: U.S. Department of Justice, Office of Justice Programs, Bureau of Justice Statistics.

Bauman, Laurie J., Ellen J. Silver, and Ruth E. K. Stein. 2006. "Cumulative Social Disadvantage and Child Health." *Pediatrics* 117:1321–28.

Baumer, Eric P. and Scott T. South. 2001. "Community Effects on Youth Sexual Activity." *Journal of Marriage and Family* 63:540–54.

Baumrind, D. and A. E. Black. 1967. "Socialization Practices Associated with Dimensions of Competence in Preschool Boys and Girls." *Child Development* 38:291–327.

Beck, Ulrich. 1995. *Ecological Enlightenment: Essays on the Politics of the Risk Society.* Atlantic Highlands, NJ: Humanities Press.

Becker, Marshall H. 1974. *The Health Belief Model and Personal Health Behavior.* Thorofare, NJ: Charles B. Slack.

Becker, Marshall H. and Irwin M. Rosenstock. 1989. "Health Promotion, Disease Prevention, and Program Retention." Pp. 284–305 in *Handbook of Medical Sociology,* edited by H. Freeman and S. Levine. 4th ed. Englewood Cliffs, NJ: Prentice Hall.

Bell, Janice F., Fredrick Zimmerman, Gunnar R. Almgren, Jonathan D. Mayer, and Colleen E. Huebner. 2006. "Birth Outcomes among Urban African American Women: A Multilevel Analysis of the Role of Racial Residential Segregation." *Social Science and Medicine* 63:3030–45.

Bell, Judith and Victor Rubin. 2007. *Why Place Matters: Building a Movement for Healthy Communities.* Oakland, CA: PolicyLink.

Bell, Wendell and M. Boat. 1957. "Urban Neighborhoods and Informal Social Relations." *American Journal of Sociology* 62:391–98.

Bell, Wendell and M. T. Force. 1962. "Urban Neighborhood Types and Participation in Formal Associations." *American Sociological Review* 21:25–34.

Bellah, Robert N., Richard Madsen, William M. Sullivan, Ann Swidler, and Steven Tipton. 1991. *The Good Society.* New York: Vintage Books.

Benbow, N. ed. 2007. *Big Cities Health Inventory: The Health of Urban America.* Washington, DC: National Association of County and City Health Officials.

Berger, R. L., J. T. McBreen, and M. J. Rifkin. 1996. *Human Behavior: A Perspective for the Helping Professions.* White Plains, NY: Longman.

Berkman, Lisa F. and L. Breslow. 1983. *Health and Ways of Living.* New York: Oxford University Press.

Berkman, Lisa F. and T.A. Glass. 2000. "Social Integration, Social Networks, Social

Support, and Health." Pp. 137–73 in *Social Epidemiology*, edited by L. F. Berkman and I. Kawachi. New York: Oxford University Press.

Berlin, Lisa J., Jeanne Brooks-Gunn, and J. Lawrence Aber. 2001. "Promoting Early Childhood Development through Comprehensive Initiatives." *Children's Services: Social Policy, Research, and Practice* 4:1–24.

Bernard, Larry C. and Edward Krupat. 1994. *Health Psychology: Biopsychosocial Factors in Health and Illness.* New York: Harcourt Brace.

Bernson, Miya. 2002. "Seasonal Affective Disorder: Shedding Light on Seasons and the Brain." *Harvard Science Review* 16:54–57.

Beyers, Jennifer M., Rolf Loeber, Per-Olof H. Wikstreom, and Magda Stouthamer-Loeber. 2001. "What Predicts Adolescent Violence in Better-Off Neighborhoods?" *Journal of Abnormal Child Psychology* 29:369–81.

Blau, Peter. 1977. *Inequality and Heterogeneity.* New York: Free Press.

———. 1994. *Structural Contexts of Opportunities.* Chicago, IL: University of Chicago Press.

Blau, Peter and Joseph Schwartz. 1984. *Crosscutting Social Circles: Testing a Macrostructural Theory of Intergroup Relations.* Orlando, FL: Academic Press.

Bobo, Lawrence and James Kluegel. 1993. "Opposition to Race Targeting: Self-Interest, Stratification Ideology or Racial Attitudes?" *American Sociological Review* 58:443–64.

Bolland, John M. 2003. "Hopelessness and Risk Behavior Among Adolescents Living in High Poverty Inner-City Neighborhoods." *Journal of Adolescence* 26:145–58.

Booth, Alan and John Edwards. 1976. "Crowding and Family Relations." *American Sociological Review* 41:308–22.

Booza, Jason C., Jackie Cutsinger, and George Galster. 2006. *Where Did They Go? The Decline of Middle-Income Neighborhoods in Metropolitan America.* Washington, DC: The Brookings Institution.

Bourdieu, Pierre. 1984. *Distinction.* Translated by Richard Nice. Cambridge, MA: Harvard University Press.

———. 1990. *The Logic of Practice.* Translated by Richard Nice. Stanford, CA: Stanford University Press.

Braddock, J. H. and J. McPartland. 1992. "Education of At-Risk Youth: Recent Trends, Current Status, and Future Needs." Commissioned Paper for the Panel on High-Risk Youth, Commission on Behavioral and Social Sciences and Education, National Research Council, Washington, DC.

Braithwaite, R. L., F. Murphy, N. Lythcott, and D. S. Blumenthal. 1989. "Community Organization and Development for Health Promotion within an Urban Black Community: A Conceptual Model." *Health Education* 20:56–60.

Braudel, Fernand. 1979. *The Structures of Everyday Life: The Limits of the Possible.* New York: Harper and Row.

Brewer, Laura. 2004. "InFocus Programme on Skills, Knowledge and Employability." Working Paper No. 19, International Labour Office, Geneva.

Brindis, Claire D. and Rupal V. Sanghvi. 1997. "School Based Health Clinics: Remaining

Viable in a Changing Health Care Delivery System." *Annual Review of Public Health* 18:567–87.

Brodeur, Paul. 2000. "School-Based Health Clinics." In *To Improve Health and Health Care 2000: The Robert Wood Johnson Anthology*, edited by Stephen L. Isaacs and James R. Knickman. San Francisco, CA: Jossey-Bass.

Brody, Elaine. 1985. "Parent Care as a Normative Family Stress." *Sociological Perspectives* 38:195–215.

Bronfenbrenner, Urie. 1979. *The Ecology of Human Development: Experiments by Nature and Design.* Cambridge, MA: Harvard University Press.

———. 1986. "Ecology of the Family as a Context to Human Development: Research Perspectives." *Developmental Psychology* 22:723–42.

Brooks, Ann-Marie, Robert S. Byrd, Michael Weitzman, Peggy Auinger, and John T. McBride. 2001. "The Impact of Low Birth Weight on Early Childhood Asthma in the United States." *Archives of Pediatric and Adolescent Medicine* 155: 401–406.

Brooks-Gunn, Jeanne, Greg J. Duncan, Pamela Kato Klebanov, and Naomi Sealand. 1993. "Do Neighborhood Influence Child and Adolescent Development?" *American Journal of Sociology* 62:353–95.

Brooks-Gunn, Jeanne, Greg J. Duncan, and J. Lawrence Aber, eds. 1997. *Neighborhood Poverty.* Vols. 1 and 2. New York: Russell Sage.

Brown, L. K., Ralph DiClemente, and Larry Reynolds. 1991. "HIV Prevention for Adolescents: Utility of the Health Belief Model." *AIDS Education and Prevention* 3:50–59.

Brown, Prudence and Harold Richman. 1997. "Neighborhood Effects and State and Local Policy." Pp. 164–81 in *Neighborhood Poverty.* Vol. 2, *Policy Implications in Studying Neighborhoods*, edited by Jeanne Brooks-Gunn, Greg Duncan, and J. Lawrence Aber. New York: Russell Sage.

Browning, Christopher R. and Kathleen A. Cagney. 2003. "Moving Beyond Poverty: Neighborhood Structure, Social Processes and Health." *Journal of Health and Social Behavior* 44: 552–71

Browning, Christopher R., Danielle Wallace, Seth L. Feinberg, and Kathleen A. Cagney. 2006. "Neighborhood Social Processes, Physical Conditions, and Disaster-Related Mortality: The Case of the 1995 Chicago Heat Wave." *American Sociological Review* 71:661–78.

Brunner, Eric J. 2000. "Toward A New Social Biology." Pp. 306–31 in *Social Epidemiology*, edited by L. F. Berkman and I. Kawachi. New York: Oxford University Press.

Buettner-Janusch, J. 1973. *Physical Anthropology: A Perspective.* New York: Wiley.

Buka, Stephen L., Theresa L. Stichick, Isolde Birdthistle, and Felton J. Earls. 2001. "Youth Exposure to Violence: Prevalence, Risks, and Consequences." *American Journal of Orthopsychiatry* 71:298–310.

Bullard, Robert. 1990. *Dumping in Dixie: Race, Class, and Environmental Equity.* Boulder, CO: Westview Press.

——— ed. 1993. *Confronting Environmental Racism: Voices from the Grassroots.* Boston, MA: South End Press.

——. 1994. *Unequal Protection: Environmental Justice and Communities of Color.* San
   Francisco, CA: Sierra Club.

Bullard, Robert D. 2000. *The Environment and Society Reader.* Boston: Allyn and Bacon.

Burge, P. S. 2004. "Sick Building Syndrome." *Occupational Environmental Medicine*
   61:185–190.

Bursik, Robert. 1986. "Ecological Stability and the Dynamics of Delinquency." Pp. 35–66 in
   Communities and Crime, edited by Albert Reiss and Michael Tonry. Chicago, IL:
   University of Chicago Press.

Burt, Martha. 1992a. *Over the Edge: The Growth of Homelessness in the 1980s.* New York:
   Russell Sage.

——. 1992b. *Practical Methods for Counting Homeless People: A Manual for States and
   Local Jurisdictions.* Washington, DC: Department of Housing and Urban
   Development.

Cagney, Kathleen and Christopher R. Browning. 2004. "Exploring Neighborhood-Level
   Variation in Asthma and Other Respiratory Diseases." *Journal of General Internal
   Medicine* 19:229–36.

Cairns, Robert B. and Beverly D. Cairns. 1994. *Lifelines and Risks: Pathways of Youth in Our
   Time.* Cambridge, England: Cambridge University Press.

Campbell, Karen and Barrett Lee. 1992. "Sources of Personal Neighbor Networks: Social
   Integration, Need or Time?" *Social Forces* 70:1077–100.

Carp, F. 1976. "Housing and Living Environments of Older People." Pp. 244–71 in
   Handbook of Aging and the Social Sciences, edited by Robert Binstock and Ethel Shanas.
   New York: Van Nostrand Reinhold.

Case, Anne, Angela Fertig, and Christina Paxson. 2005. "Lasting Impact of Childhood
   Health and Circumstances." *Journal of Health Economics* 24:365–89.

Casimir, Michael and Aparna Rao, eds. 1992. *Mobility and Territoriality: Social and Spatial
   Boundaries among Foragers, Fishers, and Pastoralists and Peripatetics.* New York: St.
   Martin's Press.

Centers for Disease Control and Prevention. 2002. "Surveillance Summaries." *Mortality and
   Morbidity Weekly Report* 51:1–64.

——. 2005. "Blood Levels, United States, 1999–2002." *Mortality and Morbidity Weekly
   Report* 54:513–16.

——. 2006. "Youth Risk Behavior Surveillance—United States 2005." *Morbidity and
   Mortality Weekly Report* 55:145–60.

——. 2007a. "Cases of HIV infection and AIDS in the United States and Dependent Areas,
   2007." *HIV/AIDS Surveillance Report* vol. 19. Atlanta, GA: Centers for Disease
   Control and Prevention.

——. 2007b. "2007 National Youth Risk." *Morbidity and Mortality Weekly Report*
   55:145–60.

——. 2008a. "HIV/AIDS among Women." *CDC HIV/AIDS Fact Sheet.* Atlanta, GA:
   Centers for Disease Control and Prevention.

——. 2008b. "Summary Health Statistics for the U.S. Population: National Health

Interview Survey, 2007." *Vital and Health Statistics* Series 10, Number 238. Hyattsville, MD: National Center for Health Statistics.

———. 2008c. "Youth Risk Behavior Surveillance—United States. Surveillance Summaries, 2007." *Morbidity and Mortality Weekly Report* 57:1–131.

———. 2009a. "Healthy Communities: Preventing Chronic Disease by Activating Grassroots Change." Atlanta, GA: Center for Disease Control and Prevention.

———. 2009b. "Youth and Tobacco Use: Current Estimates." Atlanta, GA: Center for Disease Control and Prevention.

———. 2009c. "Youth Violence: Facts at a Glance." Atlanta, GA: Center for Disease Control and Prevention.

Charles, Camille Zubrinsky. 2003. "The Dynamics of Racial Residential Segregation." *Annual Review of Sociology* 29:167–207.

Chen, P. and Wilmoth, J. M. 2004. "The Effects of Residential Mobility on ADL and IADL Limitations among the Very Old and the Old Living in the Community." *Journal of Gerontology* 59B:164–72.

Choldin, Harvey. 1978. "Urban Density and Pathology." *Annual Review of Sociology* 4:91–113.

Choldin, Harvey and Dennis Roncek. 1976. "Density, Population Potential and Pathology: A Block-Level Analysis." *Review of Public Use Data* 4:19–30.

Cloward, Richard A. and Lloyd E. Ohlin. 1960. *Delinquency and Opportunity.* New York: Free Press.

Cobb, Sidney. 1976. "Social Support as a Moderator of Life Stress." *Psychosomatic Medicine* 38:300–14.

Cockerham, William. 1999. *The Sociology of Mental Disorders.* 5th ed. Upper Saddle River, NJ: Prentice Hall.

Cockerham, William C. 2005. "Health Lifestyle Theory and the Convergence of Agency and Structure." *Journal of Health and Social Behavior* 46: 51–67.

———. 2007. *Social Causes of Health and Disease.* Malden, MA: Polity Press.

———. 2009. "Understanding the Russian Health Crisis: A Sociological Perspective." *Sociology Compass* 3: 327–340.

Cockerham, William C. and Ferris J. Ritchey. 1997. *Dictionary of Medical Sociology.* Westport, CT: Greenview Press.

Cockerham, William C., Alfred Rütten, and Thomas Abel. 1997. "Conceptualizing Health Lifestyles: Moving Beyond Weber." *Sociological Quarterly* 38:601–22.

Cockerham, William C., Thomas Abel, and Guenther Lueschen. 1993. "Max Weber, Formal Rationality and Health Lifestyles." *Sociological Quarterly* 34:413–35.

Cockerham, William C., Gerhard Kunz, and Guenther Lueschen. 1988. "Social Stratification and Health Lifestyles in Two Systems of Health Care Delivery: A Comparison of America and West Germany." *Journal of Health and Social Behavior* 29:113–26.

Cohen, Albert K. 1955. *Delinquent Boys.* New York: Free Press.

———. 1972. "Social Control and Subcultural Change." *Youth and Society* 3:259–76.

Cohen, Deborah A., Karen Mason, Ariane Bedimo, Richard Scribner, Victoria Basolo, and Thomas A. Farley. 2003. "Neighborhood Physical Conditions and Health." *American Journal of Public Health* 93:467–71.

Cohen, Lawrence and Marcus Felson. 1979. "Social Change and Crime Rate Trends: A Routine Activities Approach." *American Sociological Review* 44:588–607.

Cohen, Sheldon and Gail Williamson. 1991. "Stress and Infectious Disease in Humans." *Psychological Bulletin* 109:5–24.

Coid, J., A. Petruckevitch, G. Feder, W. S. Chung, J. Richardson, and S. Moorey. 2001. "Relation Between Childhood Sexual and Physical Abuse and Risk of Revictimisation in Women: A Cross-Sectional Survey." *Lancet* 358:450–54.

Colditz, G. A., D. DeJong, D. J. Hunter, D. Trichopoulos, and W. C. Willett, eds. 1996. "Harvard Report on Cancer Prevention. Vol. 1, Causes of Human Cancer." *Cancer Causes Control*, 7 Suppl 1.

Collins, C. A. and D. R. Williams. 1999. "Segregation and Mortality: The Deadly Effects of Racism?" *Sociological Forum* 14:495–523.

Collins, James W., Jr. and Nancy Fisher Schulte. 2003. "Infant Health: Race, Risk, and Residence." Pp. 223–32 in *Neighborhoods and Health*, edited by I. Kawachi and L. F. Berkman. New York: Oxford University Press.

Comey, Jennifer, Xavier de Souza Briggs, and Gretchen Weismann. 2008. "Struggling to Stay Out of High-Poverty Neighborhoods: Lessons from the Moving to Opportunity Experiment." Washington, DC: The Urban Institute.

Communities of Shalom. 1998. *Communities of Shalom: Churches and Communities Working Together to Rebuild and Renew Community Life.* New York: United Methodist Board of Global Ministries.

Connor, M. and P. Norman. 1996. *Predicting Health Behavior.* Open University Press, Buckingham.

Conrad, Peter. 2009. *The Sociology of Health and Illness: Critical Perspectives.* 8th ed. New York: Worth.

Cooley, Charles Horton. 1922. *Human Nature and the Social Order.* New York: Scribners.

Cooper, Clair. 1975. *Easter Hill Village.* New York: Free Press.

Corburn, Jason. 2009. *Toward the Healthy City: People, Places, and the Politics of Urban Planning.* Cambridge, MA: MIT Press.

Coser, Rose L. 1975. "The Complexity of Roles as a Seedbed of Individual Autonomy." Pp. 237–64 in *The Idea of Social Structure: Papers in Honor of Robert K. Merton*, edited by Louis Coser. New York: Harcourt Brace.

Costello-Wilson, Deanne, Harriet Friedman, Nori Minich, Avroy A. Fanaroff, and Maureen Hack. 2005. "Improved Survival Rates with Increased Neurodevelopmental Disability for Extremely Low Birth Weight Infants in the 1990s." *Pediatrics* 115:997–1003.

Crane, Jonathan. 1991. "The Epidemic Theory of Ghettos and Neighborhood Effects on Dropping Out and Teenage Childbearing." *American Journal of Sociology* 96:1226–59.

Crosse, S., M. Burr, D. Cantor, C. A. Hagen, and I. Hantman. 2001. *Wide Scope, Questionable Quality: Drug and Violence Prevention Efforts in American Schools.* Report on the Study on School Violence and Prevention. Washington, DC: U.S. Department of Education, Planning and Evaluation Service.

Cummings, Mark E., Marcie C. Goeke-Morey, and Lauren M. Papp. 2004. "Everyday Marital Conflict and Child Aggression." *Journal of Abnormal Child Psychology* 32:191–202.

Cummins, Steven and Sally Macintyre. 2006. "Food Environments and Obesity—Neighborhood or Nation?" *International Journal of Epidemiology* 35:100–104.

Cyert, R. M. and J. G. March. 1963. *A Behavioral Theory of the Firm.* Englewood Cliffs, NJ: Prentice Hall.

Darley, J. and B. Latane. 1970. *The Unresponsive Bystander: Why Doesn't He Help?* New York: Appleton-Century Crofts.

Datcher, L. 1982. "Effects of Community and Family Background on Achievement." *Review of Economics and Statistics* 64:32–41.

Davis, Brennan and Christopher Carpenter. 2009. "Proximity of Fast-Food Restaurants to Schools and Adolescent Obesity." *Research and Practice* 99:505–10.

Davis, Mike. 1990. *City of Quartz.* New York: Vintage Books.

———. 1998. *Ecology of Fear.* New York: Vintage Books.

Dean, Alfred and Nan Lin. 1977. "The Stress Buffering Role of Social Support." *Journal of Nervous and Mental Disease* 165:403–13.

Dear, Michael. 2002. "Los Angeles and the Chicago School: Invitation to a Debate." *City and Community* 1:5–32.

Dear, Michael and Jennifer Wolch. 1987. *Landscapes of Despair: From Deinstitutionalization to Homelessness.* Princeton, NJ: Princeton University Press.

Dekovic, Maja. 1999. "Risk and Protective Factors in the Development of Problem Behavior during Adolescence." *Journal of Youth and Adolescence* 28:667–85.

DeLuca, Stephanie and James E. Rosenbaum. 2003. "If Low Income Blacks are Given a Chance to Live in White Neighborhoods, Will They Stay? Examining Mobility Patterns with Quasi-Experimental Data." *Housing Policy Debate* 14:305–45.

Deutsch, M. and M. Collins. 1951. *Interracial Housing: A Psychological Evaluation of a Social Experiment.* Minneapolis, MN: University of Minnesota Press.

Dinkes, R., Kemp, J., and Baum, K. (2009). *Indicators of School Crime and Safety: 2008* (NCES 2009–022/NCJ 226343). National Center for Education Statistics, Institute of Education Sciences, U.S. Department of Education, and Bureau of Justice Statistics, Office of Justice Programs, U.S. Department of Justice. Washington, DC.

Do, D. Phuong, Brian Karl Finch, Ricardo Basurto-Davila, Chloe Bird, Jose Escarce, and Nicole Lurie. 2008. "Does Place Explain Racial Health Disparities? Quantifying the Contribution of Residential Context to the Black/White Health Gap in the United States." *Social Science & Medicine* 67:1258–68.

Dohrenwend, Bruce P. and Barbara S. Dohrenwend. 1969. *Social Status and Psychological Disorder: A Causal Inquiry.* New York: John Wiley.

——. 1981. "Life Stress and Illness: Formulation of the Issues." Pp. 1–28 in *Stressful Life Events: Their Nature and Effects*, edited by Bruce S. Dohrenwend and Barbara P. Dohrenwend. New York: Prodist.

Dohrenwend, Bruce P., Itzhak Levan, Patrick E. Shrout, Sharon Schwartz, Guedalia Naveh, Bruce G. Link, Andrew E. Skodol, and Ann Stueve. 1992. "Socioeconomic Status and Psychiatric Disorders: The Causation-Selection Issue." *Science* 255:946–52.

Downey, Liam and Marieke Van Willigen. 2005. "Environmental Stressors: The Mental Health Impacts of Living near Industrial Activity." *Journal of Health and Social Behavior* 46:289–305.

Drewnowski, A. 2004. "Poverty and Obesity." Paper presented at "Obesity and the Built Environment." Washington, DC: May 24–26.

Drewnowski, A. and S. E. Specter. 2004. "Poverty and Obesity: The Role of Energy Density and Energy Costs." *American Journal of Clinical Nutrition* 79:6–16.

Drewnowski, Adam, Colin Rehm, Chi Kao, and Harold Goldstein. 2009. "Poverty and Childhood Overweight in California Assembly District." *Health and Place* 15:631–35.

Drukker, Marjan, Charles Kaplan, Frans Feron, and Jim van Os. 2003. "Children's Health Related Quality of Life, Neighborhood Socioeconomic Deprivation and Social Capital: A Contextual Analysis." *Social Science & Medicine* 57:825–41.

Dryfoos, Joy. 1990. *Adolescents at Risk*. New York: Oxford University Press.

Durkheim, Emile. [1893] 1933. *The Division of Labor in Society*. Translated by George Simpson. New York: Free Press.

Early, David B. 2006. "The Desperate Need for New Churches." Liberty Baptist Theological Seminary and Graduate School Faculty Publications and Presentations. Liberty University, Lynchburg, VA.

Eaton, William W. 1986. *The Sociology of Mental Disorders*. 2nd ed. New York: Praeger.

Edelstein, Michael R. 2004. *Contaminated Communities: Coping with Residential Toxic Exposure*. Boulder, CO: Westview Press.

Edwards, J. 1994. *Household Crowding and Its Consequences*. Boulder, CO: Westview.

Eibl-Eibesfeldt, Irenaus. 1989. *Human Ethology*. New York: Aldine de Gruyter.

Ellaway, Anne and Sally Macintyre. 1996. "Does Where You Live Predict Health Related Behaviors? A Case Study in Glasgow." *Health Bulletin* 54:443–6.

——. 1998. "Does Housing Tenure Predict Health in the U.K. Because it Exposes People to Different Levels of Housing Related Hazards in the Home or its Surroundings?" *Health and Place* 4:141–50.

Elliott, M. 2000. "The Stress Process in Neighborhood Context." *Health Place* 6:287–99

Ensel, Walter and Nan Lin. 1991. "The Life-Stress Paradigm and Psychological Distress." *Journal of Health and Social Behavior* 32:321–41.

Escalona, S. 1982. "Babies at Double Hazard: Early Development of Infants at Biologic and Social Risk." *Pediatrics* 70:670–76.

Esch, Tobias, George B. Stefano, Gregory L. Fricchione, and Herbert Benson. 2002. "The Role of Stress in Neurodegenerative Diseases and Mental Disorders." *Neuroendocrinology Letters* 23:199–208.

Evans, Gary W. 2004. "The Environment of Childhood Poverty." *American Psychologist* 59:77–92.

Eyles, John. 1985. *Senses of Place*. Cheshire, England: Silverbrook Press.

Eyles, John and Andrea Litva. 1998. "Place, Participation and Policy: People in and for Health Care Policy." Pp. 248–69 in *Putting Health into Place: Landscape, Identity and Well-Being*, edited by Robin Kearns and Wilbert Gesler. Syracuse, NY: Syracuse University Press.

Faris, Robert E. L. and H. Warren Dunham. 1939. *Mental Disorders in Urban Areas*. New York: Hafner.

Fauth, Rebecca C., Tama Leventhal, and Jeanne Brooks-Gunn. 2007. "Welcome to the Neighborhood? Long-Term Impacts of Moving to Low-Poverty Neighborhoods on Poor Children's and Adolescents' Outcomes." *Journal of Research on Adolescence* 17:249–84.

Federal Interagency Forum on Child and Family Statistics. 2008. *America's Children: Key National Indicators of Well-Being, 2008*. Washington, DC: U.S. Government Printing Office.

———. 2009. *America's Children: Key National Indicators of Well-Being, 2009*. Washington, DC: U.S. Government Printing Office.

Feld, Scott. 1981. "The Focused Organization of Social Ties." *American Journal of Sociology* 86:1015–35.

Ferrell, Betty R. and Polly Mazanec. 2009. "Family Caregivers." Pp. 135–55 in *Geriatric Oncology: Treatment, Assessment and Management*, edited by A. Hurria and L. Balducci. New York: Springer.

Festinger, L., S. Schacter, and K. Back. 1950. *Social Pressures in Informal Groups: A Study of Social Factors in Housing*. Stanford, CA: Stanford University Press.

Finkelhor, D., H. A. Turner, R. K. Ormrod, and S. L. Hamby. 2009. "Violence, Crime, and Exposure in a National Sample of Children and Youth." *Pediatric* 124: 1411–23.

Fischer, Claude. 1975. "Toward a Subcultural Theory of Urbanization." *American Sociological Review* 80:1319–41.

———. 1976. *The Urban Experience*. New York: Harper Brace Jovanovich.

———. 1981. "The Public and Private Worlds of City Life." *American Sociological Review* 46:306–16.

———. 1982. *To Dwell among Friends*. Chicago, IL: University of Chicago.

Fischer, Claude and R. Jackson. 1976. "Suburbs, Networks, and Attitudes." Pp. 279–308 in *The Changing Face of the Suburbs*, edited by B. Schwartz. Chicago, IL: University of Chicago Press.

Fitzpatrick, Kevin M. 1997. "Fighting among America's Youth: A Risk and Protective Factors Approach." *Journal of Health and Social Behavior* 38:131–48.

Fitzpatrick, Kevin M. and Janet P. Boldizar. 1993. "The Prevalence and Consequences of Exposure to Violence among African American Youth." *Journal of the American Academy of Child and Adolescent Psychiatry* 32:424–30.

Fitzpatrick, Kevin M. and M. LaGory. 2000. *Unhealthy Places: The Ecology of Risk in the Urban Landscape.* New York: Routledge.

Fitzpatrick, Kevin M. and John Logan. 1985. "The Aging of the Suburbs, 1960–1980." *American Sociological Review* 50:106–17

Fitzpatrick, Kevin M. and Brad Myrstol. 2008. "The Jailing of America's Homeless: Evaluating the Rabble Management Thesis." *Crime & Delinquency* DOI: 10.177/0011128708322941.

Fitzpatrick, Kevin M., Bettina Piko, and Elizabeth Miller. 2008. "Suicide Ideation and Attempts among Low-Income, African American Adolescents." *Suicide and Life-Threatening Behavior* 38:552–63.

Fitzpatrick, Kevin M., Akilah Dulin, and Bettina Piko. 2009. "Bullying and Depressive Symptomatology among Low-Income, African American Youth." *Journal of Youth and Adolescence* DOI: 10.1007/s 10964-009-9426-8.

Fitzpatrick, Kevin M., Jessica Irwin, Mark LaGory, and Ferris Ritchey. 2007a. "Just Thinking About It: Social Capital and Suicide Ideation Among Homeless Persons." *Journal of Health Psychology* 12:750–60.

Fitzpatrick, Kevin M., Mark LaGory, and Ferris Ritchey. 1993. "Criminal Victimization among the Homeless." *Justice Quarterly* 10:353–68.

Fitzpatrick, Kevin M., Akilah J. Dulin, and Bettina F. Piko. 2007b. "Not Just Pushing and Shoving: School Bullying Among African American Adolescents." *Journal of School Health* 77:16–22.

Fong, E. and K. Shibuya. 2005. "Multiethnic Cities in North America." *Annual Review of Sociology* 31:285–304.

Foucault, Michel. 1973. *The Birth of the Clinic.* London, England: Tavistock.

Freedman, J. L. 1975. *Crowding and Behavior.* San Francisco, CA: Freeman.

Frumkin, Howard 2003. "Healthy Places: Exploring the Evidence." *American Journal of Public Health* 93:1451–56.

Fuller, Millard. 1995. *A Simple, Decent Place to Live.* Dallas, TX: Word Publishing.

Fullilove, Mindy T. 1996. "Psychiatric Implications of Displacement: Contributions from the Psychology of Place." *American Journal of Psychiatry* 153:1516–23.

Furumoto-Dawson, Alice, Sarah Gehlert, Dana Sohmer, Olufunmilayo Olopade, and Tina Stacks. 2007. "Early-Life Conditions and Mechanisms of Population Health Vunerabilities." *Health Affairs* 26:1238–48.

Galea, Sandro, Nicholas Freunenberg, and David Vlahov. 2005. "Cities and Population Health." *Social Science & Medicine* 60:1017–33.

Gallagher, Winifred. 1993. *The Power of Place: How Our Surroundings Shape Our Thoughts, Emotions, and Reactions.* New York: HarperCollins.

Galle, Omer R. and Walter R. Gove. 1978. "Overcrowding, Isolation and Human Behavior: Exploring the Extremes in Population Distribution." Pp. 95–132 in *Social Demography*, edited by K. E. Taeuber, L. L. Bumper, and J. A. Sweet. New York: Academic Press.

Gans, Herbert. 1967. *The Levittowners.* New York: Pantheon.

Garbarino, James, Nancy Dubrow, Kathleen Kostelny, and Carole Pardo. 1992. *Children in Danger: Coping with the Consequences of Community Violence.* San Francisco, CA: Jossey-Bass.

Garber, J. and E. McCauley. 2002. "Prevention of Depression and Suicide in Children and Adolescents." Pp. 805–20 in *Child and Adolescent Psychiatry*, edited by M. Lewis. Philadelphia: Lippincott. Williams and Wilkins.

Garmezy, Norman. 1983. "Stressors of Childhood." Pp. 43–84 in *Stress, Coping, and Development in Children*, edited by N. Garmezy and M. Rutter. New York: McGraw-Hill.

Garreau, Joel. 1991. *Edge City: Life on the New Frontier.* New York: Doubleday.

George, Valerie A. and Paulette Johnson. 2001. "Weight Loss Behaviors and Smoking in College Students of Diverse Ethnicity." *American Journal of Health Behavior* 25:115–24.

Gephart, Martha. 1997. "Neighborhoods and Communities as Contexts for Development." Pp. 1–43 in *Neighborhood Poverty.* Vol. 1, *Context and Consequences for Children*, edited by Jeanne Brooks-Gunn, Greg J. Duncan, and J. Lawrence Aber. New York: Russell Sage.

Geronimus, Arline. 1992. "The Weathering Hypothesis and the Health of African American Women and Infants." *Ethnicity and Disease* 2:207–21.

——. 2000. "To Mitigate, Resist, or Undo: Addressing Structural Influences on the Health of Urban Populations." *American Journal of Public Health* 90:867–72.

Geronimus, Arline, John Bound, Timothy Waidmann, Cynthia Colen, and Diane Steffick. 2001. "Inequality in Life Expectancy, Functional Status, and Active Life Expectancy Across Selected Black and White Populations in the United States." *Demography* 38:227–51.

Giles, Wayne H., Amy Holmes-Chavez and Janet L. Collins. 2009. "Cultivating Healthy Communities: The CDC Perspective." *Health Promotion Practice* 10: S86–87.

Goffman, Erving. 1959. *The Presentation of Self in Everyday Life.* New York: Doubleday/Anchor.

——. 1963. *Stigma: Notes on the Management of Spoiled Identity.* Englewood Cliffs, NJ: Prentice Hall.

Goldsmith, William W. and Edward J. Blakely. 1992. *Separate Societies: Poverty and Inequality in U.S. Cities.* Philadelphia, PA: Temple University Press.

Goldstein, Michael S. 1992. *The Health Movement: Promoting Fitness in America.* New York: Twayne.

Gottdiener, Mark. 1985. *The Social Production of Urban Space.* Austin, TX: University of Texas Press.

——. 1994. *The New Urban Sociology.* New York: McGraw-Hill.

Gould, Kenneth. 1998. "Response to Eric Krieg's The Five Faces of Toxic Waste: Trends in the Spread of Environmental Hazards.'" *Sociological Forum* 13:21–23.

Gove, Walter R., Michael Hughes, and Omer R. Galle. 1979. "Overcrowding in the Home: An Empirical Investigation of Its Possible Pathological Consequences." *American Sociological Review* 44:59–80.

Granovetter, Mark. 1973a. "The Strength of Weak Ties." *American Journal of Sociology* 78:1360–80.

———. 1973b. "Threshold Models of Collective Behavior." *American Journal of Sociology* 83:1420–43.

Greenberg, Michael. 1991. "American Cities: Good and Bad News about Public Health." *Bulletin of the New York Academy of Medicine* 67:17–21.

Greenberg, Michael and Dona Schneider. 1996. *Environmentally Devastated Neighborhoods: Perceptions, Policies, and Realities.* New Brunswick, NJ: Rutgers University Press.

Greene, Richard. 1997. "Chicago's New Immigrants, Indigenous Poor and Edge Cities." *Annals of the Academy of Political and Social Science* 551:178–90.

Greer, Scott. 1956. "Urbanism Reconsidered: A Comparative Study of Local Areas in a Metropolis." *American Sociological Review* 21:19–25.

———. 1960. "The Social Structure and Political Process of Suburbia." *American Sociological Review* 25:514–26.

Greer, Scott and E. Kube. 1972. "Urbanism and Social Structure: A Los Angeles Study." Pp. 34–54 in *The Urbane View,* edited by Scott Greer. New York: Oxford University Press.

Greer, Scott and P. Orleans. 1962. "The Mass and Parapolitical Structure." *American Sociological Review* 27:643–49.

Grzywacz, Joseph G. and Nadine F. Marks. 2001. "Social Inequalities and Exercise During Adulthood: Toward an Ecological Perspective." *Journal of Health and Social Behavior* 42:202–20.

Guterman, Neil B., Hyeouk C. Hahm, and Mark Cameron. 2002. "Adolescent Victimization and Subsequent Use of Mental Health Counseling Services." *Journal of Adolescent Health* 30:336–45.

Haan, Mary, George A. Kaplan, and Terry Camacho. 1987. "Poverty and Health: Prospective Evidence from the Alameda County Study." *American Journal of Epidemiology* 125:989–98.

Habitat for Humanity. 2009a. *Habitat for Humanity Ranked as Top Builder in U.S.* Atlanta, GA: Habitat for Humanity International.

———. 2009b. *Habitat for Humanity Fact Sheet.* Atlanta, GA: Habitat for Humanity International.

Hack, M., H.G. Taylor, D. Drotar, M. Schluchter, L. Cartar, L. Andreias, D. Wilson-Costello, and N. Klein. 2005. "Chronic Conditions, Functional Limitations, and Special Health Care Needs of School-Aged Children Born with Extremely Low-Birth-Weight in the 1990s." *Journal of the American Medical Association* 294:318–25.

Hagglund, K., W. Haley, J. Reveille, and G. Alarcon. 1988. "Predicting Individual Differences in Pain and Functional Impairment among Patients with Rheumatoid Arthritis." *Arthritis and Rheumatism* 32:851–58.

Haggstrom, G. W., T. J. Blaschke, and R. J. Shavelson. 1991. *After High School Then What? A Look at the Postsecondary Sorting Out Process for American Youth.* Santa Monica, CA: RAND.

Haines, Valerie and Jeanne Hurlbert. 1992. "Network Range and Health." *Journal of Health and Social Behavior* 33:254–66.

Hall, Edward. 1966. *The Hidden Dimension.* Garden City, NJ: Doubleday.

Hammond, W. R. and B. R. Yung. 1991. "Preventing Violence in At-Risk African American Youth." *Journal of Health Care for Poor and Underserved* 2:359–73.

Hanson, Margaret D. and Edith Chen. 2007. "Socioeconomic Status and Health Behaviors in Adolescence: A Review of the Literature." *Journal of Behavioral Medicine* 30:263–85.

Harris, Chauncey and Edward Ullman. 1945. "The Nature of Cities." *The Annals of the American Academy of Political and Social Science* 252:7–17.

Harvey, David. 1972. "Social Justice and Spatial Systems." *Antipode Monographs in Social Geography 1.*

———. 1997. "The Environment of Justice." Pp. 65–99 in *The Urbanization of Justice*, edited by Andy Merrifield and Erik Swyngedouw. New York: New York University Press.

Hawkins, David J. 1995. "Controlling Crime before It Happens: Risk-Focused Prevention." *National Institute of Justice Journal* 229:10–18.

Hawkins, David J. and Richard Catalano. 1992. *Communities That Care: Action for Drug Abuse Prevention.* San Francisco, CA: Jossey-Bass.

Hawkins, David J., Richard Catalano, and Janet Miller. 1992. "Risk and Protective Factors for Alcohol and Other Drug Problems in Adolescence and Early Adulthood: Implications for Substance Abuse Prevention." *Psychological Bulletin* 112:64–105.

Hawkins, David and Joseph Weis. 1985. "The Social Development Model: An Integrated Approach to Delinquency Prevention." *Journal of Primary Prevention* 6:73–97.

Hawkins, D. R. and S. Rosenbaum. 1992. *Lives in the Balance: A National, State and County Profile of America's Medically Underserved.* Washington, DC: U.S. Department of Health and Human Services.

Health Resources and Services Administration. U.S. Department of Health and Human Services. 2001. "Program Assistance Letter: Understanding the Health Care Needs of Homeless Youth." Retrieved October 10, 2009 (http://bphc.hrsa.gov/policy/pal0110.htm).

Henshaw, S. K. 2003. *U.S. Teenage Pregnancy Statistics with Comparative Statistics for Women Aged 20–24.* New York: The Alan Guttmacher Institute.

Hill, Terrence D., Catherine E. Ross, and Ronald J. Angel. 2005. "Neighborhood Disorder, Psychological Distress, and Health." *Journal of Health and Social Behavior* 46:170–86.

Hinde, Robert. 1987. *Individuals, Relationships and Culture: Links between Ethology and the Social Sciences.* New York: Cambridge University Press.

Hindelang, Michael, Michael Gottfredson, and James Garofalo. 1978. *Victims of Personal Crime: An Empirical Foundation for a Theory of Personal Victimization.* Cambridge, MA: Ballinger.

Holmes, Thomas and Richard Rahe. 1967. "The Social Readjustment Rating Scale." *Journal of Psychosomatic Research* 11:213–18.

Hood, Ernie. 2005. "Dwelling Disparities: How Poor Housing Leads to Poor Health." *Environmental Health Perspectives* 5:311–17.

Hoyert, D., M. Freedman, D. Strobino, and B. Guyer. 2001. "Annual Visit Statistics: 2000."
    Pediatrics 108:1241–55.
Hoyt, Homer. 1939. "The Structure and Growth of Residential Neighborhoods in
    American Cities." U.S. Federal Housing Administration. Washington, DC:
    Government Printing Office.
Hynes, H. Patricia and Russ Lopez. 2009. *Urban Health: Reading in the Social Built and
    Physical Environments of U.S. Cities.* Sudbury, MA: Jones and Bartlett.
Institute for the Prevention of Crime. 2008. *Homelessness, Victimization, and Crime:
    Knowledge and Actionable Recommendations.* Ottawa: Institute for the Prevention of
    Crime, University of Ottawa.
Irwin, J., M. LaGory, F. Ritchey, and K. Fitzpatrick. 2008. "Social Assets and Mental
    Distress Among the Homeless: Exploring the Effects of Social Support and Other
    Forms of Social Capital on Depression." *Social Science and Medicine* 67:1935–43.
Ittelson, W., Harold Proshansky, L. Rivlin, and G. Winkel. 1974. *An Introduction to
    Environmental Psychology.* New York: Holt, Rinehart, and Winston.
Iwarsson, S. 2005. "A Long Term Perspective on Person-Environment Fit and ADL
    Dependence Among Older Swedish Adults." *The Gerontologist* 45:327–36.
Jacobs, D. E., R. P. Clickner, J. Y. Zhou, et al. 2002. "The Prevalence of Lead-Based Paint
    Hazards in U.S. Housing." *Environmental Health Perspectives* 110:A599–606.
Jacobs, Jane. 1961. *The Death and Life of Great American Cities.* New York: Vintage.
Jacobs, Jerry. 1984. *The Mall.* Prospect Heights, IL: Waveland Press.
Jackson, S. A. and R. T. Anderson. 2000. "The Relation of Residential Segregation to All-
    Cause Mortality: A Study in Black and White." *American Journal of Public Health*
    90:615–17.
Jargowsky, Paul. 2003. "Stunning Progress, Hidden Problems: The Dramatic Decline of
    Concentrated Poverty in the 1990s." Washington, DC: Brookings.
Jargowsky, Paul A. 1997. *Poverty and Place: Ghettos, Barrios, and the American City.* New
    York: Russell Sage.
Jargowsky, Paul A. and Mary Jo Bane. 1991. "Ghetto Poverty in the United States,
    1970–1980." Pp. 235–73 in *The Urban Underclass,* edited by C. Jencks and P. E.
    Peterson. Washington, DC: Brookings Institution.
Jargowsky, Paul A. and Yoonwhan Park. 2009. "Cause or Consequence: Suburbanization
    and Crime in U.S. Metropolitan Areas." *Crime and Delinquency* 55:28–50.
Jargowsky, Paul A. and Rebecca Young. 2005. "The Underclass Revisited: A Social Problem
    in Decline." Washington, DC: Brookings Institution.
Jeffery, Robert W., Judy Baxter, Maureen M. McGuire, and Jennifer Linde. 2006. "Are Fast
    Food Restaurants an Environmental Risk Factor for Obesity?" *International Journal of
    Behavioral Nutrition and Physical Activity* 3:2.
Jessor, Richard. 1993. "Successful Adolescent Development among Youth in High-Risk
    Settings." *American Psychologist* 48:117–26.
Johnston, L. D., P. M. O'Malley, and J. G. Bachman. 2003. *Monitoring the Future: National
    Results on Adolescent Drug Use. Overview of Key Findings.* Bethesda, MD: National

Institute on Drug Abuse, U.S. Department of Health and Human Services, Public Health Service, National Institute of Health.

Johnston, R. J. 1972. "Activity Spaces and Residential Preferences: Some Tests of the Hypothesis of Sectoral Maps." *Economic Geography* 48:199–211.

Kain, John. 1968. "The Distribution and Movement of Jobs and Industry." Pp. 1–43 in *The Metropolitan Enigma*, edited by J. Q. Wilson. Cambridge, MA: Harvard University Press.

Kaiser Family Foundation. 2005. "U.S. Teen Sexual Activity." Washington, DC: Kaiser Family Foundation.

Karp, Jordan F. and Charles F. Reynolds III. 2009. "Depression, Pain, and Aging." *Focus: The Journal of Lifelong Learning in Psychiatry* 7:17–27.

Kart, Carey. 1990. *The Realities of Aging*. Boston, MA: Allyn and Bacon.

Kawachi, Ichiro. 2001. "Social Capital for Health and Human Development." *Development* 44:31–35

———. 2002. "Social Epidemiology." *Social Science and Medicine*. 54:1739–41.

Kawachi, Ichiro and Lisa F. Berkman. 2001. "Social Ties and Mental Health." *Journal of Urban Health*. 78:458–67.

Kawachi, Ichiro and Lisa F. Berkman, eds. 2003. *Neighborhoods and Health*. New York: Oxford University Press.

Kawachi, Ichiro, S. V. Subramanian and Daniel Kim, eds. 2008. *Social Capital and Health*. New York: Springer Science.

Keels, Micere, Greg J. Duncan, Stephanie DeLuca, Ruby Mendenhall, and James Rosenbaum. 2005. "Fifteen Years Later: Can Residential Mobility Programs Provide a Long Term Escape from Neighborhood Segregation, Crime, and Poverty?" *Demography* 42:51–73.

Kennedy, M. M., R. K. Jung, and M. E. Orland. 1986. *Poverty, Achievement, and the Distribution of Compensatory Education Services*. Washington, DC: Office of Educational Research and Improvement, U.S. Department of Education.

Kessler, Ronald and Harold W. Neighbors. 1986. "A New Perspective on the Relationships between Race, Social Class, and Psychological Distress." *Journal of Health and Social Behavior* 27:107–15.

Kessler, Ronald and E. Wallers. 1998. "Epidemiology of DSM-III-R Major Depression and Minor Depression among Adolescents and Young Adults in the National Comorbidity Survey." *Depression and Anxiety* 7:3–14.

Kingston, Beverly, David Huizinga, and Delbert S. Elliot. 2009. "A Test of Social Disorganization Theory in High-Risk Urban Neighborhoods." *Youth and Society* 41:53–79.

Klinenberg, Eric. 2002. *Heat Wave: A Social Autopsy of Disaster in Chicago*. Chicago: University of Chicago Press.

Klopfer, P. H. 1969. *Habitat and Territories: A Study of the Use of Space by Animals*. New York: Basic Books.

Kneebone, Elizabeth and Alan Berube. 2008. "Reversals of Fortune: A New Look at Concentrated Poverty in the 2000s." Washington, DC: Brookings.

Krieg, Eric. 1998. "The Future of Environmental Justice Research: A Response to Gould and Weinberg." *Sociological Forum* 13:33–34.

Krivo, Lauren and Ruth Peterson. 1996. "Extremely Disadvantaged Neighborhoods and Crime." *Social Forces* 75:619–50.

Krueger, Patrick M. and Virginia W. Chang. 2008. "Being Poor and Coping with Stress: Health Behaviors and the Risk of Death." *American Journal of Public Health* 98:889–96.

Kubzansky, Laura D., S. V. Subramanian, Ichiro Kawachi, Martha E. Fay, Mah-J Soobader, and Lisa F. Berkman. 2005. "Neighborhood Contextual Influences on Depressive Symptoms in the Elderly." *American Journal of Epidemiology* 162:253–60.

Kurtz, Margot E., J. C. Kurtz, Charles W. Given, and Barbara Given. 2005. "A Randomized, Controlled Trial of a Patient/Caregiver Symptom Control Intervention: Effects on Depressive Symptomatology of Caregivers of Cancer Patients." *Journal of Pain and Symptom Management* 30:112–22.

Kushel, Margot B., Sharon Perry, David Bangsberg, Richard Clark, and Andrew R. Moss. 2002. "Emergency Use Among the Homeless and Marginally Housed: Results from a Community-Based Study." *American Journal of Public Health* 92:778–84.

Kwate, Naa Oyo A., Chun-Yip Yau, Ji-Meng Loh, and Donya Williams. 2009. "Inequality in Obesigenic Environments: Fast Food Density in New York City." *Health & Place* 15:364–73.

LaGory, Mark E. 1982. "Toward a Sociology of Space: The Constrained Choice Model." *Symbolic Interaction* 5:65–78.

——. 1983. "The Social Consequences of Urban Space." Pp. 180–96 in *Remaking the City: Social Science Perspectives on Urban Design*, edited by John Pipkin, Mark LaGory, and Judith Blau. Albany, NY: SUNY Press.

——. 1993. "Spatial Structure and the Urban Experience: Ecology and the New Urban Sociology." Pp. 111–25 in *Research in Urban Sociology: Urban Sociology in Transition*, edited by R. Hutchison. Greenwich, CT: JAI Press.

——. 2009. "Social Capital." In *Encyclopedia Of Human Relationships*, edited by H. Reis and S. Sprecher. Thousands Oaks: Sage.

LaGory, Mark and Kevin Fitzpatrick. 1992. "The Effects of Environmental Context on Elderly Depression." *Journal of Aging and Health* 4:459–79.

LaGory, Mark and John Pipkin. 1981. *Urban Social Space*. Belmont, CA: Wadsworth.

LaGory, Mark, Russell Ward, and Thomas Juravich. 1980. "The Age Segregation Process: Explanations for American Cities." *Urban Affairs Quarterly* 16:59–80.

LaGory, Mark, Ferris Ritchey, Kevin Fitzpatrick, and Jessica Irwin. 2005. *A Needs Assessment of the Homeless of Birmingham and Jefferson County*. Birmingham, AL: University of Birmingham.

LaGory, Mark, Ferris Ritchey, and Jeffery Mullis. 1990. "Depression among the Homeless." *Journal of Health and Social Behavior* 31:87–101.

LaGory, Mark, Russell Ward, and Susan Sherman. 1985. "The Ecology of Aging: Neighborhood Satisfaction in an Older Population." *Sociological Quarterly* 26:405–18.

Laird, J., M. DeBell, G. Kienzl, and C. Chapman. 2007. *Dropout Rates in the United States:*

2005 (NCES 2007–059). U.S. Department of Education. Washington, DC: National Center for Education Statistics. Retrieved October 27, 2009 (http://nces.ed.gov/pubsearch).

Lang, Iain A., Ruth E. Hubbard, Melissa K. Andrews, David J. Llewellyn, David Melzer, and Kenneth Rockwood. 2009. "Neighborhood Deprivation, Individual Socioeconomic Status, and Frailty in Older Adults." *Journal of the American Geriatrics Society* 57:1776–80.

Laraia, Barbara A., Lynne Messer, Jay S. Kaufman, Nancy Dole, Margaret Caughy, Patricia O'Campo, and David A Savitz. 2006. "Direct Observation of Neighborhood Attributes in an Urban Area of the U.S. South: Characterizing the Social Context of Pregnancy." *International Journal of Health Geographics* 5:11.

Latino Health Access. 2009. "Latino Health Access." Retrieved November 11, 2009 (www.latinohealthaccess.org/index.shtml).

Latkin, Carl A. and Aaron D. Curry. 2003. "Stressful Neighborhoods and Depression: A Prospective Study of the Impact of Neighborhood Disorder." *Journal of Health and Social Behavior* 44:34–44.

Lawton, M. Powell. 1980. *Environment and Aging*. Belmont, CA: Brooks/Cole.

Lawton, M. Powell and Lucille Nahemow. 1973. "Ecology and the Aging Process." Pp. 619–74 in *The Psychology of Adult Development and Aging*, edited by Carl Eisdorfer and M. Powell Lawton. Washington, DC: American Psychological Association.

Lawton, M. Powell and B. Simon. 1968. "The Ecology of Social Relationships in Housing for the Elderly." *Gerontologist* 8:108–15.

Lawton, M. Powell and Sylvia Yaffe. 1980. "Victimization and Fear of Crime in Elderly Public Housing Tenants." *Journals of Gerontology* 35:768–79.

Layton, David W. and Paloma Beamer. 2009. "Migration of Contaminated Soil and Airborne Particulates to Indoor Dust." *Environmental Science and Technology* 43:8199–205.

Lazarus, Richard S. and Susan Folkman. 1984. *Stress, Appraisal and Coping*. New York: Springer.

LeClere, Felicia B., Richard G. Rogers, and Kimberly Peters. 1997. "Ethnicity and Mortality in the United States: Individual and Community Correlates." *Social Forces* 76:169–98.

——. 1998. "Neighborhood Social Context and Racial Differences in Women's Heart Disease Mortality." *Journal of Health and Social Behavior* 39:91–107.

Lefebvre, Henri. 1974. *La Production de L'espace* (in French). Paris: Anthropos.

——. 1991. *The Production of Space*. Oxford: Blackwell.

Lehman, Jeffrey S. and Timothy Smeeding. 1997. "Neighborhood Effects and Federal Policy." Pp. 251–78 in *Neighborhood Poverty*, vol. 1, *Context and Consequences for Children*, edited by Jeanne Brooks-Gunn, Greg Duncan, and J. Lawrence Aber. New York: Russell Sage.

Lennon, Jeffery L. 2005. "The Use of Health Belief Model in Dengue Health Education." *Dengue Bulletin* 29:217–19.

Leventhal, Tama and Jeanne Brooks-Gunn. 2000. "The Neighborhoods They Live in: The Effects of Neighborhood Residence on Child and Adolescent Outcomes." *Psychological Bulletin* 126:309–37

Levine, Felice J. and Katherine J. Rosich. 1996. *The Social Causes of Violence: Crafting a Science Agenda.* Washington, DC: American Sociological Association.

Lewis, L. B., D. C. Sloane, L. M. Nascimento, A. L. Diamant, J. J. Guinyard, A. K. Yancey, et. al. 2005. "African Americans' Access to Healthy Food Options in South Los Angeles Restaurants." *American Journal of Public Health* 95:668–73.

Lieberson, Stanley. 1961. "The Import of Residential Segregation on Ethnic Assimilation." *Social Forces* 40:52–57.

Lin, Nan. 2001. *Social Capital: A Theory of Social Structure and Action.* New York: Cambridge University Press.

Lin, Nan, Alfred Dean, and Walter Ensel. 1986. *Social Support, Life Events, and Depression.* Orlando, FL: Academic Press.

Link, Bruce G. 2008. "Epidemiological Sociology and the Social Shaping of Population Health." *Journal of Health and Social Behavior* 49:367–84.

Link, Bruce and Jo Phelan. 1995. "Social Conditions as Fundamental Causes of Disease." *Journal of Health and Social Behavior.* Extra issue: 80–94.

Lochner, Kimberly A., Ichiro Kawachi, Robert T. Brennan, and Stephen L. Burka. 2003. "Social Capital and Neighborhood Mortality Rates in Chicago." *Social Science and Medicine* 56:1797–805.

Lofland, Lynn. 1973. *A World of Strangers.* New York: Basic Books.

Logan, John R. and Harvey Molotch. 1987. *Urban Fortunes: The Political Economy of Place.* Berkeley, CA: University of California Press.

Lopez, R. 2002. "Segregation and Black/White Differences in Exposure to Air Toxics in 1990." *Environmental Health Perspectives* 110:289–95.

Lueschen, Guenther, William Cockerham, Jouke Van Der Zee, Fred Stevens, Jos Diederiks, Manual Garcia Ferrando, Alphonse D'Houtaud, Ruud Peeters, Thomas Abel, and Steffen Niemann. 1995. *Health Systems in the European Union: Diversity, Convergence, and Integration.* Munich, Germany: Oldenbourg.

Lundberg, O. 1993. "The Impact of Childhood Living Conditions on Illness and Mortality in Adulthood." *Social Science and Medicine* 36:1047–52.

Lurie, Stephen J., Barbara Gawinski, Deborah Pierce, and Sally J. Rousseau. 2006. "Seasonal Affective Disorder." *American Family Physician* 74:1521–24.

Lyndon Baines Johnson Library and Museum. 1965. President Lyndon B. Johnson's Commencement Address at Howard University: "To Fulfil These Rights." Retrieved April 28, 2010 (www.lbjlib.utexas.edu/johnson/archives.hom/speeches.hom/650604.asp).

Macintyre, Sally, Anne Ellaway, and Steve Cummins. 2002. "Place Effects on Health: How Can We Conceptualize, Operationalize, and Measure Them?" *Social Science and Medicine* 55:125–39.

Macintyre, Sally, Laura McKay, and Anne Ellaway. 2005. "Are Rich People or Poor People

More Likely to Be Ill? Lay Perceptions, by Social Class and Neighbourhood, of Inequalities in Health." *Social Science and Medicine* 60:313–17.

Magnusson, A. 2000. "An Overview of Epidemiological Studies on Seasonal Affective Disorder." *Acta Psychiatrica Scandinavica* 101:176–84.

Maslow, Abraham. 1954. *Motivation and Personality.* New York: Harper and Row.

Massey, Douglas S. 1990. "American Apartheid: Segregation and the Making of the Underclass." *American Journal of Sociology* 96:329–58.

———. 2001. "Residential Segregation and Neighborhood Conditions in U.S. Metropolitan Areas." Pp. 391–434 in *America Becoming: Racial Trends and Their Consequences,* edited by N. J. Smelser, W. J. Wilson, and F. Mitchel. Washington DC: National Academy Press.

Massey, Douglas S. and Nancy Denton. 1993. *American Apartheid: Segregation and the Making of the Underclass.* Cambridge, MA: Harvard University Press.

Mather, M. and Adams, D. 2006. *A KIDS COUNT/PRB Report on Census 2000: The Risk of Negative Child Outcomes in Low-Income Families.* KIDS COUNT & Population Reference Bureau.

Matte, Thomas D., Michaeline Bresnahan, Melissa D. Begg, and Ezra Susser. 2001. "Influence of Variation in Birth Weight within Normal Range and within Sibships on IQ at Age 7 Years: Cohort Study." *British Medical Journal* 323:310–14.

Matthews, B., F. Baker, and R. Spillers. 2003. "Family Caregivers and Indicators of Cancer-Related Distress." *Psychology, Health and Medicine* 8:45–56.

Mayes, Frances. 1997. *Under the Tuscan Sun.* New York: Broadway Books.

McCord, Colin and Harold Freeman. 1990. "Excess Mortality in Harlem." *New England Journal of Medicine* 322:173–77.

———. 2009. "Excess Mortality in Harlem." Pp. 30–38 in *The Sociology of Health and Illness: Cultural Perspectives.* 8th ed., edited by Peter Conrad. New York: Worth.

McEwen, Rhonda N. 2007. "Tools of the Trade: Drugs, Law and Mobile Phones." Presented at American Society of Information Science and Technology Conference, October, Milwaukee, WI.

McKnight, J. and J. Kretzmann. 1990. *Building Communities from the Inside Out.* Evanston, IL: Center for Urban Affairs and Policy Research, Northwestern University.

McLuhan, Marshall. 1965. *Understanding Media: The Extension of Man.* New York: McGraw-Hill.

McNeil, Linda M., Eileen Coppola, Judy Radigan, and Julian Vasquez Heilig. 2008. "Avoidable Losses: High-Stakes Accountability and the Dropout Crisis." *Education Policy Analysis Archives* 16:1–48.

Meadows, Donella, Dennis Meadows, Jordan Randers, and William Behrens. 1972. *The Limits to Growth: A Report to the Club of Rome's Project on the Predicament of Mankind.* New York: Universe Books.

Means, Richard K. 1975. *Historical Perspectives on School Health.* Thorofare, NJ: Charles B. Slack.

Melnyk, B. M., Z. Moldenhauer, J. Tuttle, T. G. Veenema, D. Jones, and J. Novak. 2003a. "Improving Child and Adolescent Mental Health: An Evidence-Based Approach." *Advance for Nurse Practitioners* 11:47–52.

Melnyk, Bernadette M., Holly E. Brown, Dolores C. Jones, Richard Kreipe, and Julie Novak. 2003b. "Improving the Mental Psychosocial Health of U.S. Children and Adolescents: Outcomes and Implementation Strategies from the National KySS Summit." *Journal of Pediatric Health Care* 17:1–24.

Mercado, Susan, Kirsten Havemann, Mojan Sami, and Hiroshi Ueda. 2007. "Urban Poverty: An Urgent Health Issue." *Journal of Urban Health* 84:i7–i13.

Merrifield, Andy and Erik Swyngedouw, eds. 1997. *The Urbanization of Injustice.* New York: New York University Press.

Merton, Robert. 1968. *Social Theory and Social Structure.* New York: Free Press.

Michelson, William. 1976. *Man and His Urban Environment.* Reading, MA: Addison Wesley.

Milgram, Stanley. 1972. "The Experience of Living in Cities." *Science* 167:1461–68.

Miller, Walter B. 1958. "Lower-Class Culture as a Generating Milieu of Gang Delinquency." *Journal of Social Issues* 14:5–19.

Millstein, S., C. Irwin, N. Adler, L. Cohn, S. Kegeles, and M. Dolcini. 1992. "Health-Risk Behaviors and Health Concerns among Young Adolescents." *Pediatrics* 89:422–28.

Mirowsky, John and Catherine Ross. 1989. *Social Causes of Psychological Distress.* New York: Aldine.

———. 2003. *Social Causes of Psychological Distress,* 2nd ed. New York: Aldine de Gruyter.

Mitchell, Carey and Mark LaGory. 2002. "Social Capital and Mental Distress. In an Impoverished Community." *City and Community* 1:95–216.

Mitchell, R. 1971. "Some Social Implications of High Density Housing." *American Sociological Review* 36:18–29.

Montgomery, S. B., J. G. Joseph, M. H. Becker, D. G. Ostrow, R. C. Kersher, and J. P. Kirscht. 1989. "The Health Belief Model in Understanding Compliance with Preventive Recommendations for AIDS: How Useful?" *AIDS Education and Prevention* 1:303–23.

Moos, R. H., P. L. Brennan, K. K. Schutte, and B. S. Moos. 2005. "Older Adults' Health and Changes in Late-Life Drinking Patterns." *Aging and Mental Health* 9:49–59.

Morenoff, Jeffrey and Marta Tienda. 1997. "Underclass Neighborhoods in Temporal and Ecological Perspective." *Annals of the Academy of Political and Social Science* 551:59–72.

Morland K., S. Wing, and A. Diez Roux. 2002. "The Contextual Effect of the Local Food Environment on Residents' Diets: the Atherosclerosis Risk in Communities Study." *American Journal of Public Health* 92:1761–67.

Mortimer K. M., L. M. Neas, D. W. Dockery, S. Redline, and I. B. Tager. 2002. "The Effect of Air Pollution on Inner-City Children with Asthma." *European Respiratory Journal* 19:699–705.

Moy, Ernest, Elizabeth Dayton, and Carolyn M. Clancy. 2005. "Compiling the Evidence: The National Healthcare Disparities Reports." *Health Affairs* 24:376–87.

Moyers, Bill. 2009. "Bill Moyers Journal, October 16, 2009: Community Health Crusade." Retrieved December 15, 2009 (www.pbs.org/moyers/journal/10162009/profile2. html).

Munch, Richard. 1988. *Understanding Modernity*. London: Routledge.

National Alliance of Gang Investigators Associations. 2009. "National Gang Threat Assessment, 2008." Washington, DC: Bureau of Justice Assistance, Department of Justice.

National Assembly on School-Based Health Care. 2008. "National Census Statistics." Retrieved July 20, 2009 (http://ww2.nasbhc.org/census/census_sbhcNatstats.asp).

National Association of Community Health Centers. 2009. *America's Health Centers*. Bethesda, MD.

——. 2009. *Health, United States, 2008*. Hyattsville, MD: National Center for Health Statistics.

National Association of County and City Health Officials. 2009. *Building Healthy Communities: Lessons Learned from CDC's Steps Program*. Washington, DC: National Association of County and City Health Officials.

National Center on Family Homelessness. 2009. *America's Youngest Outcasts: State Report Card on Child Homelessness*. Newton, MA: National Center on Family Homelessness.

National Center for Health Statistics. 1998. *Health, United States, 1998*. Hyattsville, MD: National Center for Health Statistics.

National Coalition for the Homeless. 2008. *NCH Fact Sheet #13*. Washington, DC: National Coalition for the Homeless.

National Research Council. 1993. *Losing Generations: Adolescents in High-Risk Settings*. Washington, DC: National Academy Press.

Nawar, E. W., R. W. Niska, and J. Xu. 2007. *National Hospital Ambulatory Medical Care Survey: 2005 Emergency Department Summary. Advance Data from Vital and Health Statistics, no. 386*. Hyattsville, MD: National Center for Health Statistics.

Nelson, G. D. and P. B. Moffit. 1988. "Safety Belt Promotion: Theory and Practice." *Accident Analysis and Prevention* 20:27–38.

Nelson, Melissa C., Penny Gordon-Larsen, Yang Song, and Barry M. Popkin. 2006. "Built and Social Environments Associations with Adolescent Overweight and Activity." *American Journal of Preventative Medicine* 31:109–17.

Newman, David. 1997. *Sociology: Exploring the Architecture of Everyday Life*. Thousand Oaks, CA: Pine Forge.

Newman, Oscar. 1973a. "Defensible Space: Crime Prevention through Urban Design." *Ekistics* 36:325–32.

——. 1973b. *Defensible Space: Crime Prevention Through Urban Design*. New York: Macmillan.

Nored, Ron. 1999. "B.E.A.T.ing the Odds." *Birmingham News*. March 21, pp. 1c, 5c.

Novac, S., J. Hermer, E. Paradis, and A. Kellen. 2006. *Justice and Injustice: Homelessness, Crime, Victimization, and the Criminal Justice System*. Toronto: Centre for Urban and Community Studies, University of Toronto, and the John Howard Society of Toronto.

O'Campo, Patricia, Ravi P. Rao, Andrea C. Gielen, Wendy Royalty, and Modena Wilson. 2000. "Injury-Producing Events among Children in Low-Income Communities: the Role of Community Characteristics." *Journal of Urban Health* 77:34–49.

Office of Substance Abuse Prevention. 1991. *The Future by Design: A Community Framework for Preventing Alcohol and Other Drug Problems Through a Systems Approach.* Washington, DC: U.S. Government Printing Office.

Organization for Economic Cooperation and Development, Paris, France, OECD Health Data 2007 (copyright).

Osofsky, J. D., S. Wewers, D. M. Hann, and A. C. Fick. 1993. "Chronic Community Violence: What Is Happening to Our Children?" *Psychiatry* 6:36–45.

Oswald, Frank, Hans-Werner Wahl, Oliver Schilling, Carita Nygren, Agneta Fange, Andrew Sixsmith, Judith Sixsmith, Zsuzsa Szeman, Signe Tomsone, and Susanne Irwarssson. 2007. "Relationship Between Housing and Healthy Aging in Very Old Age." *The Gerontologist* 47:97–107.

Ozer, E. J., M. H. Richards, and W. Kliewer, eds. 2004. "Protective Factors in the Relation Between Community Violence Exposure and Adjustment in Youth [Special Section]." *Journal of Clinical Child and Adolescent Psychology.* 33:434–505.

Palen, John. 1997. *The Urban World.* New York: McGraw-Hill.

Palmer, Raymond F., Stephen Blanchard, and Robert Wood. 2009. "Proximity to Point Sources of Environmental Mercury Release as a Predictor of Autism Prevalence." *Health and Place* 15:18:24.

Park, Robert, Ernest Burgess, and Roderick McKenzie. 1925. *The City.* Chicago, IL: University of Chicago Press.

Partridge, E. 1958. *Origins. A Short Etymological Dictionary of Modern English.* London: Routledge, Kegan, and Paul.

Pearlin, Leonard I. 1989. "The Sociological Study of Stress." *Journal of Health and Social Behavior* 30:241–56.

Pearlin, Leonard I. and Carmi Schooler. 1978. "The Structure of Coping." *Journal of Health and Social Behavior* 19:2–21.

Peck, Magda G. and Elice D. Hubbert, eds. 1994. *Changing the Rules: Medicaid, Managed Care and MCH in U.S. Cities. Special Report 1.* Omaha, NE: City Match.

Perkins, Douglas, Barbara Brown, and Ralph Taylor. 1996. "The Ecology of Empowerment: Predicting Participation in Community Organizations." *Journal of Social Issues* 52:85–110.

Peters, John M., Edward Avol, W. James Gauderman, William S. Linn, William Navidi, Stephanie J. London, Helen Margolis, Edward Rappaport, Hita Vora, Henry Gong Jr., and Duncan C. Thomas. 1999. "A Study of Twelve Southern California Communities with Differing Levels and Types of Air Pollution II: Effects on Pulmonary Function." *American Journal of Respiratory and Critical Care Medicine* 159:768–75.

Peterson, Ruth D. and Lauren J. Krivo. 2005. "Macrostructural Analyses of Race, Ethnicity, and Violent Crime: Recent Lessons and New Directions for Research." *Annual Review of Sociology* 31:331–56.

Petschauer, Peter. 1997. *Human Space: Personal Rights in a Threatening World.* Westport, CT: Praeger.

Pickett, K. E. and M. Pearl. 2001. "Multilevel Analyses of Neighbourhood Socioeconomic Context and Health Outcomes: A Critical Review." *Journal of Epidemiology and Community Health* 55:111–22.

Piko, Bettina and Kevin M. Fitzpatrick. 2003. "Gender Differences in Depression among Adolescents: A Risk and Protective Factors Approach." *American Journal of Orthopsychiatry* 73:44–54.

Piko, Bettina F., Kevin M. Fitzpatrick, and Darlene Wright. 2005. "A Risk and Protective Factors Framework for Understanding Externalizing Problem Behavior among Hungarian and American Youth." *European Journal of Child and Adolescent Psychiatry* 14:95–103.

Popkin, Susan J., Bruce Katz, Mary K. Cunningham, Karen D. Brown, Jeremy Gustafson, and Margery Austin Turner. 2004. *A Decade of HOPE VI: Research Findings and Policy Challenges.* Washington, DC: Urban Institute.

Porteous, J. Douglas. 1977. *Environment and Behavior: Planning and Everyday Urban Life.* Reading, MA: Addison-Wesley.

Putnam, Robert. 1993. "The Prosperous Community: Social Capital and Public Life." *American Prospect* 25:26–28.

Putnam, Robert D. 2000. *Bowling Alone.* New York: Simon & Schuster.

Rabito, Felicia A., Charles Shorter, and LuAnn E. White. 2003. "Lead Levels among Children Who Live in Public Housing." *Epidemiology* 14:263–68.

Rankin, Bruce H. and James M. Quane. 2002. "Social Context and Urban Adolescent Outcomes: The Interrelated Effects of Neighborhoods, Families, and Peers on African American Youth." *Social Problems* 49:79–100.

Raudenbush, Stephen W. and Anthony S. Bryk. 2002. *Hierarchical Linear Models: Applications and Data Analysis Methods.* 2nd ed. Thousand Oaks, CA: Sage.

Regoeczi, Wendy C. 2003. "When Context Matters: A Multilevel Analysis of Neighborhood Crowding on Aggression and Withdrawal." *Journal of Environmental Psychology* 23:457–70.

———. 2008. "Crowding in Context: An Examination of the Differential Responses of Men and Women to High Density Living Environments." *Journal of Health and Social Behavior* 49:254–68.

Reichmann, Nancy E., Julien O. Teitler, and Erin R. Hamilton. 2009. "Effects of Neighborhood Racial Composition on Birthweight." *Health and Place* 15:814–21.

Reiss, Albert. 1959. "Rural-Urban and Status Differences in Interpersonal Contacts." *American Journal of Sociology* 65:182–95.

Reitzes, Donald, Elizabeth Mutran, and Hollowell Pope. 1991. "Location and Well-Being among Retired Men." *Journals of Gerontology* 46:S195–203.

Relph, Edward C. 1976. *Place and Placelessness.* London: Pion.

———. 1985. "Geographical Experiences as Being in the World." Pp. 15–31 in *Dwelling Place and Environment: Towards a Phenomenology of Person and World*, edited by D. Seamon and R. Mugerauer. Boston, MA: M. Nijhoff.

Repetti, Rena L., Shelly E. Taylor, and Teresa E. Seeman. 2002. "Risky Families: Family Social Environments and the Mental and Physical Health of Offspring." *Psychological Bulletin* 128:330–66.

Reschovsky, James and Sandra Newman. 1991. "Home Upkeep and Housing Quality of Older Homeowners." *Journals of Gerontology* 46:S288–97.

Richards, Marcus, Rebecca Hardy, Diana Kuh, and Michael Wadsworth. 2001. "Birthweight and Cognitive Function in the British 1946 Birth Cohort: Longitudinal Population Based Study." *British Medical Journal* 322:199–203.

Richters, John and Pedro Martinez. 1993. "The NIMH Community Violence Project: Volume 1. Children as Victims of and Witnesses to Violence." *Psychiatry* 56:3–6.

Ricketts, E. and R. Mincy. 1990. "Growth of the Underclass: 1970–1980." *Journal of Human Resources* 25:137–45.

Riva, Mylène, Lisa Gauvin, and Tracie A. Barnett. 2007. "Toward the Next Generation of Research into Small Area Effects on Health: A Synthesis of Multilevel Investigations Published Since July 1998."*Journal of Epidemiology and Community Health* 61: 853–61.

Robert, Stephanie A. 1999. "Socioeconomic Position and Health: The Independent Contribution of Community Socioeconomic Context." *Annual Review of Sociology* 25:489–516.

Robert Wood Johnson Foundation, Commission to Build a Healthier America. 2009. "Beyond Health Care: New Directions to a Healthier America." Princeton, NJ: Robert Wood Johnson Foundation.

Robinson, John P. and Geoffrey Godbey. 1997. *Time for Life: The Surprising Ways Americans Use Their Time.* College Park, PA: Pennsylvania State University Press.

Rochell, Anne. 1998. "Folk Artist's Heart Not Yet at Home in New Surroundings." *Atlanta Journal and Constitution*, June 7, p. M8.

Roodman, D. M. and N. Lenssen. 1995. "A Building Revolution: How Ecology and Health Concerns are Transforming Construction." Worldwatch Paper 124, Worldwatch Institute, Washington, D.C.

Rosenberg, M. 1965. *Society and the Adolescent Self-Image.* Princeton, NJ: Princeton University Press.

Rosenstock, Irwin. 1966. "Why People Use Health Services." *Milbank Memorial Fund Quarterly* 44:94–124.

——. 1990. "The Health Belief Model: Explaining Health Behavior through Expectancies." Pp. 39–62 in *Health Behavior and Health Education*, edited by K. Glanz, F. M. Lewis, and B. K. Rimer. San Francisco, CA: Jossey-Bass.

Ross, Catherine E. 2000. "Neighborhood Disadvantage, Disorder, and Health." *Journal of Health and Social Behavior* 41:177–87.

Ross, Catherine E. and John Mirowsky. 2001. "Neighborhood Disadvantage, Disorder, and Health." *Journal of Health and Social Behavior* 42:258–76.

Roubenoff, Ronenn and Virginia A. Hughes. 2000. "Sacropenia: Current Concepts." *Journals of Gerontology: Medical Sciences* 55: M716–M724.

Royal Society Study Group. 1992. *Risk: Analysis, Perception and Management.* London: Royal Society.

Rubinowitz, Leonard S. and James E. Rosenbaum. 2000. *Crossing the Class and Color Lines: From Public Housing to White Suburbia.* Chicago, IL: University of Chicago Press.

Sager, Alan. 1983. "Why Urban Voluntary Hospitals Close." *Health Services Research* 18:451–81.

Saha, Robin. 2009. "A Current Appraisal of Toxic Wastes and Race in the United States–2007." Pp. 237–60 in *Urban Health: Readings in the Social Built, and Physical Environments of U.S. Cities,* edited by H. Hynes and R. Lopez. Sudbury, MA: Jones and Bartlett.

Salzinger, Suzanne, Daisy S. Ng-Mak, Richard S. Feldman, Chi-Ming Kam, and Margaret Rosario. 2006. "Exposure to Community Violence Processes That Increase the Risk for Inner-City Middle School Children." *Journal of Early Adolescence* 26:232–66.

Sameroff, Arnold J., Ronald Seifer, Alfred Baldwin, and Clara Baldwin. 1993. "Stability of Intelligence from Preschool to Adolescence: The Influence of Social and Family Risk Factors." *Child Development* 64:80–97.

Sampson, Robert J. 1988. "Local Friendship Ties and Community Attachment in Mass Society: A Multilevel Systemic Model." *American Sociological Review* 53:766–79.

——. 1997. "The Embeddedness of Child and Adolescent Development: A Community-Level Perspective on Urban Violence." Pp. 31–77 in *Violence and Childhood in the Inner City,* edited by Joan McCord. Cambridge, England: Cambridge University Press.

——. 2003. "The Neighborhood Context of Well-Being." *Perspectives in Biology and Medicine* 46: S53–64.

Sampson, Robert J. and J. L. Lauritsen. 1994. "Violent Victimization and Offending: Individual-, Situational-, and Community-Level Risk Factors." Pp. 1–114 in *Understanding and Preventing Violence: Social Influences* Vol. 3, edited by A. J. Reiss, Jr. and J. A. Roth. Washington, DC: National Academy Press.

Sampson, Robert J. and William Julius Wilson. 1995. "Toward a Theory of Race, Crime, and Urban Inequality." Pp. 37–54 in *Crime and Inequality,* edited by John Hagan and Ruth Peterson. Stanford, CA: Stanford University Press.

Sampson, Robert J. and William Julius Wilson. 2005. "Toward a Theory of Race, Crime, and Urban Inequality." Pp. 177–89 in *Race, Crime and Justice: A Reader,* edited by Shaun L. Gabbidon and Helen Taylor Greene. New York: Routledge.

Sampson, Robert J., Jeffery D. Morenoff, and Thomas Gannon-Rowley. 2002. "Assessing 'Neighborhood Effects': Social Processes and New Directions in Research." *Annual Review of Sociology* 28:443–78.

Sampson, Robert J., Stephen Raudenbush, and Felton Earls. 1997. "Neighborhoods and Violent Crime: A Multilevel Study of Collective Efficacy." *Science* 277:918–24.

Sampson, Robert J., Patrick Sharkey, and Stephen W. Raudenbush. 2008. "Durable Effects of Concentrated Disadvantage on Verbal Ability Among African American Children." *The National Academy of Sciences of the USA* 105:845–52.

Samuels and Associates. 2007. "Key Lessons from California Schools Working to Change School Food Environments." California Project LEAN, the Partnership for the Public's Health and the Center for Weight and Health, University of California, Berkeley. Los Angeles: The California Endowment.

Sassen, Saskia. 2000. *Cities in a World Economy*. Thousand Oaks, CA: Pine Forge.

Satariano, William A. 2006. *Epidemiology of Aging: An Ecological Approach*. Sudbury, MA: Jones and Bartlett Publishers.

Schlitt, J. 1994. *State Initiatives to Support School-Based Health Centers: A National Survey Report*. Washington, DC: Robert Wood Johnson Foundation.

Schoenberg, S. P and P. L. Rosenbaum. 1980. *Neighborhoods That Work: Sources for Viability in the Inner City*. New Brunswick, NJ: Rutgers University Press.

Schulz, Amy J., David R. Williams, Barbara A. Israel, and Lora Bex Lempert. 2002. "Racial and Spatial Relations as Fundamental Determinants of Health in Detroit." *Milbank Quarterly* 80:677–707.

Schumpeter, Joseph. [1934] 1961. *The Theory of Economic Development*. New York: Oxford University Press.

Schwarz, Donald F., Jeanne A. Grisso, Carolyn Miles, John H. Holmes, and Rudolph L. Sutton. 1993. "An Injury Prevention Program in an Urban African American Community." *American Journal of Public Health* 83:675–80.

Sharma, Leena, September Cahue, Jing Song, Karen Hayes, Yi-Chung Pai, and Dorothy Dunlop. 2003. "Physical Functioning Over Three Years in Knee Osteoarthritis: Role of Psychosocial, Local Mechanical and Neuromuscular Function." *Arthritis & Rheumatism* 48:3359–3370.

Shaw, Clifford and Henry McKay. 1942. *Juvenile Delinquency and Urban Areas*. Chicago, IL: University of Chicago Press.

Shaw, M. 2004. "Housing and Public Health." *Annual Review of Public Health* 25:397–418.

Shevky, Eshref and Wendell Bell. 1955. *Social Area Analysis*. Stanford, CA: Stanford University Press.

Shihadeh, Joseph and Graham Ousey. 1998. "Industrial Restructuring and Violence: The Link between Entry-Level Jobs, Economic Deprivation, and Black and White Homicide." *Social Forces* 77:185–206.

Shinn, M., J. S. Schteingart, N. C. Williams, J. Carlin-Mathis, N. Bialo-Karagis, R. Becker-Klein, and B. C. Weitzman. 2008. "Long Term Associations of Homelessness with Children's Wellbeing." *American Behavioral Scientist* 51:789–809.

Shonkoff, Jack P. and Deborah Phillips. 2000. *From Neurons to Neighborhoods: The Science of Early Childhood Development, ed. National Research Council, Institute of Medicine*. Washington, DC: National Academic Press.

Shrum, W. and N. Cheek. 1987. "Social Structure during the School Years: Onset of the Degrouping Process." *American Sociological Review* 52:218–23.

Simmel, Georg. [1905] 1964. "The Metropolis and Mental Life." Pp. 409–24 in *The Sociology of Georg Simmel*, edited by K. Wolff. New York: Free Press.

Simon, Herbert. 1957. *Models of Man*. New York: Wiley.

Sims, Mario and Yolanda Rainge. 2002. "Urban Poverty and Infant Health Disparities Among African Americans and Whites in Milwaukee." *Journal of the National Medical Association* 94:472–79.

Sims, Mario, Tammy L. Sims, and Marino A. Bruce. 2007. "Urban Poverty and Infant Mortality Rate Disparities." *Journal of the National Medical Association* 99:349–56.

Smedley, Brian D. and S. Leonard Syme, eds. 2000. *Promoting Health: Intervention Strategies from Social and Behavioral Research*. Washington, DC: National Academies Press.

Smedley, Brian, Adrienne Y. Stith, and Alan Ray Nelson, eds. 2003. *Unequal Treatment: Confronting Racial and Ethnic Disparities in Health Care*. Washington, DC: National Academy Press.

Smith, Christopher, J. 1988. *Public Problems: The Management of Urban Distress*. New York: Guilford Press.

Snow, David and Leon Anderson. 1993. *Down on Their Luck: A Study of Homeless Street People*. Berkeley, CA: University of California Press.

Soldo, Beth and Charles Longino. 1988. "Social and Physical Environments for the Vulnerable Aged." Pp. 103–33 in *America's Aging: The Social and Built Environment in an Aging Society*. Committee on an Aging Society. Washington, DC: National Academy Press.

Spencer, Thomas. 2008. "Village Creek Rebounds." *Birmingham News*, September 5.

Srole, Leo, T. S. Langer, S. T. Michael, M. K.Opler, and Thomas A. C. Rennie. 1962. *Mental Health in the Metropolis: The Midtown Manhattan Study*. New York: McGraw-Hill.

Sternfeld, B., L. Ngo, W. A. Stariano, and I. B. Tager. 2002. "Associations of Body Composition with Physical Performance and Self-Reported Functional Limitations in Elderly Men and Women." *American Journal of Epidemiology* 156:110–21.

Stevens, Gregory D. 2006. "Gradients in the Health Status and Developmental Risks of Young Children: The Combined Influences of Multiple Social Risk Factors." *Maternal and Child Health Journal* 10:187–99.

Stokols, D. 1972. "A Social Psychological Model of Human Crowding Phenomena." *Journal of the American Institute of Planners* 38:72–82.

Subramanian, S. V., D. Acevedo-Garcia, and T. L. Osypuk. 2005. "Racial Residential Segregation and Geographic Heterogeneity in Black/White Disparity in Poor Self-Rated Health in the U.S.: A Multilevel Statistical Analysis." *Social Science and Medicine* 60:1667–79.

Subramanian, S. V., Kelvyn Jones, and Craig Duncan. 2003. "Multilevel Methods for Public Health Research." Pp. 65–111 in *Social Epidemiology*, edited by L. F. Berkman and I. Kawachi. New York: Oxford University Press.

Substance Abuse and Mental Health Services Administration, Office of Applied Studies.

2008. *Results from the 2007 National Survey on Drug Use and Health: National Findings* (NSDUH Series H-34, DHHS Publication No. SMA 08–4343). Rockville, MD.

Sundstrom, Eric. 1986. "Privacy in the Office." Pp. 177–202 in *Behavioral Issues in Office Design*, edited by Jean Wineman. New York: Van Nostrand Reinhold.

Sundstrom, Eric and Irving Altman. 1974. "Field Study of Dominance and Territorial Behavior." *Journal of Personality and Social Psychology* 30:115–25.

Sutherland, E. H. and D. Cressey. 1960. *Principles of Criminology*. Philadelphia, PA: Lippincott.

Suttles, Gerald. 1968. *The Social Order of the Slum: Ethnicity and Territory in the Inner City*. Chicago, IL: University of Chicago Press.

Tausig, Mark. 1986a. "Measuring Life Events." Pp. 71–93 in *Social Support, Life Events, and Depression*, edited by Nan Lin, Alfred Dean, and Walter Ensel. New York: Academic Press.

———. 1986b. "Prior History of Illness in the Basic Model." Pp. 267–80 in *Social Support, Life Events, and Depression*, edited by Nan Lin, Alfred Dean, and Walter Ensel. New York: Academic Press.

Taylor, Dorceta. 2009. *The Environment and the People in American Cities, 1600s–1900s: Disorder, Inequality, and Social Change*. Durham, NC: Duke.

Taylor, Ralph B. 1988. *Human Territorial Functioning: An Empirical Evolutionary Perspective on Individual and Small Group Territorial Cognitions, Behaviors, and Consequences*. New York: Cambridge University Press.

Taylor, Ralph B. and Jeanette Covington. 1988. "Neighborhood Changes in Ecology and Violence." *Criminology* 26:553–89.

Thoits, Peggy A. 1983. "Dimensions of Life Events that Influence Psychological Distress: An Evaluation and Synthesis of the Literature." Pp. 33–103 in *Psychosocial Stress: Trends in Theory and Research*, edited by H. B. Kaplan. New York: Academic.

———. 1985. "Social Support and Psychological Well-Being: Theoretical Possibilities." Pp. 51–72 in *Social Support: Theory, Research, and Application*, edited by Irwin G. Sarason and Barbara R. Sarason. Dordrecht, Netherlands: Martinus-Nijhoff.

———. 1995. "Stress, Coping, and Social Support Processes: Where Are We? What Next?" *Journal of Health and Social Behavior* Extra issue: 53–79.

Timms, Duncan. 1971. *The Urban Mosaic*. Cambridge, England: Cambridge University Press.

Tönnies, F. [1887] 1957. *Community and Society*. Translated and edited by Charles Loomis. East Lansing, MI: Michigan State University Press.

Trojanowicz, Robert and Bonnie Bucqueroux. 1994. *Community Policing*. Cincinnati, OH: Anderson Publishing.

Tuan, Yi Fu. 1977. *Space and Place: The Perspective of Experience*. Minneapolis, MN: University of Minnesota Press.

———. 1982. *Segmented Worlds and Self*. Minneapolis, MN: University of Minnesota Press.

Turnbull, Colin. 1961. *The Forest People*. New York: Simon & Schuster.

Turner, R. Jay. 1983. "Direct, Indirect, and Moderating Effects of Social Support upon

Psychological Distress and Associated Conditions." Pp. 105–55 in *Psychological Stress: Trends in Theory and Research*, edited by H. B. Kaplan. New York: Academic Press.

Turner, R. Jay, Blair Wheaton, and Donald A. Lloyd. 1995. "The Epidemiology of Social Stress." *American Sociological Review* 60:104–25.

Umberson, Deborah. 1987. "Family Status and Health Behaviors: Social Control as a Dimension of Social Integration." *Journal of Health and Social Behavior* 28:306–19.

U.S. Bureau of the Census. 2000. Summary File 1, Detailed Tables, Table SF1 and SF4, Alabama. Washington, DC: U.S. Government Printing Office.

——. 2001. *At-Risk Conditions of U.S. School-Age Children*. Washington, DC: U.S. Government Printing Office.

——. 2002. *Statistical Abstract of the United States, 2002*. Washington, DC: U.S. Government Printing Office.

——. 2007. *American Community Survey, 1-Year Estimates*. Washington DC: U.S. Government Printing Office

U.S. Department of Commerce. Office of Consumer Goods. 2005. "2005 Sporting and Athletic Goods Outlook." Retrieved August 14, 2009 (www.ita.doc.gov/td/ocg/outlook05_sports.pdf).

U.S. Department of Education. 2009. "American Recovery and Reinvestment Act of 2009: Title I, Part A Funds for Grants to Local Education Agencies." Retrieved July 22, 2009 (www.ed.gov/policy/gen/leg/recovery/factsheet/ title-i.html).

U.S. Department of Health and Human Services. 1998. *Health, United States 1998*. Washington, DC: U.S. Government Printing Office.

——. 2000. *Healthy People 2010*. Volume 1. Washington, DC: U.S. Government Printing Office.

——. 2009a. "Deaths: Final Data for 2006." *National Vital Statistics Report*. Vol. 57. Washington, DC: U.S. Government Printing Office.

——. 2009b. Agency for Health Care Research and Quality "What is Health Care Quality and Who Decides?" Carolyn M. Clancy's Testimony before Committee on Finance, Subcommittee on Health Care, and United States Senate 3–19–2009.

U.S. Department of Housing and Urban Development. Office of Community Planning and Development. 2009. *The 2008 Annual Homeless Assessment Report to Congress*. Washington, DC: U.S. Government Printing Office.

U.S. Department of Housing and Urban Development. Office of Policy Development and Research. 2003. *Moving to Opportunity for Fair Housing Demonstration Program: Interim Impacts Evaluations*. Washington, DC: U.S. Department of Housing and Urban Development.

U.S. Department of Justice. 1996. *Creating Safe and Drug-Free Schools: An Action Guide*. Washington, DC: Office of Juvenile Justice and Delinquency Prevention.

U.S. Environmental Protection Agency. 1997. "A Review of Clorpyrifos Poisoning Data." Washington, DC: Office of Pesticide Programs, U.S. Environmental Protection Agency.

———. 1999. "Why Should You Be Concerned about the Quality of the Air that You Breathe?" Washington, DC: U.S. Environmental Protection Agency. Online at (www.epa.gov/iaq/).

U.S. General Accounting Office. 1987. *School Dropouts: Survey of Local Programs.* Washington, DC: U.S. General Accounting Office.

U.S. National Advisory Commission on Civil Disorders. 1968. *Report of the National Advisory Commission on Civil Disorders.* Washington, DC: U.S. Government Printing Office.

U.S. Office of Management and Budget. 2007. OMB Bulletin No. 08–01 *Update of Statistical Area Definitions and Guidance on Their Uses.* Washington D.C. Retrieved August 14, 2009 (www.whitehouse.gov/omb/assets/omb/bulletins/ fy2008/b08-01.pdf).

Veenstra, Gerry, Issac Luginaah, Sarah Wakefield, Stephen Birch, John Eyles, and Susan Elliott. 2005. "Who You Know, Where You Live: Social Capital, Neighbourhood and Health." *Social Science and Medicine* 60:2799–818.

Verbrugge, Lois. 1989. "The Twain Meet: Empirical Explanations of Sex Differences in Health and Mortality." *Journal of Health and Social Behavior* 30:282–304.

Volkart, E. H. 1951. *Introduction to Social Behavior and Personality.* New York: Social Sciences Research Council.

Wachholz, S. 2005. "Hate Crimes Against the Homeless: Warning-out New England Style." *Journal of Sociology and Social Welfare* 32:141–63.

Walter, Heather J., Roger D. Vaughan, Bruce Armstrong, Roberta Y. Krakoff, Lorraine Tiezzi, and James F. McCarthy. 1995. "School-Based Health Care for Urban Minority Junior High School Students." *Archives of Pediatric and Adolescent Medicine* 149:1221–25.

Wang, M. C., S. Kim, A. A. Gonzalez, K. E. MacLeod, and M. A. Winkleby. 2007. "Socioeconomic and Food-Related Physical Characteristics of the Neighborhood Environment are Associated with Body Mass Index." *Journal of Epidemiology and Community Health* 61:491–98.

Wang, Y. and Q. Zhang. 2006. "Are American Children and Adolescents of Low Socioeconomic Status at Increased Risk of Obesity? Changes in the Association Between Overweight and Family Income between 1971 and 2002." *American Journal of Clinical Nutrition* 84:707–16.

Ward, Russell. 1984. *The Aging Experience: An Introduction to Social Gerontology.* New York: Lippincott.

Ward, Russell, Mark LaGory, and Susan Sherman. 1986. "Fear of Crime among the Elderly as Person/Environment Interaction." *Sociological Quarterly* 27:327–41.

Ward, Russell, Mark LaGory, and Susan Sherman. 1988. *The Environment for Aging: Social, Interpersonal and Spatial Contexts.* Tuscaloosa, AL: University of Alabama Press.

Webber, Melvin. 1964. "The Urban Place and the Nonplace Urban Realm." Pp. 79–153 in *Explorations into Urban Structure,* edited by M. M. Webber, J. W. Dyckman, D. L. Foley, A. Z. Guttenberg, W. L. C. Wheaton, and C. B. Wurster. Philadelphia: University of Pennsylvania Press.

Weber, Max. [1922] 1978. *Economy and Society,* 2nd Vol, edited by G. Roth and C. Wittich. Berkeley, CA: University of California Press.

Wehr, Thomas and Norman Rosenthal. 1989. "Seasonality and Affective Illness." *American Journal of Psychiatry* 146:829–39.

Wellman, Barry. 1979. "The Community Question: The Intimate Networks of East Yorkers." *American Journal of Sociology* 84:1201–31.

——. 1999. *Networks in the Global Village: Life in Contemporary Communities.* Boulder, CO: Westview.

Wenzel, S. L., B. D. Leake and L. Gelberg. 2001. "Risk Factors for Major Violence Among Homeless Women." *Journal of Interpersonal Violence* 16:739–52.

Werner, Emmy E. 1990. "Protective Factors and Individual Resilience." Pp. 97–116 in *Handbook of Early Childhood Intervention*, edited by S. J. Meisels and J. P. Shonkoff. New York: Cambridge University Press.

Westin, A. F. 1967. *Privacy and Freedom.* New York: Atheneum.

Wheaton, Blair. 1983. "Stress, Personal Coping Resources, and Psychiatric Symptoms: An Investigation of Interactive Models." *Journal of Health and Social Behavior* 24:208–29.

——. 1985. "Models for the Stress-Buffering Functions of Coping Resources." *Journal of Health and Social Behavior* 26:352–64.

Wheeler, L. 1967. *Behavioral Research for Architectural Planning and Design.* Terre Haute, IN: Ewing Miller.

Whitbourne, Susan Krauss. 2008. *Adult Development and Aging: Biopsychosocial Perspectives.* 3rd ed. Hoboken, NJ: John Wiley & Sons.

Whiteis, David G. 1992. "Hospital and Community Characteristics in Closure of Urban Hospitals, 1980–87." *Public Health Reports* 107:409–16.

——. 1997. "Unhealthy Cities: Corporate Medicine, Community Economic Under-development, and Public Health." *International Journal of Health Services* 27:227–42.

Whyte, William H. 1956. *The Organization Man.* Garden City, NY: Doubleday.

——. 1990. *City: Rediscovering the Center.* New York: Anchor Books.

Wilkinson, Richard. 1996. *Healthy Societies: The Afflictions of Inequality.* New York: Routledge.

Williams, David R. 1996. "Introduction: Racism and Health, A Research Agenda." *Ethnicity and Disease* 2:126–41.

Williams, David R. and Chiquita Collins. 2001. "Racial Residential Segregation: A Fundamental Cause of Racial Disparities in Health." *Public Health Reports* 116:404–16.

Wilson, E. O. 1975. *Sociobiology: The New Synthesis.* Cambridge, MA: Harvard University Press.

Wilson, J. Q. and G. E. Kelling. 1982. "Broken Windows: The Police and Neighborhood Safety." *Atlantic Monthly*, March.

Wilson, William Julius. 1980. *The Declining Significance of Race: Blacks and Changing American Institutions.* Chicago, IL: University of Chicago Press.

——. 1987. *The Truly Disadvantaged.* Chicago, IL: University of Chicago Press.

——. 1996. *When Work Disappears: The World of the New Urban Poor.* New York: Vintage Press.

Wilson, William J. and Richard P. Taub. 2007. *There Goes the Neighborhood: Racial, Ethnic, and Class Tensions in Four Chicago Neighborhoods and their Meaning for America.* New York: First Vintage Books.

Winkleby, M. A., H. C. Kramer, D. K. Ahn, and A. N. Varady. 1998. "Ethnic and Socioeconomic Differences in Cardiovascular Disease Risk Factors." *Journal of the American Medical Association* 280:356–62.

Winslow, Emily B. and Daniel S. Shaw. 2007. "Impact of Neighborhood Disadvantage on Overt Behavior Problems During Early Childhood." *Aggressive Behavior* 33:207–19.

Wirth, Louis. 1938. "Urbanism as a Way of Life." *American Journal of Sociology* 44:1–24.

Wittman, F. D. 1990. "Environmental Design to Prevent Problems of Alcohol Availability: Concepts and Prospects." Pp. 232–44 in *Research, Action, and the Community: Experiences in the Prevention of Alcohol and Other Drug Problems.* OSAP Prevention Monograph-4. Rockville, MD: U.S. Department of Health and Human Services.

Woldoff, Rachel A. 2002. "The Effects of Local Stressors on Neighborhood Attachment." *Social Forces* 81:87–116.

Wolfe, David A., Peter G. Jaffe, and Claire V. Crooks. 2006. *Adolescent Risk Behaviors: Why Teens Experiment and Strategies to Keep Them Safe.* New Haven, CT: Yale University Press.

Wright, J., B. Rubin, and J. Devine. 1998. *Beside the Golden Door: Policy, Politics and the Homeless.* New York: Aldine de Gruyter.

Wright, Rosalind J. and Edwin B. Fisher. 2003. "Putting Asthma into Context: Community Influences on Risk, Behavior and Intervention." Pp. 233–62 in *Neighborhoods and Health,* edited by I. Kawachi and L. F. Berkman. New York: Oxford University Press.

Xue, Yange, Tama Leventhal, Jeanne Brooks-Gunn, and Felton J. Earls. 2005. "Neighborhood Residence and Mental Health Problems of Five to Eleven Year Olds." *Archives of General Psychiatry* 62:554–63.

Yancey, William. 1971. "Architecture, Interaction, and Social Control." *Environment and Behavior* 3:3–21.

Zarit, Steven H., Patricia C. Griffiths, and Stig Berg. 2004. "Pain Perceptions of the Oldest Old: A Longitudinal Study." *Gerontologist* 44:459–68.

Zukin, Sharon. 1991. *Landscapes of Power: From Detroit to Disney World.* Berkeley, CA: University of California Press.

Index

Adolescence 144, 169; *see also* youth
African American: access to health
   care 131; health risks 135;
   neighborhoods 2, 57, 105, 118,
   175; poverty 61, 71, 133
Aging: buildings 39; high poverty
   ghetto areas 179; persons 87–8;
   residential areas 96; suburbs 103;
   see also elderly; mental health;
   physical health
Andrulis, Dennis 136
Aneshensel, Carol S. 122
Ardrey, Robert 24
Assimilation 32, 75
At-risk populations 18–19, 131, 160,
   166
Athanasiou, Robert 38

Baldassare, Mark 34
Balshem, Martha 87
Bane, Mary Jo 8
Barker, Roger 16

Beck, Ulrich 10, 12, 155
Behavior settings 16, 29
Bell, Wendell 58
Birmingham 16, 44, 98, 128, 182
Blau, Peter 38
Boat, M. 58
Booth, Alan 34
Bourdieu, Pierre 86–7
Bracho, America 154
Bronfenbrenner, Urie 89
Brooks-Gunn, Jeanne 137
Building Healthy Communities 164,
   180
Burt, Martha 114

Campbell, Karen 71
Capital: human 94, 164, 182;
   physical 163–4, 188; social 94–5,
   139, 164
Capitalism 61, 63–5, 67–8, 81
Caregiver burden 147, 183
Catalano, Richard 177

Chicago: city of 65, 97–8, 161, 168; Gautreaux Assisted Housing Program 160
Chicago School 61, 106, 121–2
Child abuse 139
Children 34–5, 92, 138–45; *see also* youth
Choice: constraints 28, 68, 72, 135, 152; density 70–1, 74, 76; field 69; theories 69
Choldin, Harvey 33
Church: B.E.A.T. (Bethel Ensley Task Force) 179; Central Presbyterian Church 115; Communities of Shalom (United Methodist) 181; Congregations for Public Health 182; Cooperative Downtown Ministries 116, 118, 181; as protection 113, 116, 144, 154, 180
Churchill, Winston 17
Cockerham, William C. 85
Communalism 72, 76
Community: attachment 58–9; community health clinics (CHC) 173; development 20, 112, 116, 160, 164; identity 54; policing 176–7
Congruence (mental and experiential) 29
Contact opportunities 59
Contagion effect 75
Context: effect of 19, 57–8, 63, 156
Continuum of care 158
Cooper, Clair 37
Coping 41, 53, 85, 94
Cosmopolitan community 74, 77

Crane, Jonathan 75
Crime: juvenile 142; prevention 175–6
Crowding 33–5, 46, 123, 127, 129

Darley, J. 53
Dear, Michael 61, 68
Deinstitutionalization 68
Density: age 150; density-intensity hypothesis 34; household 34, 123; neighborhood 33, 123; patterns 26
Detachment 71, 73–5, 80
Deviance: *see* crime; lifestyles
Differential association theory 15
Docility hypothesis 35, 151
Dropout 75, 103, 117–18, 144–5, 154, 160
Drug: culture 140; prevention 118–19
Durkheim, Emile 32, 36
Dursban 2–3

Ecological: actors 17, 19, 121, 126, 137, 146; foci 137
Ecology of: fear 66–8, 188; health 16, 18–19, 43, 95, 101, 112; opportunity 65
Edwards, John 34
Eibl-Eibesfeldt, Irenaus 33
Elderly 88, 146–52
Environment: definition of 7; perceived 148–9, 151; person–environment fit 29, 126, 148
Environmental: controllability 29; discrimination 105; justice 66, 105–6; press 148–9

Environmental Protection Agency (EPA) 2, 48, 162
Ethology 23
Exchange value 31, 64

Faith-based initiatives 114–16, 179–84
Family as protection 109
Festinger, L.S. 37
Fischer, Claude 54, 99
Freedman, J.L. 34
Fuller, Miller 114, 180

Gallagher, Winifred 48
Gangs 15, 23
Gans, Herbert 38
Genovese, Kitty 53
Geronimus, Arlene 135
Ghetto: *see* inner city
Granovetter, Mark 76
Greer, Scott 58

Haan, Mary 133
Habitat for Humanity 144, 179
Habitus 86–7, 96
Hall, Edward 24, 26, 33, 56
Harvey, David 50, 66
Hawkins, David J. 109, 177
Hazard: physical 104, 138, 162; social 150; waste 65, 80, 104–5; zone 133, 163, 187; *see also* pollution
Health: beliefs 17–19, 83–4, 86, 95, 99, 100–1; compromising behavior 87–9, 99, 108–9, 121, 177; education 84, 167, 170; improving behavior 87; lifestyles 15, 17–18, 85, 88, 91, 95; promotion 49, 117, 164–5, 171, 180–2, 184; psychosocial resources 83; risks 11, 88–91; services 81, 84, 143, 174, 178
Healthy Cities Project (HCP) 184–5
Healthy Communities project 185
Hippocrates 82
Hispanics 13, 121, 135
Holley, Lonnie 21–2
Home space: definition of 46; exterior 46–7; interior 47, 49–50, 126–7
Homeless 126–30
Homophily 70–1
Houston 105, 181

Individual distance 24, 26
Inequality: income 92; spatial 67
Infant mortality 6, 135, 140, 141
Inner city 7–9, 39–40, 61–3, 103

Jargowsky, Paul 8, 62, 132–3
Johnson, Lyndon 110

Latane, B. 53
Lawton, M. Powell 148
Lead poisoning 50, 120
Lee, Barrett 71
Lefebvre, Henri 30
Lehman, Jeffrey S. 159
Life: chances (*Lebenschancen*) 64, 85–8, 95–6, 99, 136; choices (*Lebenfuhrung*) 86–7; events 91–3, 109, 111; expectancy 15, 92, 134

Lifestyles (*Lebensstil*) 86
Limited liability 73
Lin, Nan 93
Location models 59
Lofland, Lynn 45, 56
Logan, John R. 30, 64
Los Angeles 67, 98, 161, 169, 181

Malsow, Abraham 38–9
Mastery 93, 148
Mayes, Frances 44
McKay, Henry 107
McLuhan, Marshall 5
Mechanical solidarity 32
Mental health: Alzheimer's disease
    147; dementia 147; depression
    130, 143, 147, 151–2; and place
    18–19, 91, 122–3
Mental map 8, 19, 69, 137
Merton, Robert 76
Michelson, William 29
Milgram, Stanley 52–3, 55
Minorities 103–4, 130–1, 134–5; *see
    also* African American and
    Hispanics
Molotch, Harvey 30, 64
Morbidity 91, 129, 134–5, 183
Mortality 4, 6–7, 36, 91, 133–4; *see
    also* infant mortality

Nahemow, Lucille 148
Neighborhood: crime prevention
    175–8; disadvantage 17, 83,
    95–100, 136, 138, 140; high
    poverty 33, 61–3, 145, 186;
    mobilization 80, 161, 182–3;
    neighboring 37, 73, 112;

participation 12–13, 40, 106; as
    protection 15, 112–16; role of 39,
    57–9, 111–12, 170; sick 133–4
Newman, Sandra 150
New York City 4, 74, 98, 161;
    Harlem 11; Kew Gardens 53
Nored, Reverend Ron 178–9
Nutrition 85, 119, 167, 169, 186

Organic solidarity 32

Pearlin, Leonard 91
Physical health 90–1, 96, 104, 120
Place: approaches to health 6, 20,
    168, 178, 185, 187; attachment to
    22–3, 30–1, 44–5, 58, 98, 149;
    awareness of 148–9; definition of
    7–8; distinct from space 7, 15–16,
    30–1, 64; experience 25;
    multidimensionality 7, 11, 15–16,
    23, 28, 188
Placelessness 42, 59, 65, 126,
    129–30
Policy 159–60, 184–5
Pollution: air 6, 51, 104; noise 11,
    42, 60, 104, 127; toxic waste 42,
    65, 104, 127, 186; water 2, 104,
    132, 162
Poverty: concentration of 6–7, 61–3,
    132; subculture of 39; urban 62,
    102–3, 151, 158–9
Prevention: disease 83–4; dropout
    117–18
Prevention programs: Block Home
    Program 176–7; Central Health
    Center (Atlanta) 116;
    Neighborhood Watch 175–6;

Operation Identification 176; Safe Block Project 118; Safe and Drug Free Schools 166–7; substance abuse 166–7; violence 166, 170, 176
Privacy 32–3, 46–7, 127
Protective factors 88–91, 94, 110
Putnam, Robert 163

Quality of life 71, 80, 107, 136

Racism 105, 155, 170
Reitzes, Donald 151
Relocation effects 66, 147, 161, 172
Relph, Edward 30, 32
Removal strategies 159–60, 172
Reschovsky, James 150
Resource machine, city as 69, 113, 132
Resources: psychological 35, 91, 93; psychosocial 17, 83, 91; social 12, 15, 93–5
Revitalization 177, 181
Richman, Harold 161
Risk: definition of 10; environment 107, 134–5; factors 89–90, 119, 155; society 10, 17, 78, 162; spaces 11–12, 151; taking behavior 81, 86, 129, 165, 168
Routine activities theory 108
Roxbury 4, 11

Santa Ana, California 154–5
Sapir-Whorf hypothesis 25
Satisficing behavior 69–70
School: prevention programs 117–18, 166, 169–70; as protection 88–90, 92–3, 117; role of 117–18, 164–5; school-based clinics (SBC) 168–9, 178
Schwartz, Joseph 38
Seasonal Affective Disorder (SAD) 49
Segregation: age 19, 150; class 9, 14; ethnic 62, 74–5, 96, 130–5; racial 9, 14, 133, 159
Self: esteem 90, 93; home as reflection of 22, 31–2, 44–7
Shakers 49
Shaw, Clifford 107
Simmel, Georg 33
Slum: definition of 12; emergence of 60–1
Smeeding, Timothy 159
Social: affiliation 36–7; areas 57–9, 63; capital 94–7, 100, 105–6, 110–11, 163–4; climate 58–9, 65, 69, 71, 73–4, 87; ecology 89, 136; linkages 76; organization 12–13, 39, 112; structure 4, 27–8, 75–6, 81; theories 56, 82–3, 85, 88–9, 95–6
Social support: actual 93, 110–11; formal 24, 92–3, 108, 113–14, 171; informal 92–3, 108, 110, 112; perceived 93, 111; psychosocial 91–4, 127–9
Social ties 36, 69–74, 94
Socialization patterns 75–8
Socioeconomic status (SES) 85, 92, 107, 122, 187
Space: action 127–8; architectural 45, 48, 68–9; defensible 38–40; distinct from place 7, 16, 30, 64;

Space (*cont*):
    interaction 36–8, 54–6; personal 24–5, 33
Spatial: arrangements 26, 36, 70; behavior 23–6; boundaries 55; imprisonment 148; needs 31; organization 54; segmentation 47; structure 18, 44, 57, 78
Srole, Leo 122
STDs (sexually transmitted diseases) 138, 165; HIV/AIDS 120, 135, 142
Stokols, D. 29
Stress: stressors 80, 91–4, 110–11, 129
Subcultures, health-related 99–100
Substance abuse 109, 118, 120–1, 129
Suburbs 6–8, 14, 29, 151, 160
Sundstrom, Eric 32
Sutherland, E.H. 75
Suttles, Gerald 39

Taylor, Ralph 24, 26, 37, 48, 55
Territory: behavior 17, 23–5, 27–9, 31, 40; definition of 23–4; functioning 24, 29, 40, 55, 59, 98; functions of 24; territoriality 23–5
Thomas, W.I. 25
Tönnies, F. 112
Trust 72, 97, 100
Tuan, Yi Fu 30, 45, 47, 68
Turnbull, Colin 26

Unemployment 61–2, 100, 145–6
Urban: ecology 44, 65, 67, 98–9, 186; environment 115, 123, 126; experience 44; health penalty 6–7, 100, 119, 136; mosaic 56, 59, 64; poverty 62, 158–9; renewal 116
Urbanism 52, 56, 74, 112, 172
Urbanization 6, 44, 50, 68–9
Use value 31, 64

Victimization 108, 127–9, 142–3
Village Creek: *see* Birmingham
Violence: exposure 90, 121, 142; prevention 166, 170, 176

Weak ties 41, 73–5, 95, 136
Weathering hypothesis 135
Webber, Melvin 5
Weber, Max 85–6
Wilkinson, Richard 18, 66–7, 92, 155, 187
Wilson, E.O. 24
Wilson, J.Q. 96
Wilson, William Julius 8–9, 12, 39, 61, 159, 188
Wirth, Louis 51–4, 68, 70, 74, 112
Wolch, Jennifer 68

Yoshioka, G. 38
Youth 76–7, 121, 137–8, 165

Zukin, Sharon 64